THIRTY MILLION THEORIES OF GRAMMAR

Thirty Million Theories of Grammar

JAMES D. McCAWLEY

THE UNIVERSITY OF CHICAGO PRESS

The University of Chicago Press, Chicago 60637
Croom Helm Ltd., London SW11

Library of Congress Cataloging in Publication Data

McCawley, James D.
   Thirty million theories of grammar.

   Bibliography: p.204.
   Includes index.
   1. Generative grammar—Addresses, essays, lectures.
2. Semantics—Addresses, essays, lectures.   I. Title.
P158.M39   1982   415   82-40319
ISBN 0-226-55619-0   AACR2

CONTENTS

ACKNOWLEDGEMENTS

The author wishes to acknowledge The Asahi Press, Tokyo and The MIT Press, Cambridge, Massachusetts for granting permission to use the material in Chapters 1 and 2, respectively.

INTRODUCTION

'You can't order linguini with clam sauce.
If you want clam sauce, you gotta order spaghetti.'
  (Unidentified waitress, San Diego, California,
  February 1970.)

This volume consists of four articles by me—two previously published in journals and two previously available only in working papers volumes—that are devoted to some significant extent to critiques of 'interpretive' and 'lexicalist' approaches to syntax and semantics, that is, of work by Chomsky since 'Remarks on nominalization' (1970) and by other linguists, especially Chomsky's students, which is more or less within the frameworks within which Chomsky has worked since the late 1960s.

I emphasize, however, that these articles are not concerned with a supposed single issue often spoken of as 'generative semantics versus interpretive semantics'. The terms 'generative semantics' and 'interpretive semantics' are names not of two contrasting positions on a single issue, nor of two poles on a continuum of positions, but of two packages of positions on a fairly large number of issues, each package corresponding to the views held (actually or in popular caricature) by representative members of two communities of linguists in about 1970 (George Lakoff, Haj Ross, Paul Postal, and I being representative members of the 'generative semantic' community, and Noam Chomsky, Ray Jackendoff, and Joseph Emonds being representative members of the 'interpretive semantic' community).

Neither of these communities was completely homogeneous, no member of either community retained exactly the same set of views for very long, the loci of the disputes between the two communities changed rapidly, often in mid-article, and the relationships among the views that at any moment were packaged together as 'generative semantics' or as 'interpretive semantics' were generally far more tenuous than representative members of either community led people (including themselves) to believe. One of my chief goals in writing the articles collected here has been to take apart the various packages and to demonstrate where possible the independence of the views that comprise the package.

The title of this volume is a conservative estimate of the number of viable combinations of answers to the questions that I take up here.[1] I arrived at the figure of thirty million by computing 2^{25} and rounding downwards: I deal here with easily forty issues, each of which admits at least two possible positions, and I doubt that weeding out the inconsistent, incoherent, or blatantly false combinations of positions would reduce the number of combinations by a factor of more than a few powers of 2. Beyond the probable understatement in the number, the title involves the inaccuracy of applying the term 'theory' to simply a set of positions on issues, when the term is most often used (though not so often defined) to refer not to just a set of propositions but to an ontology combined with a conception of what propositions are meaningful and what their relationship to possible facts is. A number of the issues discussed in the articles below provide distinctions among 'theories' in this narrower sense. In any case, whether what I provide below is indirectly a survey of thirty million theories or of only three hundred, the number of significantly different sets of positions that can be taken on the issues discussed here is considerably greater than the number of names that have been given to conceptions of how meaning and form are organized and are related to one another and to context. It is the issues and not the named sets of views that form the subject matter of this book.

According to the vulgarized version of Sir Karl Popper's 'Falsificationist' philosophy of science that is popular among linguists, each of those issues is in principle resolvable by matters of fact that will falsify one or other of the competing views.[2] Many of the issues are indeed widely believed to have been resolved in this way. The trouble with this conception of the resolution of scientific controversies is that there is no reliable way of telling what a falsification falsifies. False factual consequences are never deduced from just a theory but only from a large number of premises, many of them hidden,[3] of which some are parts of the theory that the investigator is testing, some are parts of other theories whose subject matter the given test impinges on (for example, if you test an astronomical theory by making predictions about what one will see through a telescope pointed at a particular place in the heavens, you must rely on theories of optics, of the medium through which the light is passing, and of visual perception), and others of which relate to the correctness of the assumed statement of the facts (for example, the proposition that your telescope really has the magnification that you think it does). A falsification demonstrates that at least one of the premises from which the false factual proposition has been deduced is false, but it gives no clue as to which one(s) the blame should be pinned on. Thus falsifications do not conclusively eliminate the theoretical propositions that they are designed to test: they only provide estimates of the price that one must pay in order to retain those propositions. The philosophies of science developed by Lakatos (1970) and Feyerabend (1975) acknowledge that any theoretical idea can be maintained at some price. Much of this book is devoted to what Feyerabend calls 'counter-induction': the search for ideas that can provide environments in which allegedly refuted ideas are viable (that is, in which the price of accepting them becomes affordable), in the way that Galileo's theory of motion provided an environment in which the proposition that the earth rotates on its axis was viable.

This book begins with a review article on Chomsky's *Studies on Semantics in Generative Grammar* (*SSGG*) which was written in 1973 and first published in *Studies in English Linguistics, 3*, 209-311 (1975). Chomsky's *SSGG* consists of his influential article 'Remarks on nominalization', in which he first advanced the 'X-bar' conception of syntactic categories and his 'lexicalist' account of nominalizations, and two articles devoted mainly to attacks on generative semantics as he conceived of it. In my review I point out that whether nominalizations must be entered in the lexicon of English is independent of whether a nominalization transformation is required, that the 'transformationalist' analysis that Chomsky attacks is a straw man, and that most of the facts which he takes as evidence against that analysis in fact provide support for an alternative 'transformationalist' analysis that is much closer to that offered by Lees 1960.[4] Since the papers in *SSGG* were written fairly early in the development of Chomsky's non-transformational approach to grammar, and since not even Chomsky, let alone I, could predict what significance some of the ideas he expressed or hinted at in *SSGG* would have in subsequent work, I have added to this review article a particularly generous supply of annotations (enclosed in square brackets to keep them distinct from the original notes) so as to relate my discussion of *SSGG* to many issues that have subsequently acquired importance.

The next article, 'How to get an Interpretive Theory of Anaphora to Work', appeared in *Linguistic Inquiry, 7*, 319-41 (1976) under the title 'Notes on Jackendoff's theory of anaphora'. I have restored the title under which I circulated a preliminary version of it, on the grounds that the earlier title is more informative: the article is concerned not just with evaluating Jackendoff's specific system of semantic interpretation rules but with determining what facets of his approach can be retained in an analysis that accounts for a number of phenomena for which his rules make false predictions. As in the discussion of anaphora in my review of *SSGG*, I make a point of keeping separate the issues of what underlies personal pronouns and other anaphoric devices, what determines the form they take, and what role coreference can play in the action of linguistic rules. The 'classical' transformational treatment of anaphora (for example, Ross 1967a), in which all anaphoric devices are derived from constituents identical to and coreferential with their antecedents and take their form from syntactic features of the underlying constituent, involves answers to all three of these questions. Arguments for 'interpretive' treatments of anaphora have often mistakenly taken facts relating to one of the questions as necessarily having a bearing on all three, perhaps because of a belief that propriety demands that one be either 'consistently interpretivist' or 'consistently transformationalist' and avoid any 'mixed position'. In my current view, 'mixed' positions are mixed only in relationship to packages of answers that, largely through historical accident, have taken on the status of landmarks.

The third article, 'Language Universals in Linguistic Argumentation' was my forum lecture at the 1978 Linguistic Institute, held at the University of Illinois at Champaign-Urbana; it received semi-publication in that university's working papers series (*Studies in the Linguistic Sciences*, *8*, no. 2, 205–19, 1979). It deals with the role that the notion 'language universal' has played in the argumentation of transformational grammarians, especially with arguments in which conclusions are justified on the basis of the claim that they allow one to maintain language universals that alternative analyses would conflict with. I find the bulk of such arguments worthless, since the putative universals generally are merely features accidentally shared by analyses that the investigator for some reason happens to like. The investigator's preferred type of analysis is always available at a price, and in advancing the putative universal he is only expressing his commitment to pay that price and to bully his fellow linguists into paying it too. However, there are also worthwhile arguments based on considerations of language universals, especially those in which an analysis is supported by verifying the pattern of interlinguistic variation that it predicts, on the assumption that linguistic rules purport to identify the possible loci of linguistic variation.

The final paper in the volume, 'The Nonexistence of Syntactic Categories', is an extensively revised and expanded version of a paper read at the Second Annual Michigan State Linguistic Metatheory Conference (May 6–7, 1977) and circulated in the volume of conference papers. In it, I dispute a large number of assumptions about syntactic categories, which generative semanticists and interpretive semanticists have shared, and show that it is only in virtue of these assumptions (especially the assumption that syntactic categories remain constant throughout derivations) that there is any conflict between the claims of generative semanticists that there are extremely few syntactic categories, and the claims of interpretive semanticists that there are a large number of categories. I develop an alternative approach in which the notion of syntactic category as such is rejected in favor of the recognition of a set of factors, some of which are not syntactic in nature, that can play roles in various kinds of syntactic phenomena. The resulting conception of syntax is shown to provide the basis for a picture of language acquisition that is far less mysterious than the picture generally assumed in transformational grammar.

While I will disagree below with many ideas that adherents of Chomsky's (revised) extended standard theory ((R)EST) hold dear, I emphasize that I am by no means hostile to all developments within (R)EST. For example, I regard the following as fairly well established:

1. Points relating to complementizers and COMP position:
   (a) complementizers are sisters of their clauses;
   (b) in WH-movement in English, items are moved into 'COMP position', that is, into a position that could otherwise be occupied by a complementizer.
2. Points relating to syntactic categories:
   (a) a fairly large number of syntactic category distinctions must be drawn;
   (b) the syntactic category of an item is a complex of components, of which one is the lexical category of the head of the item;
   (c) there is a category distinction between lexical items and phrasal constituents of which they are heads, for example, N vs. $\bar{\text{N}}$, A vs. $\bar{\text{A}}$.
3. Points relating to the cycle and cyclic domains:
   (a) NPs, as well as Ss and/or $\bar{\text{S}}$s, are cyclic domains;[5]
   (b) there is a principle of strict cyclicity.

My differences with (R)EST in these areas relate to specific issues that go beyond those listed above. For example, with regard to the first category listed above, I consider the case for successive-cyclic WH-movement to be extremely weak and the problems created by successive-cyclic WH-movement to outweigh its alleged benefits, and I reject the putative language universal (Bresnan 1970) that WH-movement always substitutes the moved item for a complementizer.[6] With regard to the second category, I have several reasons for rejecting the conception of 'base rules' with which X-bar syntax is usually combined, as well as its double and triple bars (for me, NP is not N plus bars and $\bar{\text{N}}$ and $\bar{\text{V}}$ can nest *ad libitum*, for example $[_{\bar{\text{N}}}$ $[_{\bar{\text{N}}}$ $[_{\bar{\text{N}}}$ *book on Copernicus*] *by Kuhn*] *that you recommended*] or $[_{\bar{\text{V}}}$ $[_{\bar{\text{V}}}$ $[_{\bar{\text{V}}}$ *work*] *hard*] *all day*]$)$, and I reject many of the putative categories that have figured in X-bar syntax (for example, M, Aux, QP). With regard to the third category listed above, I lean towards the position that ALL constituents are cyclic domains,[7] I recognize as cyclic domains many constituents that do not exist in REST analyses (see, for example, the explanation of why passive *be* follows all other auxiliary verbs given in McCawley 1981a), and I accept a different version of strict cyclicity than that which Chomsky has generally assumed (for example, for me postcyclic transformations can apply to embedded clauses).

Except for 'The Nonexistence of Syntactic Categories', which I rewrote completely for this volume, and §2.2 of 'How to Get an Interpretive Theory of Anaphora to Work', which I have replaced by a newly written section that avoids a major error that I made in the original, the versions of my papers that are included here are lightly edited but heavily annotated. With those two exceptions, changes in the texts of the previously published papers are confined to stylistic improvements (including the omission of some superfluous notes and the addition of a couple of extra examples); however, I have added numerous new notes in which I make retractions and clarifications or comment on subsequent work. The new notes, as well as the rewritten section of Chapter 2, are enclosed in square brackets to make them easily distinguishable from the original material.

To keep the number of added notes from becoming astronomical, I have not included retractions and clarifications in all the places where they are appropriate, particularly in the earliest work in this volume, my review article on *Studies on semantics in generative grammar*. I will accordingly list here some points on which either I have changed my mind since the early 1970s or my thinking has become more consistent since then, in lieu of still more added notes that would be quite repetitive.

First, I now regard my earlier use of 'V' as a symbol for 'predicate' (as in (13) of §4.6.1 of Chapter 1) as extremely misleading and now restrict 'V' to the lexical category 'verb' (as opposed to noun, adjective, preposition, and perhaps some other things); I now use '0' for 'predicate' without determinate lexical category, as in (10) of §2 of Chapter 4.

Second, in many places I was much less concerned with justifying details of constituent structure than I now am and accordingly failed to bring in considerations that now lead me to set up such constituent structures as [$_{NP}$ *the* [$_\bar{N}$ [$_\bar{N}$ *discovery of Uranus*] *by Herschel*]].

Third, I have become much more consistent than I had been in taking linguistic structures not to be strings but topological objects such as trees and thus in taking the question of underlying constituent structure to have more substance and importance than the question of underlying constituent order. I accordingly reject notational schemes (such as the standard schemes for formulating transformations) in which the often totally irrelevant factors of constituent order and adjacency are made necessary parts of the formulations of all transformations; in fact I doubt that adjacency is ever relevant to syntactic phenomena other than those that are in part also morphological phenomena, for example, cliticization.[8]

Fourth, as is suggested in the third point, I now regard the case that I offered (1970c) for deep VSO word order in English as very weak because of my gratuitous assumption that there IS a deep constituent order, my reliance in some of the arguments on the notational system for transformations that even in 1970 I regarded as pernicious, and my failure to identify the role of grammatical relations in some of the phenomena that I discussed; I now consider the VSO order that appears in structures that I propose in Chapter 1 to be simply a makeshift way of indicating the grammatical relations between predicates and arguments (see in this connection note 11 to Chapter 4).

Fifth, another idea that I assume more consistently now than in some of my earlier work is that rules of grammar are derivational con- straints rather than operations, that is I take the rules of a grammar to be conditions on what can occur in various stages of derivations and on how different stages of derivations may or must differ from each other. I accordingly reject the metaphor of the grammar as a sentence factory (or as a blueprint for an imaginary sentence factory) and am quite happy to consider possibilities that from the point of view of that metaphor are quite outlandish, for example, a conception of grammar in which there are 'phrase structure rules' specifying what are possible surface constituent structures but no rules specifying what are possible deep constituent structures. The arrow that figures in my formulations of rules for how consecutive derivational stages may differ serves only for the purpose of orientation, like the arrow on a map that points north, and it does not imply that what follows the arrow owes its existence to what precedes it. (The arrow on the map tells you that Detroit is north of Toledo, not that you have to go through Toledo to get to Detroit.)

Finally, much of what I say in this volume reflects my rejection of the notion of a language as being a set of sentences and the notion of 'grammaticality' as a property of sentences in and of themselves. Accordingly, I am interested in identifying factors that affect the interpretation and acceptability of sentences but have no interest at all in classifying those factors as grammatical or extra-grammatical. For me the question of whether an odd-sounding sentence is 'grammatical' or not is a question not about the language but about the linguist who asks the question, in the sense that his answer tells me something about his conception of linguistics but nothing about the language (cf. McCawley 1976a). I hang my head in shame at seeing how many times I have spoken of sentences as being 'grammatical' or 'ungrammatical' in the review of *SSGG*; in those passages, the reader should take 'un-grammatical' as simply an informal English equivalent for the asterisk, which I use to indicate that the sentence (with an intended interpretation that I hope will always be obvious) possesses the kind of anomaly that I happen to be talking about at that moment.

To the acknowledgements with which the individual papers in this volume are provided, I wish only to add expressions of appreciation to Ray Jackendoff, whose course at the 1980 Linguistic Institute at the University of New Mexico assisted me considerably in identifying and exploring quite a few issues that I take up in the newly added notes, and to Geoff Pullum, who gave me valuable suggestions for the improvement of this introduction, and to voice my gratitude to the many students at the University of Chicago who, through their incisive questions and comments in classes where I have discussed the topics with which I deal here, have helped me to achieve a much better understanding of those topics than I otherwise could have attained.

Notes

1.   Since certain highly literate friends of mine have misinterpreted the title as a reproach to interpretive semanticists for failure to narrow down the set of possible theories sufficiently, I should emphasize that no such suggestion lurks behind my choice of a title. I am rather reproaching interpretive semanticists and generative semanticists alike for failing to recognize issues that ought to have been matters of controversy but so far have not been.

2.   See Lakatos (1970: 180–4) for a clear account of the differences between Popper's actual views and those which are often mistakenly attributed to him.

3.   See Musgrave (1976: 200–2) for the role of the hidden assumption that water is not a combustion product in what for several years was widely held to be a conclusive refutation of oxygen chemistry and confirmation of phlogiston chemistry. Hidden assumptions, as in this case, are often false propositions which are so obviously true that no one bothers to mention them.

4.   See, however, note 17 to Chapter 1, where I argue that the surface constituent structure of nominalizations conflicts with the implications both of Chomsky's non-transformational analysis and of the 'updated Lees' transformational analysis.

5.   'S̄' here is to be understood *de re* rather than *de dicto*: I regard the constituents that are labeled S̄ by X-bar syntacticians as cyclic domains, though I am neutral with regard to whether a category distinction between S and S̄ need be drawn.

6.   Epée (1976) points out that in Duala-dependent questions, a WH-moved expression is put after rather than in place of the complementizer (which in some cases is a morpheme that introduces yes–no questions and in others is the Duala analog of the *that* complementizer) and Wachowicz (1974) observes that in Polish two or more interrogative expressions can occur in a single 'COMP position'. Since in Polish as in English, constituents of dependent questions cannot be relativized or questioned, this shows that Chomsky's (1973: 244–7) putative explanation of the English fact must be rejected: if the reason why such expressions as *the book which Al asked who wrote* are impossible is that successive-cyclic WH-movement would allow them to be derived only via an intermediate stage involving a doubly-filled COMP position, then languages such as Polish that allow multiple WH expressions in COMP position should allow relativization out of dependent questions. Rudin (1981) gives a similar argument based on Bulgarian facts.

7.   This position is argued for in Williams (1974) and is in effect assumed in Montague grammar, as I argue in McCawley (1977b). See Pullum (1976: 97–100) for criticism of Williams's proposal; I regard Pullum's objections as posing a more serious problem for Williams's claim that only 'root' transformations can be post-cyclic than for his proposal that all constituents are cyclic domains.

8.   On this point, see also Pullum (1980b).

1 REVIEW ARTICLE ON NOAM A. CHOMSKY, *STUDIES ON SEMANTICS IN GENERATIVE GRAMMAR* *

1

This volume, henceforth *SSGG*, which reprints three papers[1] written by Chomsky between 1967 and 1970, is concerned with developments in transformational grammar since the appearance of *Aspects of the theory of syntax* in 1965. It takes up a large number of issues on which Chomsky's position has either changed or become more specific since then and contains much criticism of other lines of development in transformational grammar, especially that one which has become known as generative semantics.

A reader of *SSGG* who has read nothing later than *Aspects* may be amazed at the extent to which Chomsky's ideas have changed, but I think it is inevitable that any serious proponent of the *Aspects* theory would rapidly come to give up one or other of the major tenets of that theory. While *Aspects* accepted a distinction between syntactic rules and semantic interpretation rules (henceforth SIRs), it also accepted tenets that made it hard to maintain such a distinction: that only the deepest stage of syntactic derivations was relevant to meaning, and that 'syntax' was to be interpreted so broadly that, for example, selectional restrictions were matters of syntax rather than (or perhaps, in addition to) semantics. In the years immediately following the emergence of the *Aspects* theory, deep structures rapidly got deeper (and closer to what could be taken as constituting semantic structure), until a point was reached where it was reasonable to question the assumption that syntax and semantics are distinct. 'Generative semanticists' such as Postal, Lakoff, Ross, and myself found the syntax/semantics dichotomy the most dispensable of our premises and proceeded to reject it. 'Interpretive semanticists' such as Chomsky and Jackendoff, on the other hand, clung to the distinction between syntax and semantics and rejected some of the premises of the arguments that led to deep structures that approximated semantic structures, notably the assumptions that deep structure determines meaning and that selectional restrictions are a matter of syntax.

Since this dilemma became apparent (about 1967) and linguists began to choose horns, further areas of divergence have arisen. For example, while there was general agreement about the notion of 'grammaticality' in 1967, generative semanticists have come to dispute the notion that one can speak coherently of a string of words (or even a surface phrase-marker) as being grammatical or ungrammatical or having a degree of grammaticality and now hold that a surface structure can be 'grammatical' only relative to the meaning that it is supposed to convey and the (linguistic and extra-linguistic) context in which it is used. Thus, strictly speaking, generative semanticists are not engaged in 'generative grammar'. Chomsky, on the other hand, has greatly expanded the range of sentences which he would call 'grammatical' but semantically unacceptable and thus, while maintaining a notion of grammaticality of sentences, applies it very differently than he did in 1965. The fact that the differences between these two lines of development have been increasing as time passes makes it difficult to be fair in reviewing anything even a couple of years old in which an interpretive semanticist criticizes generative semantics or vice versa: changes in the assumptions on both sides have been rapid, often not explicitly acknowledged, sometimes perhaps unconscious, which renders it impossible to be very sure what X assumed in his 1968 criticism of Y's 1967 paper or what it would have been reasonable for X to assume in 1968 that Y had assumed in 1967. I will not try very hard to be fair, since (for the reason just mentioned) fairness would require going into tiresome detail about ephemeral and insignificant points of history. I will concentrate rather on making clear the issues touched on in this volume or raised by it which, on the basis of all the hindsight now available to me, seem the most important and which are most germane to current controversies. However, I have cast the review in the form of a fairly detailed commentary since I think that it will thereby serve best the interests of readers who wish to give *SSGG* a careful and intensive reading such as it deserves.

2

2.1.

The first paper, 'Remarks on nominalization' (pp. 11-61, henceforth 'Nominalization'), is devoted to arguments that nominalizations[2] do not involve an embedded S but rather have deep structures that differ in only minor ways from their surface structures. Chomsky's proposals cover only action and property nominalizations (*their refusal of my offer*; *John's honesty*); he mentions other kinds of nominalizations such as agent and object nominalizations (*the discoverer of radium*; *Dostoevskii's writings*) only in the process of criticizing proposed transformational analyses of nominalizations. I will comment in §2.2.3 on the importance of this gap in Chomsky's proposals.

'Nominalization' begins with a brief description of Chomsky's conception of a grammar; this part of the paper is noteworthy only for the offhand way in which he refers to 'semantic rules that assign to each paired deep and surface structure generated by the syntax a semantic interpretation' (p. 12) and thus quietly adopts the controversial idea (which plays no role in 'Nominalization' but is central to the other two papers in *SSGG*) of SIRs which refer to surface structure. There then follows some discussion (pp. 13–15) of how one chooses among alternative analyses, in which Chomsky speaks of 'enrichment of one component of the grammar' combined with 'simplification in other parts' and cautions the reader that 'we have no *a priori* insight into the "trading relations" between the various parts'. Significantly, there is no mention of SIRs in this section; indeed, except for a brief passage on p. 56, there is no reference to SIRs in relation to choice among grammars, even though in many cases the alternatives discussed differ radically as to what SIRs they would require. While Chomsky states explicitly that there is no *a priori* basis for preferring a simplification in one component of a grammar over a simplification in another, his practise strongly suggests that he thinks that simplification of syntactic rules must take precedence over simplification of SIRs.

Chomsky illustrates this section with discussion of alternative analyses of *John felt sad*: one which sets up a deep structure involving an embedded sentence (*John felt* [*John be sad*]$_s$), and one in which there is no embedded sentence and *feel* may be followed in deep structure by items of the category 'Pred'.[3] He speaks of the one analysis as 'extend[ing] the transformational component' and the other as 'extend[ing] the base'. However, as far as I can determine, both analyses would involve the same transformations (since he would anyway need Equi-NP-deletion and the copula-deletion observed in *Spiro makes me angry*) and, unless the existence of the rule VP → V Pred which he assumes elsewhere hinges on the analysis of *feel*, the same 'categorial rules' also; the difference between them thus appears to be confined to the lexicon.

2.2.1.

Chomsky now proceeds to contrast Poss-ing complements with nominal-izations and to sketch two classes of analyses of nominalizations which are roughly parallel to the two analyses of *John felt sad*: LEXICALIST analyses, in which there is no embedded S but the base component allows for NPs containing the subject, object, etc. of a corresponding S; and TRANSFORMATIONALIST analyses, in which there is an embedded S whose main verb or predicate adjective provides the source of the surface head noun. Under a 'lexicalist' position, the relationship between the nominalization and any related sentence is relegated to the lexicon, for example, there is a single dictionary entry for the verb *refuse* and the noun *refusal*, with a single statement of what can be the subject, the object, etc. Chomsky states that

> In the earliest work on transformational grammar (cf. Lees (1960)), the correctness of the transformationalist position was taken for granted; and in fact, there was really no alternative as the theory of grammar was formulated at the time. However, the extension of grammatical theory to incorporate syntactic features (as in Chomsky (1965, chapter 2)) permits a formulation of the lexicalist position, and therefore raises the issue of choice between the alternatives. (p. 17)

As far as I can see, however, a lexicalist analysis was just as easily formulable in the theory of *Syntactic structures* as in that of *Aspects*: as long as the theory allows subscripted curly brackets, it allows rules such as[4]

$$(1) \quad \begin{Bmatrix} V \\ N \end{Bmatrix}_1 \rightarrow \textit{refuse} \begin{Bmatrix} \phi \\ \textit{-al} \end{Bmatrix}_1 \text{ /NP\_NP}$$

Chomsky now takes up three classes of differences between nominalizations and Poss-ing complements: PRODUCTIVITY — essentially every declarative clause has a corresponding Poss-ing complement, whereas there are heavy restrictions, both systematic and idiosyncratic, on what nominalizations exist; SEMANTIC REGULARITY — the meaning of a Poss-ing complement is that of the corresponding clause, whereas the meanings of nominalizations are related to those of corresponding clauses in highly idiosyncratic ways; and INTERNAL STRUCTURE — nominalizations have the constituent structure of ordinary NPs and allow articles, quantifiers, the plural morpheme, and prenominal adjectives, whereas Poss-ing complements allow none of these.

In discussing productivity, Chomsky states that transformationally derived structures can occur as Poss-ing complements but cannot serve as the basis for nominalizations.[5] He contrasts (2-3), which involve Tough-movement, Subject-raising, and Predicate-raising or something such, with (4-5):

(2) (a)   John's being easy to please
     (b)   John's being certain to win the prize
     (c)   John's amusing the children with his antics
(3) (a)   *John's easiness/ease to please
     (b)   *John's certainty to win the prize
     (c)   *John's amusement of the children with his stories
(4) (a)   John's being eager to please
     (b)   John's being certain that Bill will win the prize
     (c)   John's being amused at the children's antics
(5) (a)   John's eagerness to please
     (b)   John's certainty that Bill will win the prize
     (c)   John's amusement at the children's antics

The lexicalist hypothesis correctly predicts the ungrammaticality of (3): if nominalizations do not contain an embedded S, then the structure to which Tough-movement, Subject-raising, or Predicate-raising would apply is not present and their application in (3) would not be possible. Moreover, under a transformationalist analysis, unless the nominalization rule(s) (that is, the rules which move the verb or adjective out of the embedded sentence and make it the head N of the NP) are precyclic,[6] the rules of the cycle would be applicable to the embedded sentence before the nominalization rules destroyed that sentence, and thus nominalizations of sentences derived by cyclic transformations (thus, all the examples in (3)) ought to be possible.

This would yield an excellent argument for the lexicalist hypothesis if it could be combined with a demonstration that the lexicalist hypothesis also implies that (5) are grammatical. However, the lexicalist hypothesis evidently implies that (5a) should be ungrammatical, since (5a) involves an application of Equi-NP-deletion.[7] The facts thus appear to conflict with both hypotheses: the lexicalist hypothesis implies that all nominalizations of structures derived by cyclic rules are ungrammatical; the transformationalist hypothesis implies that they are all grammatical; but in reality some of them are grammatical and some ungrammatical. Thus, either hypothesis can be salvaged only by supplementing it by some principle that correctly predicts *which* transformationally derived structures have nominalizations.

Chomsky in fact proposes later in 'Nominalization' a descriptive device which allows him to formulate his rules so that they imply that (3) are all ungrammatical and (5) all grammatical. Specifically, he allows rules to differ with regard to whether they apply just to Ss or to both Ss and NPs. For example, he divides passivization into two operations:

'Agent-postposing', which moves a subject NP into the 'empty' NP position in [*by* Δ], and a rule moving the first NP following the verb into subject position. He holds Agent-postposing to be applicable both in Ss and in such NPs as *the destruction of the city by the enemy* and suggests that the second component of passivization may be identifiable with the 'NP-preposing' which converts *the picture of John's* into *John's picture*. Thus, for Chomsky *the city's destruction by the enemy* is not a nominalization of a passive but rather a nominalization in which at least one (and perhaps both) of the components of passivization have applied TO THE NP. While he discusses no other examples in 'Nominalization' of transformations which apply to both Ss and NPs, it is clear that he could so formulate Equi-NP-deletion and thus have his rules imply that (5a) is grammatical, and that is in fact what he proposes later in the book (footnote 34 of 'Some empirical issues . . .'). A similar formulation could be given to reflexivization, and his rules would correctly imply that (6) was grammatical.

(6)   Vassily's denunciation of himself

It should be emphasized, however, that it is then the rules and not the lexicalist hypothesis that have these implications. If transformations are allowed to differ freely as to whether they apply just to Ss or to both Ss and NPs, then there is nothing in principle to prevent Tough-movement, Subject-raising, or Predicate-raising from applying to NPs as well as to Ss and thus any or all of (3) being grammatical. Thus, unless some constraints are placed on the possibility of a transformation having both S and NP as its domain, the lexicalist hypothesis has no implications about the grammaticality of (3).

The only way I can see for Chomsky to get his theory to have the implications about (3) and (5) that he says it has is for him to (i) reject his analysis of *the city's destruction by the enemy* and (ii) either reject Reflexivization and Equi-NP-deletion as transformations (that is, allow deep structures containing reflexive pronouns and subjectless infinitives and treat the anomaly of **Himself loves me* and **Max believes to be a criminal* as corresponding to failure of obligatory SIRs to apply and/or violation of output constraints; Chomsky (1973) in fact eventually embraces that position) or exclude the possibility of *movement* transformations that apply to both NPs and Ss: it appears that the cyclic transformations whose outputs do not correspond to nominalizations are the movement transformations;[8] or at least, that is the case if one rejects Chomsky's analysis of *the city's destruction by the enemy*.

2.2.2

Let me at this point digress into the analysis of passives which Chomsky proposes in 'Nominalizations'. The NP phenomenon and the S phenomenon which Chomsky says may be combinable in a single rule of NP-preposing have little in common. Ss allow a 'stranded preposition' but (as observed by Lees (1960: 67)) NPs do not:

(7) (a)   John was approved of by the director.
    (a$'$)   *John's approval of by the director
    (b)   The proposal was agreed to by their lawyer.
    (b$'$)   *The proposal's agreement to by their lawyer

Moreover, as Postal (personal communication) has pointed out, (7a$'$, b$'$) cannot be ruled out by an output constraint, since there are relatively acceptable NPs of the same surface shape, for example, (8) is far more acceptable than are (7a$'$, b$'$):

(8)   The only person who I bought pictures of by Max is Tony.

The composite rule would thus require a formulation such as (9), in which two rules are combined that have no more resemblance to each other than either has to Dative-movement.

$$
(9) \quad \left\{ \begin{array}{ccc} \# & \phi & V \\ & the & N \end{array} \ (\text{Prep}) \right\} \quad NP
$$

1	2	3	4	5
→1	5	3	4	ϕ

Chomsky's Agent-postposing rule involves the [by Δ] $_{\text{Manner}}$ of *Aspects*. It is open not only to the many objections raised by, for example, Lakoff (1965) but also to the further objection that nominalizations do not allow manner adverbs at all.

(10)   *The enemy's destruction of the city ruthlessly.

The *raison d'être* of Chomsky's uniform Agent-postposing rule is evidently that it allows one to maintain that all *by*-phrases containing the underlying subject arise the same way. An alternative would be to propose (following Lakoff, Postal, and Fillmore) that *by* is present in subject NPs in both active and passive clauses, that the whole subject prepositional phrase is moved in passivization, and that prepositions that remain in subject position are eventually deleted. I can see no grounds for believing that the *by* of *the destruction of the city by the enemy* has anything to do with passivization or any component of passivization.[9]

2.2.3

Before I take up Chomsky's other two classes of arguments for a lexicalist treatment of nominalizations and against a transformationalist treatment, I should say a word about the diversity of the analyses that the word 'transformationalist' covers. The term covers both analyses in which the deep structure of the nominalization consists of just the embedded sentence and analyses in which it consists of the embedded sentence plus other material. The analyses of Lees (1960), if altered so as to bring them into conformity with the *Aspects* theory, are of the latter type: Lees's matrix sentence contributed a determiner and optionally a plural morpheme and/or relative clauses to the nominalization, which means that the most natural way of recasting his analyses into the *Aspects* framework is to set up a deep structure in which the sentence to be nominalized is part of a 'full' NP, say, a relative clause modifying an 'abstract' head noun, which may be accompanied by any of the other matter that can appear in the deep structure of a NP. The one other extensive transformationalist treatment of nominalizations prior to the writing of 'Nominalization', that of Lakoff (1965), does not make really explicit what is supposed to underlie nominalizations, though it gives informal expressions such as '*those whom we imprisoned* ⇒ *our prisoners*', which also suggest a deep structure in which the sentence to be nominalized is a relative clause, with a determiner and a noun also present.

The nominalization transformations discussed by Lees and Lakoff were POSTLEXICAL, that is they applied to structures whose terminal elements were morphemes of the language in question rather than some kind of semantic units. The possibility of prelexical transformations was raised in Gruber (1965), and in McCawley (1968a) I proposed that the facts discussed by Lakoff are more naturally accounted for by treating the nominalization transformation(s) as prelexical than by invoking Lakoff's exception features and postlexical transformations. Lakoff had noted that there are both verbs which idiosyncratically lack some nominalization and NPs which behave in every other respect like nominalizations except that there is no corresponding verb or adjective for them to be nominalizations of:

(11) (a)   He killed Schwartz.
      (a′)   Schwartz's killer
      (b)   He threatened Schwartz.
      (b′)   *Schwartz's threatener
(12) (a)   John transgressed against the law.
      (a′)   John's transgression against the law
      (b)   *China aggressed against India.
      (b′)   China's aggression against India

He treated *threaten* as irregularly not allowing the Agent-nominalization transformation and *aggress* as irregularly requiring that either the Agent-nominalization transformation (yielding *aggressor*) or the action nominalization transformation apply to it. I proposed that irregular paradigms such as (11) and (12) correspond rather to sporadic gaps in the lexicon (for example, there is a word meaning 'act of initiating conflict' but no related word meaning 'initiate conflict'), that there is a single nominalization transformation (which raises the embedded predicate of NP 'x such that $f(x)$' into head noun position of that NP, adding to it some mark of what the role of the x was in $f(x)$), that that transformation is prelexical and applies without restriction, that ungrammatical structures such as (11b′) and (12b) are simply those which call for a word that does not occur in the dictionary, and that the relation between, for example, *kill* and *killer* is expressed in a complex dictionary entry which lists *-er* as the realization of the agent nominalization marker when it is combined with *kill* (*threaten*, by contrast, does not allow any realization of that marker, not even zero realization).[10]

Chomsky's discussion of his second major argument for a lexicalist treatment of nominalizations and against a transformationalist treatment is of necessity somewhat vague, since it deals with details of the relationship between nominalizations and their meanings and none of the existing transformationalist treatments had had much to say on that topic. He gives a list of 14 verb-related nouns and simply says that they have 'their individual ranges of meaning and varied semantic relations to the base forms' and concludes that 'To accommodate these facts within the transformational approach (assuming, as above that it is the grammatical relations in the deep structure that determine meaning) it is necessary to resort to the artifice of assigning a range of meanings to the base form, stipulating that with certain semantic features the form must nominalize and with others it cannot' (p. 19). The kind of treatment that Chomsky objects to here is objectionable for precisely the same reason that his own treatment is: each contributes nothing towards an understanding of the question of what nominalizations are possible (though perhaps accidentally non-occurring) and what relationships between a nominalization and its meaning are possible. Either treatment says that the relationship between nominalizations and their meanings is pure chaos. Perhaps nothing is really systematic, as Chomsky seems to suggest; however, it takes more to establish that than a list of 14 words and a comment that their meanings are wildly diverse.[11]

Chomsky's terms 'lexicalist' and 'transformationalist' set up a false dichotomy, though one which is inherent in his assumption that all syntax is postlexical. The one thing about nominalizations which virtually all generative grammarians are agreed on is that the morphemic makeup and semantic content of nominalizations must be listed in their lexicon of a grammar. That conclusion, however, does not imply that in the relationship between nominalizations and their meanings all hell breaks loose. By rejecting Chomsky's dichotomy, it is possible to avoid treating the relationship of words (including nominalizations) to their meanings as totally idiosyncratic. Each language has certain prelexical transformations (see McCawley (1971a) for evidence that they can differ from one language to another), and rather than all logically conceivable combinations of semantic material being candidates for inclusion in a dictionary, only those which can arise from well-formed semantic structures through the application of those rules would be possible; any combination of semantic material which could so arise would correspond to a 'possible lexical item', and an analysis of nominalizations would be required not merely to provide dictionary entries for all existing nominalizations but to correctly predict which non-occurring ones are accidentally excluded and which ones systematically excluded. One big advantage of such a treatment over any 'lexicalist' treatment is that it would explain the absence of a subject NP in agent nominalizations and of an object NP in object nominalizations: *The inventor of dynamite* (**by Nobel*); *Newton's writings* (**of treatises*) *on theology*. The only kinds of nominalizations which Chomsky explicitly discusses are action and property nominalizations, which normally take exactly the same NPs as do corresponding verbs or adjectives and for which a single dictionary entry giving the nominalization and the related verb or adjective, with a single statement of selectional and strict subcategorization properties, has at least some plausibility. It would take great ingenuity in the employment of curly and angular brackets (though nothing in the way of linguistic insight) to combine action, agent, and object nominalizations and a related verb into a single dictionary entry that gives the strict subcategorization properties of all. By contrast, a treatment involving a prelexical nominalization rule could explain the absence of various NPs by setting up underlying structures in which the missing NP corresponds to a bound variable, for example, 'event x such that (Newton write$_x$ a treatise on theology)', 'person x such that (x invent dynamite)', 'work x on theology such that (Newton write x)': the bound variable rules out the possibility of *Nobel, treatise*, etc. filling the position in question.

A long footnote to this section of 'Nominalization' contains the only passage in which Chomsky explicitly discusses transformationalist analyses in which more than just an embedded S underlies the nominalization. He finds the proposal that *John's intelligence* is derived from the same underlying structure as *The fact that John is intelligent* or *The extent to which John is intelligent* dubious for the following reasons: (i) 'It is difficult to find a natural source for the nominal . . . in such sentences as *John's intelligence is his most remarkable quality*'; (ii) 'we can say *John's intelligence, which is his most remarkable quality, exceeds his foresight*; but the appositive clause, on this analysis, would have to derive from **the extent to which John is intelligent is his most remarkable quality*' (p. 20). Since the example in (i) allows the paraphrase 'That John is as intelligent as he is is his most remarkable quality', the structure underlying *That John is as intelligent as he is* would be the obvious source to propose for this sense of *John's intelligence*. The deletion which such a source would make necessary is independently required, as observed by Elliott (1971: 53) and Kuroda (1970:386) in their discussion of sentences like:

(13) (a) It's appalling what I have to put up with. (= . . . that I have to put up with what I have to put up with)

(b) You'll never believe who Susan is going to marry. (= . . . that Susan is going to marry who she's going to marry)[12]

(c) Jones annoyed me by the abrupt manner in which he left. (= . . . by leaving in the abrupt manner in which he left)

(d) I surprised John by the degree to which I understood astronomy. (= by understanding astronomy to the degree to which I understand it)

See McCawley (1975a) for further instances of this kind of deletion, which I have dubbed TELESCOPING. Actually, to me Chomsky's asterisked example *The extent to which John is intelligent is his most remarkable quality* is grammatical and an instance of Telescoping. Regarding (ii), I dispute Chomsky's data. I find that his example displays an oddness which is absent if the roles of main clause and appositive clause are reversed:

(14) (a) John's intelligence, which exceeds his foresight, is his most remarkable quality.

  (b) ?John's intelligence, which is his most remarkable quality, exceeds his foresight. (Chomsky's example)

This difference runs systematically through the examples that Elliott and I have analysed as involving Telescoping:

(15) (a) Frank's height, which is 6′ 8″, amazes me.
  (b) ?Frank's height, which amazes me, is 6′ 8″.
(16) (a) McGovern criticized Nixon for what he had said, which is that we should invade Bolivia.
  (b) ?What Nixon said, which McGovern criticized him for, is that we should invade Bolivia.
(17) (a) Schwartz criticized *Tropic of Cancer* for its length, which is 287 pages.
  (b) ?The length of *Tropic of Cancer*, which Schwartz criticized it for, is 287 pages.
  (b′) ?The length of *Tropic of Cancer*, for which Schwartz criticized it, is 287 pages.

Chomsky's lexicalist analysis of nominalizations provides no clue as to why there should be any difference in grammaticality between the (a)-examples and the (b)-examples. However, a treatment along the lines which I have suggested does. The source that I would need for *John's intelligence is his most remarkable quality* in fact allows insertion of the appositive clause:

(18) That the degree to which John is intelligent, which exceeds the degree to which he has foresight, is as great as it is is his most remarkable quality.

On the other hand, the structure underlying *John's intelligence exceeds his foresight* would not accommodate an appositive clause formed out of 'That the degree to which John is intelligent is as great as it is is his most remarkable quality'. Thus, provided that the presence of the appositive clause does not inhibit Telescoping, which I admit has not yet been demonstrated, the hypothesis that *John's intelligence* has (at least) two underlying structures, one a degree expression and the other a proposition containing that degree expression, implies that clauses with the degree interpretation of the nominalization may modify occurrences of the nominalization with the factive-degree interpretation, but not vice versa.

Chomsky's third class of arguments for a lexicalist treatment of nominalizations and against a transformationalist treatment in fact provide only an argument against a transformationalist treatment in which the deep structure of the nominalization consists of nothing but the embedded sentence. Chomsky states that 'It is difficult to see how a transformational approach to derived nominals can account for the fact that the structures in which they appear as well as their internal structure and, often, morphological properties are those of ordinary noun phrases' (p. 21). However, the most obvious recasting of Lees's treatment of nominalizations into the *Aspects* framework implies that nominalizations will have exactly the properties that Chomsky mentions, that is, the deep structure can have all the material that NPs ordinarily allow, and the nominalization transformation simply adjoins the verb of the embedded sentence to the 'abstract' head noun of the NP, leaving the determiner, etc. of the NP undisturbed and leaving the NPs of the embedded sentence as postadjuncts to the derived head noun.

Actually, only a transformationalist analysis of nominalizations can provide an explanation (as opposed to just a description, which either kind of treatment permits) of the occurrence of articles, etc. in nominalizations. Under the treatment of nouns presented in Bach (1968), all non-predicate nouns originate in the predicate position of relative clauses, for example, *the anthropologist* is derived from *the x [x is an anthropologist]*$_s$. In this case, ALL non-predicate NPs are nominalizations: the predicate element of the relative clause is put into head-noun position of the NP by what appears to be the same operation as nominalization. The NPs in which the nominalization transformation applies appear to be those which have a referential index, as opposed to those which consist simply of a proposition. Nominalizations denote persons, objects, events, 'extents', etc., whereas Poss-ing complements do not. (NB: the distinction must be drawn between a nominalization denoting an event and a Poss-ing complement denoting the proposition that such an event has occurred.) Whatever analysis of articles and quantifiers one adopts, if the rules that create and/or move them are sensitive to the presence of referential indices, they will be applicable to both nominalizations and 'ordinary' NPs but not to complements.[13]

2.3.1

Chomsky devotes the remainder of 'Nominalization' (pp. 21 ff.) to a relatively unstructured exposition of his lexicalist proposal, combined with numerous objections to transformationalist treatments of the phenomena in question. The most central topic of this part of 'Nominalizations' is the base rules which he proposes. After a couple of preliminary statements and revisions, he arrives at the following rules:

(19) $S \rightarrow \bar{\bar{N}}\bar{\bar{V}}$

   $\bar{\bar{X}} \rightarrow [Spec, \bar{X}] \bar{X}$

   $\bar{X} \rightarrow X \ldots$

   $[Spec, \bar{N}] \rightarrow$ (Prearticle *of*) Article (Postarticle)

   Article $\rightarrow [\pm def, (\bar{\bar{N}})]$

where X is a variable ranging over the set $\{N, Adj, V\}$ and the dots are to be filled in by some formula such as $(\bar{N})$ $(PP)_0$ (S). The single and double bars in these formulas are, as Chomsky notes, reminiscent of the superscripts that appeared in Harris (1946). The square brackets are taken as enclosing (unordered) sets of feature specifications; Chomsky rejects (p.48) the distinction accepted in *Aspects* between 'category' and 'feature' (which he says 'had a certain technical artificiality') and takes all node labels to be complexes of feature specifications. 'Nominalizations' thus calls for proliferation of the already (since *Aspects*) ubiquitous syntactic features; however, it presents even less evidence for feature representations than did *Aspects*, which itself contained remarkably little.[14] 'Spec(ifier)' refers to determiners in the case of $\bar{N}$, auxiliaries in the case of $\bar{V}$, and degree expressions in the case of $\bar{A}$, Chomsky does not indicate here that the various kinds of 'Specifier' have anything more in common than that in English they precede what they are combined with. They do not have even that in common in Japanese, where auxiliaries follow main verbs and determiners precede nouns, or in Swahili and Malay, where auxiliaries precede main verbs and determiners follow nouns.[15] Later in *SSGG* (§ 6.5.3 of 'Some empirical issues'), Chomsky refers the reader to unpublished papers by Bowers and Selkirk for discussion of 'syntactic relations between qualifiers of adjectives and determiners of nouns' (that is of [Spec, $\bar{A}$] and [Spec, $\bar{N}$]) and remarks that 'There are also certain semantic similarities among specifiers. For example, the generic–specific property of sentences is partially determined by choice of determiners and verbal auxiliaries (specifiers of nouns and verbs, respectively, in this framework), and it has often been noted that tense systems share certain of the referential functions of determiners'. The first point is not a similarity: one would not say that main verbs are similar to the plural inflection of nouns just because both are involved in determining the aspect of the clause (cf. Vendler 1957). None of Chomsky's vague allusions to similarities between different kinds of 'specifier' mentions any rule which would treat the three kinds of specifier alike; it would surprise me if there is such a rule. Chomsky appears to have committed himself to a syntactic category which plays no role in syntax.[16]

The rule for Article in (19) deserves some comment. According to Chomsky's notation, the rule means that 'Article' consists of a feature specification [+ def] or [− def] either by itself or attached to a $\bar{\bar{N}}$ node. In the examples discussed by Chomsky, however, this feature specification is not the definiteness of the NP but is indeed independent of the definiteness of the NP. For example, he takes *A proof by John of the theorem* as having both *John* (which is 'definite') and [− def] in article position. The 'Agent-postposing' rule shifts the NP but leaves the extra [± def] behind to be realized as an article. What Chomsky is adopting here thus amounts to the proposal of Emonds (1970) that in underlying structure there can be 'doubly filled' positions. The only alternative to this position which Chomsky even considers is one in which all possessives (including subjects of nominalizations) originate in relative clauses with the verb *have*, for example, **the invasion of Egypt which Israel had*. While Chomsky is right to dismiss that specific proposal as absurd, it was an oversight for him to ignore variants of this proposal in which a more plausible verb is deleted, for example, *the invasion of Egypt which Israel carried out*; see Postal (MS) for arguments in support of such an analysis. More importantly, Chomsky does not even mention the possibility that in deep structure the subject of a nominalization might FOLLOW it (that is the possibility that *the attempt by Nixon to silence the press* may be more basic than *Nixon's attempt to silence the press*), which would render 'double filling' unnecessary. There is an obvious reason why Chomsky would not like that proposal, namely that if he accepted it, the only way he could say that clauses and NPs have parallel deep structures, which is basic to his lexicalist position, would be to postulate deep structures with verb-initial order, which I gather he is not willing to do.[17] However, setting up deep structures with 'doubly filled positions' is such a sharp departure from previous assumptions in transformational grammar that I am amazed that Chomsky should adopt it without even a word of comment: this is a sufficiently important matter that it deserves explicit statement of what revisions Chomsky is making in his theory, what the alternatives are, and why he makes the specific choice among the alternatives that he does (that is, why he would rather allow 'doubly filled positions' in deep structure than either accept deep verb-initial word order for English or accept deep structures in which NPs and clauses are not 'parallel').[18]

Actually, Chomsky's proposed deep structures of NPs and of clauses are not 'parallel': the following pair of trees, of which he says that 'The internal structure of the nominal . . . mirrors that of the sentence' (p.53), fail to match in anything other than what is under the $\bar{\bar{N}}$ and $\bar{\bar{V}}$ nodes.

(20)　(a)

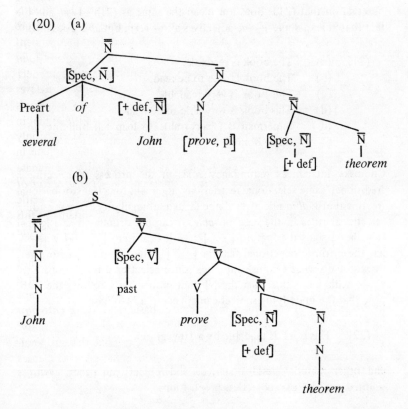

(b)

Chomsky is inconsistent as to what it is that NPs are supposed to be parallel to: he speaks in many places of parallelism between Ss and NPs but gives phrase structure rules in which NP and VP are treated alike and differently from S.[19]

2.3.2

Aside from the phrase structure rules, the only part of a lexicalist grammar which Chomsky discusses in any detail is redundancy rules; remarkably, virtually no details of the lexicon are discussed and no examples of dictionary entries are given. Chomsky presents an analysis of *readable, expendable*, etc. in terms of redundancy rules, after arguing against deriving sentences containing them from structures with an embedded sentence whose verb is *read, expend,* etc. (pp. 55-7). His arguments are actually directed against one specific such analysis: that *V-able* has the same source as *able to be V-ed*, and I completely agree with him that such a derivation is not generally possible; to Chomsky's observation that (21a) does not mean the same as (21b), I can add the fact that at least some *V-able* adjectives allow *very*, but *able* does not:[20]

(21)   (a)   The book is readable.

       (b)   ?The book is able to be read.

       (c)   This book is very readable.

       (d)   *This book is very able to be read.

      (d')   Superman is (*very) able to leap tall buildings in a single bound.

Chomsky introduces redundancy rules in the process of rejecting a traditional 'same selectional restrictions' argument for a transformational treatment of *V-able* adjectives: 'in so far as a subregularity exists regarding selectional rules in the case of *-able*, it can be formulated as a lexical rule that assigns the feature [X _] to a lexical item [V-*able*] where V has the intrinsic selectional feature [_ X]'. This rule-schema, however, does not do what Chomsky intends, since selectional restrictions have to do with more than just the NP that immediately follows the verb; note that the underlying subject can appear in a *by*-phrase:

(22)   This book is readable by a 10-year-old.

and other material besides 'subject' and 'object' can occur, even (as pointed out by Ross) objectless prepositions:

(23)   (a)   Linguistics papers are mailable in plain brown envelopes.
       (b)   Blowouts are avoidable only by changing the tires periodically.[21]
       (c)   The existence of stranded prepositions is not accountable for under Schwartz's assumptions.

The metarule would thus have to be along the lines of 'if V has the selectional feature $[X \_ Y Z]$ or $[X \_ W Y Z]$, where X and Y are single NP matrices and W is a preposition matrix, then *V-able* has the selectional feature $[Y \_ Z (by X)]$ or $[Y \_ W Y Z (by X)]$ respectively'. Such a redundancy rule resembles a transformation, a transformation not in the sense of Chomsky but of Harris: a statement that if a deep structure (for Harris, a surface structure) of such-and-such form is well-formed, then so is the corresponding one of the form so-and-so. It is important to note that these rules are not transformations in Chomsky's sense, since the implicans and implicatum are both deep structures; as Chomsky notes, the existence of a derived structure *Bill believes John to have left* does not imply that **John is believable to have left* is possible. Chomsky would have to modify his base rules, incidentally, to allow adjectives to be followed by objectless prepositions, as in (23c), which diminishes the parallelism he sees between the base rules for N, V, and A.

Chomsky's second example of redundancy rules appears in his discussion of (24), which he indicates (p. 59) demands a lexicalist treatment, so that he must take *NP grows tomatoes* to be a base form and reject his earlier claim that (25a) has an underlying structure representable as (25b):[22]

(24)   the growing of tomatoes
(25)   (a)   John grows tomatoes.
       (b)   John [+ cause] [tomatoes grow]$_s$.

Chomsky proposes that the relationship between *John grows tomatoes* and *Tomatoes grow* should be expressed by 'redundancy rules which are, in this case, universal, hence not part of the grammar of English but rather among the principles by which any grammar is interpreted. These principles specify that an intransitive verb with the feature [+ cause] *becomes* transitive and that its selectional features are systematically revised so that the *former* subject *becomes* the object' (p. 59, emphasis added). There is clearly an inconsistency here, since a redundancy rule cannot make an intransitive verb become transitive.

I gather that what he means is that verbs such as transitive *grow* have dictionary entries that contain the feature [+ cause] but no selectional features relating to the object, and that for every selectional feature [X _] of the corresponding intransitive verb, the feature [_ X] is added to the dictionary entry of the transitive verb. One technical problem connected with this which Chomsky does not mention is that of how to tell what the 'corresponding' intransitive verb is, for example, to tell that causative *sink* corresponds to '(of a marine craft) go to the bottom of a fluid body by the force of gravity' and not to 'descend':

(26)   (a)   They sank the submarine.
        (b)   *They sank Bill's head.

It appears that the dictionary entry for the causative verb must be 'tied' to the dictionary entry of the appropriate sense of the intransitive verb. This, incidentally, presents less of a problem for an analysis which postulates an embedded sentence with the intransitive verb: no transfer of selectional features is needed, sentences with the transitive verb would involve an application of Predicate-raising which adjoins the embedded intransitive verb to the verb of causation of the main clause, and the dictionary entry of (each sense of) the intransitive verb can indicate whether it allows the verb of causation to have a realization (even by zero) and if so, what; if none, then the derivation can not yield any possible surface structure.

It is unfortunate that in these two analyses involving redundancy rules Chomsky did not expand on his conception of the role of redundancy rules in grammar. In both cases he does things with redundancy rules which were not done in his previous works. Chomsky's expanded conception of the role of redundancy rules obviously opens up the possibility of many analyses in which redundancy rules do the work that had previously been done by a transformation.[23]

2.4

I will devote the rest of my review of 'Nominalization' to miscellaneous things in its second part which are worthy of comment.

2.4.1

In his discussion of a supposed counterexample to his claims (pp. 27-9), Chomsky proposes an extension of linguistic theory which, while he does not either make it very explicit or give it adequate justification, has since proved to be necessary to make sense of certain phenomena

(Hankamer 1972, Cole 1974), namely 'analogical rules'. He claims that (27) is ungrammatical for all speakers but that some speakers allow it as an analogical variant of something grammatical (he suggests that it is formed on analogy with the Poss-ing complement *his criticizing the book before he read it*):

(27)   his criticism of the book before he read it

Specifically, Chomsky points out that speakers who accept (27) do not accept it in the following combinations:

(28)   (a)   *His criticism of the book before he read it is to be found on p. 15.
       (b)   *I studied his criticism of the book before he read it carefully. [*carefully* here is to modify *study*, not *read*]

I suspect that what he wanted to say is that 'speakers who accept (27)' accept it only in a context where a Poss-ing complement would be possible, but he neglected to state what sentences 'speakers who accept (27)' accept. Whether the generalization that I take it he intended constitutes an argument for an analogical rule depends on whether Chomsky's framework allows a transformation that turns a Poss-ing complement into the corresponding nominalization: if such a rule is possible, then there is no need to have an analogical rule. Chomsky's remarkable willingness to accept a significant theoretical innovation ('analogical rules' are really a kind of 'transderivational constraint', in the sense of Lakoff (1973)) in a case where he probably did not really need it may be the result of his attitude towards the data: he considers (27) to be only 'pseudo-grammatical' and indeed speaks of 'failure [on the part of speakers who accept (27)] to take note of a certain distinction of grammaticalness'. His attitude appears to be that theoretical innovations need no particular justification if they can be relegated to 'performance'. It should be noted, though, that the phenomena that led Hankamer and Cole to propose analogical rules are by no means matters of 'performance.'[24]

2.4.2

Chomsky touches on arguments that have been given or could be offered for underlying identity of various categories, for example, Lakoff's (1965) arguments that verbs and adjectives belong to a single underlying category, and Bach's (1968) arguments that that category also encompasses nouns. His discussion suggests that he does not appreciate what the real issues are.[25] On p. 31 he says that rule-exception features such as figure in Lakoff's arguments

> could be used to establish, say, that all verbs are derived from under-lying prepositions. If one wishes to pursue this line of reasoning, he might begin with the traditional view that all verbs contain the copula, then arguing that *John visited England* . . . is of the same form as *John is in England*, where *visit* is a preposition of the category of *in* that obligatorily transforms to a verb incorporating the copula. Thus we are left with only one 'relational' category, prepositions.

All serious arguments about categories have been concerned with pin-pointing the differences between superficially different categories and have generally made the Occamesque assumption that categories should be made no more different than they have to be. Lakoff and Bach argued that there is no need to postulate any difference between Verb, Adjective, and Noun as regards what deep-structure configurations they can appear in (that is, they can all be taken as in the 'predicate' position of a clause which has one to three NPs, each supplied with a preposition) and that the differences between them can be attributed largely to a small number of rules which one of the categories undergoes or fails to undergo, for example, verbs are not subject to copula-insertion but adjectives and nouns are; nouns are subject to the nominalization rule which lifts them out of a relative clause to become head of a NP. If a deep category difference need not be drawn, it is largely a matter of taste what one calls the resulting category. When Chomsky labels the conclusion of his parody of Lakoff an 'absurdity', he appears to be concerned with terminology (that the category containing verbs is called 'Preposition') rather than with the substance of the conclusion (that verbs and pre-positions combine into deep structures in the same way).[26] I find it amusing that Chomsky then presents some of the same facts with which Bach had argued that V, Adj, and N belong to a single deep category[27] as part of a *reductio ad absurdum* argument which he prefaces with the words, 'The argument based on distributional similarities of verbs and adjectives collapses when we recognize that nouns share the same distributional properties' (p. 34).

2.4.3

Chomsky gives a long list of NPs (pp. 30–1) which he considers to be evidence that NPs can contain roughly the same combinations of prepositional phrases, sentential complements, etc. which occur in VPs and which he thus takes as supporting the third of the phrase structure rules (19). These NPs are relevant to the controversy about what the right phrase structure rules are to the extent that they allow or resist analyses in which the noun corresponds to the predicate element of a clause, and the prepositional phrases, etc. to the other constituents of that clause (for example, the analysis of *The author of "Scorched earlobes"* as a nominalization of *x authed "Scorched earlobes"*, with a hypothetical verb **auth*; the analysis of *Marcia is the sister of my oboe teacher* as having an underlying structure in which *sister* is in the position of a transitive verb, *my oboe teacher* is in object position, and some rule adjoins the object NP to the predicate). Chomsky has done an excellent job of compiling a corpus of NPs for which it is hard to come up with or defend such analyses. I hope that generative semanticists will devote more attention than we have so far to exploring the semantic structure of these examples and determining whether there are viable alternatives to treating *a war of aggression against France*; *John's advantage over his rivals*; etc., as having deep structures that are virtually the same as their surface structures, as Chomsky proposes. I admit that I have not gotten very far in analyzing them.

Chomsky provides very little commentary on his corpus of NPs, confining himself to brief statements of why he finds the proposal of **auth* unconvincing and why he rejects certain analyses involving reduced relative clauses. He says that 'the plausibility of [Lakoff's approach to *author*] diminishes when one recognizes that there is no more reason to give this analysis for [*the author of the book*] than there is for *the general secretary of the party, the assistant vice-chancellor of the university,* and similarly for every function that can be characterized by a nominal phrase' (p. 32). These expressions are not as parallel as Chomsky indicates:[28]

(29)   (a)   Benedict Arnold College has an excellent assistant vice-chancellor.

       (a')   **Scorched earlobes* has an excellent author.

       (b)   Benedict Arnold College has an assistant vice-chancellor who plays the mandolin.

       (b')   **Scorched earlobes* has an author who plays the mandolin.

       (c)   How long was he the assistant vice-chancellor of Benedict Arnold College?

       (c')   **How long was he the author of Scorched earlobes?*

The differences would be partially explained by setting up underlying structures with embedded sentences that differ aspectually: *author* involving an embedded 'accomplishment' clause (in the sense of Vendler (1957), and *assistant vice-chancellor* a 'state' clause.

Chomsky considers the (implausible) proposal that (30) are derived from underlying structures involving relative clauses based on (31) and argues that there is more reason instead to derive (31) from structures that contain the NPs (30):[29]

(30) (a)   the question whether John should leave
     (b)   the prospects for peace
     (c)   the excuse that John had left
(31) (a)   The question is whether John should leave.
     (b)   The prospects are for peace.
     (c)   The excuse was that John had left.

However, the analysis which he proposes for (31) creates more problems than it supposedly solves. He sets up the same sort of underlying structure for (31) as he does for cleft sentences: there is a 'dummy' predicate element Δ and a rule that replaces Δ by a constituent of the subject NP, that is (31b) arises from *The prospects for peace be* Δ by replacement of Δ with *for peace*. But this proposal would leave no way to derive (32a, b), since there are no NPs such as (32a', b'):

(32) (a)   The question under discussion is whether John should leave.
     (a')   *The question under discussion whether John should leave
     (b)   Bill's only excuse was that he was tired.
     (b')   *Bill's only excuse that he was tired

It also creates serious problems for integrating linguistic description with an analysis of reference and presupposition: (30a) presupposes that what is at issue is whether John should leave, but (31a) asserts it; (31b) refers to prospects in general (it is not even possible to say *Some prospects are for peace*) whereas (30b) does not.

2.4.4

Chomsky touches briefly on the proposal (Lakoff 1965, Fillmore 1966) that at an early stage of derivations all NPs have prepositions and that there are rules of preposition deletion whereby the preposition of the subject is always deleted and the preposition of the object sometimes (mainly when it is *of*) deleted, the deleted prepositions being those which appear in nominalizations. Chomsky notes that *of* is not always deleted (for example, *She approves of him*) and hence 'we would have to postulate an idiosyncratic feature *F* that subdivides verbs into those that do and those that do not undergo *of*-deletion' (p. 42). Chomsky assumes here that only *of* is deleted; however, there are cases where other prepositions are deleted:

(33) (a)   Dick's desire for/*of power
      (a′) Dick desires (*for) power.
      (b)   John's resemblance to/*of Bill
      (b′) John resembles (*to) Bill.
      (c)   Israel's attack on/*of Syria
      (c′) Israel attacked (*on) Syria.
      (d)   Edith's trust in/?of her instincts
      (d′) Edith trusts (in) her instincts.

Thus, at least four other prepositions can participate in the preposition-zero alternation that Preposition-deletion was set up to account for, and whether *to/for/on/in* is deleted is evidently an idiosyncracy of the verb or adjective; thus, the sort of 'arbitrary bifurcation' which Chomsky deplores here ('An arbitrary bifurcation of the lexicon is the worst possible case, of course') appears to be necessary independently of *of*. Chomsky's alternative (setting up *deny* without any preposition but *approve of* with *of* in the lexicon) involves just as arbitrary a bifurcation.[30]

2.4.5

In a footnote to his discussion of his proposed abolition of the distinction between 'category' and 'feature' (p. 48). Chomsky touches on the question of what the 'bearer' of a referential index is. Chomsky introduced indices in *Aspects* as features attached to nouns; in McCawley (1968b), I argued on the basis of examples such as (34a) that they must be features of the NP rather than of the noun,[31] since they are ignored when (as in *one*-pronominalization) identity of the noun and not identity of the NP is crucial:

(34) (a)   John bought a red hat and Bill bought a brown one.

Chomsky objects that I have made the unwarranted assumption that *hat* in (34a) would have to have an index under the *Aspects* approach.

He appears to be envisioning the possibility that some NPs contain indices and others (like *a real hat* in (34a)) do not. However, if indices are to have the function for which they were introduced in *Aspects* (that is to determine whether Reflexivization, Equi-NP-deletion, etc. is possible between two otherwise identical NPs), even NPs which allow *one*-pronominalization will require indices:

(34)   (b)   A fat man who hates himself was talking to a thin one.
       (c)   A tall Armenian forced a short one to shoot the Polish ambassador.

2.4.6

Chomsky's discussion of compounds with *self-* contains interesting examples which clearly demonstrate the inadequacy of the most simple-minded 'transformationalist' approach, namely to derive them all through reflexivization plus object-incorporation. However, his observation that *self-addressed envelope* 'does not mean that the envelope was addressed to itself' does not rule out the kind of derivation he is arguing against: the subject of *address* is the sender, and *self* clearly refers to the sender. I thus see no objection to an underlying structure along the lines of 'an envelope such that *x* addressed it to *x*'. The same is true of (35), about which Chomsky raised the same objection:

(35)   (a)   This is clearly a self-inflicted wound.
       (b)   John's remarks are self-congratulatory.
       (c)   John's actions are self-destructive.

This prophecy is self-fulfilling would require a different treatment, since it does not refer to the prophet fulfilling himself and (as Chomsky points out) it is senseless to say that the prophecy fulfilled the prophecy; my best guess is that this is some kind of causative structure ('the prophecy cause (the prophecy be fulfilled)') with ordinary raising and reflexivization ('the prophecy caused itself to be fulfilled'). A similar analysis may also be appropriate for Chomsky's example *Confrontations between students are self-generating*, though it is a less clear case, since (as Chomsky observes) it refers to confrontations generating OTHER confrontations; it may involve the extended use of a reflexive which appears in such examples as *You linguists can never get along with yourselves*. According to the treatment that I am suggesting here, certain *self* adjectives may involve idiosyncratic deletions, but the use of *self* is subsumed under a general process of reflexivization. Chomsky's position appears to be that if the relation between *self* adjectives and their meanings is at all idiosyncratic, then it is totally idiosyncratic.

2.4.7

As part of his argument for eliminating the category/feature distinction, Chomsky mentions that various transformationally inserted elements function as NPs, verbs, etc. and that the use of a feature representation for node labels allows him to build such labeling into the insertion rule without creating new non-terminal nodes (which, for reasons that are not clear to me, he wants to avoid). He does not mention the arbitrariness that this involves: surely it is no accident that his rule inserting *do it* specifies *do* as a verb and *it* as a NP rather than vice versa. His discussion brings in a number of examples due to Ross (see now Ross (1972a)) but misses the point of them: according to Ross's analysis, the problem of assigning *do* and *it* to appropriate categories does not arise, since the *do* of

(36)   John apologized more meekly than it had ever been done before.

is an underlying main verb with an object complement (Ross argues that all occurrences of 'action' verbs are in the complement of *do* in deep structure) and the *it* arises through pronominalization of the complement of *do* under identity with the complement of the (eventually deleted) *do* of the first clause. In the later two papers in *SSGG*, Chomsky takes seriously the problem of avoiding arbitrary labeling and adopts Emonds's position that rules of the cycle can only put material in places where the base rules allow material of that type to appear.[32] Incidentally, Chomsky fails to observe a major problem which (36) presents for his analysis: since he assumes that Passive is in the cycle and evidently does not admit precyclic rules, passive in (36) would have to apply to the *than*-clause before his *do-it* pronominalization could apply to the whole sentence; thus at the point of the derivation where *it* would have to become the subject through passivization, the rule that creates the *it* in the first place could not yet have applied.

3

3.1.1

'Deep structure, surface structure, and semantic interpretation' (pp.62–119), henceforth *DS*[4]*I*) divides into two roughly equal portions. The first is devoted to exposition of something ('the standard theory') roughly the same as the theory of *Aspects* and to criticism of various positions (some of which have never been seriously advocated) that are or might be imagined to be in conflict with either the theory of *Aspects* or its tradition of syntactic analysis, the second to a discussion of certain problems which Chomsky says cause difficulties for the standard theory and to the exposition of an alternative, later christened 'the extended standard theory', which differs from the standard theory by lacking the condition that deep structure determines meaning, that is, semantic interpretation rules are now allowed to refer to derived syntactic structures.

The following notation and terminology from Chomsky's discussion of the standard theory pop up in many passages quoted below. A grammar conforming to the standard theory contains a context-free phrase structure grammar and a set of transformations; these two sets of rules define a class of sequences of P-markers $\Sigma = (P_1, P_2, \ldots, P_n)$: the phrase structure grammar determines what can be the P_1 of such a sequence, and each subsequent P is obtained from the preceding one by applying one of the transformations to it. The transformations are of two types: 'lexical' transformations, which replace something (Chomsky leaves it open as to exactly what) by a lexical item, and 'non-lexical' transformations; in each 'derivation' $(P_1, \ldots, P_n)$, there is some stage P_i such that the transformations involved in getting from P_1 to P_i are all 'lexical' and those involved in getting from P_i to P_n are all 'non-lexical'. P_i is called a DEEP STRUCTURE.

3.1.2

The parade of supposed challengers of the standard theory begins with a straw man:

> Suppose that one were to counterpose to the 'syntactically based' standard theory a 'semantically based' theory of the following sort. Whereas the standard theory supposes that a syntactic structure Σ is mapped onto the pair (P, S) (P a phonetic and S a semantic represent-ation), the new theory supposes that S is mapped onto Σ, which is then mapped onto P as in the standard theory. (p. 69)

Chomsky dismisses this alternative as differing only terminologically from the standard theory, as would practically any advocate of anything that has been called a 'semantically based' theory. Chomsky's exposition misleadingly suggests that the difference between 'syntactically based' and 'semantically based' theories is one of 'directionality', of what comes 'first' in some sense or other. The term 'semantically based grammar' has in reality been used to mean a grammatical theory in which the closest analogue to the base component of *Aspects* is a set of rules specifying what semantic representations are well-formed. The question of what stage(s) of a derivation require rules specifying what is well-formed at that stage is one about which there is real disagreement; the question of 'directionality' is not.[33]

Next comes another straw man:

> Suppose that in forming $[(P_1, \ldots, P_n)]$, we construct P_1 which is, in fact, the semantic representation of the sentence, and then form $P_2, \ldots, P_i$ by rules of lexical insertion, replacing a substructure Q which is the semantic representation of a lexical item I by I. For example, if P_1 contains $Q = $ *cause-to-die*, the lexical entry for 'kill' will permit Q to be replaced by I = 'kill'. (p. 72)

The conception of semantic representation which this proposal would require is what might be called a 'sprouting deep structure': a deep structure as in the *Aspects* tradition, with each lexical item replaced by a tree which has semantic units as terminal node labels and in some sense represents the meaning of the lexical items.[34] To my knowledge, such a conception of semantic structure has never been seriously proposed. Indeed, the only prior allusion to it in the literature may be the demonstration in McCawley (1968a) that semantic representation must involve a different constituent structure from what the above proposal would demand, for example, that the 'ALIVE' of a decomposition *kill* = CAUSE-BECOME-NOT-ALIVE cannot be just a constituent of or a feature of a complex 2-place predicate but must be predicated of the purported referent of the object of *kill*.

I was thus mystified to find Chomsky saying, in a footnote to this passage, that 'systems of this sort have been developed by McCawley'. Indeed, the whole point of McCawley (1968a), one of the papers that Chomsky cites, was that the rules relating lexical items to semantic structures of sentences in which they are used cannot be just matchings of a word with its meaning but must also include rules that alter constituent structure. Upon comparing the text with that which appeared in Steinberg and Jakobovits (1971), however, I find that this misattribution is due to a misplaced piece of type: the footnote should not have been to the passage just discussed but to the next paragraph, in which Chomsky discusses a theory that can correctly be attributed to me. Specifically, Chomsky considers the possibility of modifying the theory just discussed by dropping the requirement that all applications of 'lexical transformations' precede all applications of 'non-lexical' transformations, thus allowing for the possibility of 'prelexical transformations' such as were discussed in McCawley (1968a). Chomsky states that 'As I have so far formulated the alternatives, it is not at all clear that they are genuine alternatives. It must be determined whether the interpolated "non-lexical" transformations are other than inverses of rules of semantic interpretation, in the standard theory' (p. 73). This is a blatant example of the 'wild card fallacy': the fallacy of assuming that it makes sense to ask whether my jack beats your joker. In none of his many writings has Chomsky made any concrete claims as to what can be a SIR. His remark thus amounts to the admonition that 'prelexical transformations' may be reducible to 'rules of semantic interpretation' once Chomsky has provided a concept for the latter term to apply to. His remark is of course true, but hardly something that can be used to support the 'standard theory'; rather, it is an illustration of a respect in which the standard theory is not a theory but a program for a theory. What is at issue is the distinction between 'transformation' and 'SIR'; showing that my 'transformations' or 'derivational constraints' can be reduced to Chomsky's SIRs not only does not support such a distinction but casts doubt on it.

Chomsky discusses briefly the case analyses of Fillmore (1968). I am at a loss as to why Chomsky includes this in a compendium of supposed attacks on the standard theory, since Fillmore stated quite explicitly (1968: 16-7) that his proposals involved no extension of the *Aspects* theory but rather a restriction of it: a systematic use of a descriptive device which the *Aspects* theory allowed but the *Aspects* tradition had employed only haphazardly, namely nodes with labels which designate 'grammatical functions'.[35] The obvious interpretation of Fillmore's proposal in terms of Chomsky's 'standard theory' paradigm is that the case representations are Fillmore's analogue to deep structure and that it fails to conform to the standard theory solely to the extent that some of the rules relating case representations to surface structures are not 'meaning-preserving' (for example, *Bees are swarming in the garden* and *The garden is swarming with bees* have the same case representation but differ in meaning) and thus Fillmore's analogue to deep structure cannot be the sole input to the SIRs. However, despite the fact that the case representations fit Chomsky's criterion for 'deep structure' (that is, that level serves as a boundary between 'lexical' operations and 'non-lexical' operations), Chomsky takes something else to be Fillmore's analogue to deep structure, namely the output of

Fillmore's 'subject selection rules'. My first guess as to why Chomsky does this was that it is because he places less importance on his 'official' criterion for 'deep structure' (that is, that it follows all 'lexical' operations and precedes all 'nonlexical' ones) than on the criterion that deep structure is the level of derivation that determines what the 'grammatical relations' are, and because he holds that 'subject' and 'object' are grammatical relations but 'agent', 'patient', and 'instrument' are not. An alternative interpretation is suggested by the discussion in the last paper of *SSGG* (pp. 172-9), in which Chomsky holds that Fillmore's case representations 'are not phrase-markers at all' (and thus presumably cannot be deep structures), on the grounds that the items in case representations are unordered.[36]

3.1.3

Chomsky now turns to some real attacks on the *Aspects* theory and/or the *Aspects* tradition of analysis. He first takes up my argument (1968b) that if surface structure and meaning are related via an *Aspects*-type deep structure, the principle governing the distribution of *respective* and *respectively* must be subjected to an otherwise unnecessary division into two rules, one a transformation and the other a SIR, and that deep structure is thus objectionable on exactly the same grounds on which the taxonomic phoneme is objectionable.

It is probably not worth the effort to go through the details of my argument and Chomsky's critique, which combine to form a real comedy of errors. The argument that I gave is badly bungled, though not incorrigibly so: see McCawley (1972) for an acceptable treatment of *respective(ly)* along the general lines of my original argument. Stripped to essentials, my argument took the form: (i) *respective* and *respectively* must originate the same way in syntactic derivations; (ii) not all cases of *respective(ly)* can be taken as arising through a generalized form of conjunction reduction; (iii) therefore, all cases of *respective(ly)* must arise through something other than conjunction reduction, and the only apparent candidate would be a rule which applies to a structure consisting of a quantifier and an expression containing two or more occurrences of the variable which the quantifier binds, attaching *respective(ly)* to occurrences of that variable; (iv) all clauses containing *respective(ly)* can in fact be assigned a semantic structure containing a quantifier and a bound variable, as in (iii); (v) but such a uniform analysis of *respective(ly)* is not available if one accepts *Aspects*-type deep structures, since the *Aspects* theory (or is it the *Aspects* tradition?) would force one to have a transformation deriving, for example, *John and Harry love Mary and Alice respectively* from a conjoined structure which also underlies *John loves Mary and Harry loves Alice*, which would necessarily be a different rule from the (semantic interpretation) rule which relates *Those men love their respective wives* to a representation containing a quantifier and the propositional function 'x loves x's wife'. The respects in which my argument was bungled are that: (a) I did not adequately justify (i); this could be corrected easily enough by pointing out that *respective* and *respectively* can cooccur in a sentence such as (1a), from which it follows that one cannot be derived by conjunction reduction but the other present in base structures, since failure to apply conjunction reduction would then yield the ungrammatical (1b):

(1) (a) Tom and Dick gave their respective girlfriends candy and flowers respectively.
     (b) *Tom gave his respective girlfriend candy and Dick gave his respective girlfriend flowers.

and noting also that the function of *respectively* and *respective* in (1a) is the same as in (2a) and (2b) respectively:

(2) (a) Tom and Dick love Mary and Alice respectively
     (b) Those men love their respective wives.

(b) The analysis of (2a) which I proposed in my supposed demonstration of (iv) was absurd,[37] since it would not be applicable to *respectively*-structures in which one of the conjuncts either is not an NP or is a syntactically derived constituent, for example,

(3) (a) George and Martha love and hate yogurt respectively.
     (b) Sam and Mike will die young and will be sent to prison respectively.

(c) I made unjustified assumptions as to what the *Aspects* theory would require as the deep structure of the sentences in question; in fact the theory has few implications as to what can be the deep structure of any particular sentence. Strangely, Chomsky's critique of my argument completely overlooks (b) and concentrates on exposing a supposed equivocation in my argument. However, the supposed equivocation actually involves two things which I never identified with each other: the '*respectively*-transformation' of the analysis which I rejected in step (ii) and the '*respectively*-transformation' which I argued for in step (iii). Chomsky ascribes to me a position involving the one analysis for some examples and the other analysis for other examples and finds (correctly but irrelevantly) that that position does not involve a unitary '*respectively*-transformation'.[38]

Up to this point, DS^4I has concentrated on linguistic metatheory and has given very little attention to linguistic facts. From this point, where Chomsky takes up Lakoff's (1968a) analysis of instrument adverbs, onwards, the quantity and inherent interest of the facts cited is higher by a large factor. Unfortunately, however, Chomsky often presents arguments in such fragmentary or abbreviated form that it is difficult to determine what the relationship of the facts to the conclusion is. For example, he contests Lakoff's claim that (4a) has an underlying structure with the main verb *use*, like that of (4b), on the grounds that the differences in meaning among the sentences (5) 'suggest a difference in the meaning of the sentences from which the adverb is omitted' (p. 82):

(4) (a) Seymour sliced the salami with a knife.
    (b) Seymour used a knife to slice the salami.
(5) (a) John carelessly broke the window with a hammer.
    (b) John broke the window carelessly with a hammer.
    (c) John carelessly used a hammer to break the window.
    (d) John used the [a?] hammer carelessly to break the window.

If he is saying that the existence of a meaning difference between two sentences containing a certain item implies that the sentences obtained by leaving that item out must differ in meaning, he is wrong; surely the existence of meaning differences among the sentences (6) does not imply that *To please John is easy* and *John is easy to please* differ in meaning:

(6) (a) Only John is easy to please.
    (b) John is only easy to please.
    (c) Only to please John is easy.
    (d) To please John is only easy.

To get any kind of argument about (4a–b) out of the meaning differences among (5a–d), it is necessary to bring in what the meaning differences among (5a–d) are and how *carelessly* fits into the semantic structure of the sentences in which it appears. Chomsky clearly has answers to these questions (indeed, he gives a partial answer to the second question in a footnote on the next page), but he would have to make them and their relationship to (5a–d) explicit in order to end up with an intelligible argument.

Chomsky proposes, contra Lakoff, that *with* is not derived from *use* but rather that (4b) has an underlying structure:

(7)   Seymour use a knife$_i$ for [Seymour slice the salami with the knife$_i$].

He proposes that the deletion rule which applies in (8a–c) (and perhaps also in *Meat is good to eat*) applies to (7) to yield (8d):

(8)   (a)   Seymour used this table to lean the ladder against.
       (b)   Seymour used this table to write the letter on.
       (c)   Seymour used this car to make his getaway in.
       (d)   Seymour used a knife to slice the salami with.

For Lakoff this ought not to be possible, since it would require an underlying structure 'Seymour use a knife for [Seymour use the knife for [Seymour slice the salami]]' and would thus be excluded by Lakoff's constraint against *use . . . use*. This fact is not as serious an objection as Chomsky suggests; it may indicate merely that Lakoff made the wrong choice when he arbitrarily took *Seymour used a knife to slice the salami* rather than *Seymour used a knife in slicing the salami* as reflecting the underlying structure of (4a). The two sentences are not in fact synonymous: the former gives the purpose for which the knife was used, whereas the latter gives the way in which the knife was used. To the extent that the meaning difference is clear, it appears to me that it is *use in* and not *use (for) to* that paraphrases *with*. Analogues to (8) with *use in* are ungrammatical, as are versions in which the deletion does not apply:

(9)   (a)   *Seymour used this table in leaning the ladder against (it).
       (b)   *Seymour used this table in writing the letter on (it).
       (c)   *Seymour used this car in making his getaway in (it).
       (d)   *Seymour used a knife in slicing the salami with (it).

It would appear, thus, that the oddity of (9d) must be attributed not to a constraint against *use . . . use* such as Lakoff proposed, but to a constraint against the S of *use x in S* containing a reference to *x*. Indeed, I have grave doubts that Lakoff's constraint against *use . . . use* is correct: combined with his other proposals, it would appear to exclude the sentences (10), which are all much better than the sort of examples (11) that Lakoff's constraint was supposed to exclude:

(10) (a)   Melvin broke the window with a chisel, using a hammer.

     (b)   Melvin used a hammer in breaking the window with a chisel.

     (c)   ?Melvin used a hammer in using a chisel in breaking the window.

     (d)   Melvin used a hammer in breaking the window using a chisel.

(11) (a)   *Melvin broke the window with a chisel with a hammer.

     (b)   *Melvin used a hammer to use a chisel to break the window.

     (c)   *Melvin used a hammer to break the window with a chisel.

     (d)   *With a hammer, Melvin used a chisel to break the window.

However, a derivation of *V with NP* from *use NP in V-ing* does not suffice to explain what *with X* can be combined with, since (Hudson, personal communication) there are *use NP in V-ing* combinations which do not allow paraphrases with *with NP*, for example, *He used a lot of tact in asking her to leave* and *He used the handle in lifting the pail.* There is as yet no satisfactory account of what instrumental expressions MEAN, and until there is one it will be impossible to determine whether Lakoff's account of them is a reasonable approximation to the truth (as I suspect) or a blind alley (as Chomsky evidently regards it).

3.1.4

The first half of *DS⁴I* closes with what Chomsky regards as a strong argument 'against any variety of semantically based grammar (what is sometimes called "generative semantics")[39] that has been discussed or even vaguely alluded to in the linguistic literature' (p. 89). Chomsky says that 'If the concept "semantic representation" ("reading") is to play any role at all in linguistic theory, then [(12a–c)] must have the same semantic representation' (p. 85):

(12) (a)   John's uncle
      (b)   the person who is the brother of John's father or
             mother or the husband of the sister of John's mother
             or father
      (c)   the person who is the son of one of John's grandparents
             or the husband of a daughter of one of John's grand-
             parents but is not his father.

He then considers sentences obtained by using (12a–c) in the complement
of *realize*:

(13) (a)   Bill realized that the bank robber was John's uncle.
      (b)   Bill realized that the bank robber was the person who
             is the brother of John's father or mother or the husband
             of the sister of John's mother or father.
      (c)   Bill realized that the bank robber was the person who
             is the son of one of John's grandparents or the husband
             of a daughter of one of John's grandparents but is not
             his father.

and states that (13a–c) 'are not paraphrases; it is easy to imagine
conditions in which each might be true and the other two false. Hence
if the concept "semantic representation" (or "reading") is to play any
serious role in linguistic theory, [(13a–c)] must have different semantic
representations.' This, he claims, forces a 'semantically based theory'
into a contradiction: (13a–c) would have to be derived from underlying
structures which differ only with regard to a certain NP, and since the
three choices for that NP 'have the same semantic representation',
(13a–c) would have to have the same semantic representation, which
contradicts the earlier conclusion that they must have different semantic
representations.

  The only linguistic theory that this argument proves anything about
is Chomsky's own. This is one of the rare places where Chomsky makes
any claims about semantic representation. His claim that (12a–c) must
have the same semantic representation[40] is far from universally accepted;
indeed, to accept it one would have to believe that the semantic representation of an NP is a function associating each possible world with
the NPs referent in that world and that the semantic representation of
an S is a function associating each possible world with the S's truth
value in that world. However, the term 'semantic representation' is
not usually used that way, and generative semanticists have explicitly

adopted a quite different conception of semantic representation; see, for example, my arguments (1970a, 1972) that (*p and q*) *and r* and *p and* (*q and r*) must be treated as distinct semantic representations (likewise 'Exists$_x$ Exists$_y$ Fxy' and 'Exists$_y$ Exists$_x$ Fxy') even though they are deductively equivalent, and my observation (1970b: 183) that distinct self-contradictory sentences generally require distinct semantic representations even though they correspond to the same mapping of worlds onto truth values (namely $v(w, p) = F$ for all worlds w).

Thus, given the conception of semantic representation which generative semanticists have actually assumed, (12-13) need not constitute an example of the type that Chomsky claimed they did: there is no reason why (12a-c) should not make distinct contributions to the semantic representation of sentences containing them, and the fact that (13a-c) are not true under the same conditions merely reflects the fact that from '*x* realizes *p*' and 'if *p*, then *q*', one cannot infer '*x* realizes *q*'.[41] The question of whether a valid argument can be given against generative semantics on the lines attempted by Chomsky divides into sub-questions: (i) are there pairs of (surface) sentences S_1 and S_2 such that S_1 and S_2 have the same meaning but '*x* realizes S_1' and '*x* realizes S_2' can differ in meaning? and (ii) if such examples exist, what does that imply? I know of no plausible examples of such pairs; indeed, in all cases where I am reasonably sure that S_1 and S_2 have the same meaning, I find '*x* realizes S_1 but he doesn't realize S_2' contradictory:

(14) (a) Ted realizes that Marty and Zelda are engaged, but he doesn't realize that Zelda and Marty are engaged.

(b) Jack realizes that the population of Tokyo is over 10 million, but he doesn't realize that Tokyo has more than 10 million inhabitants.

(c) Harold realizes that every man loves a woman, but he doesn't realize that for every man there is a woman such that he loves her.

However, even if such a pair exists, it is not obvious that that would show any linguistic theory to be inadequate. It would show that in semantic structure *realize* corresponds not (as I have hitherto assumed) to a relationship between a person and a proposition but to a relationship between a person and something else: perhaps a surface structure, perhaps a paired surface structure and semantic representation, perhaps an entire derivation. That in itself would not imply anything about the issues on which Chomsky and generative semanticists differ; in particular, it does not imply anything about how early or late in derivations lexical insertion takes place. The fact that a surface structure involves lexical items and that the alternatives just mentioned involve a semantic structure that contains a surface structure should not lead one to conclude that lexical insertion would have to take place at the level of semantic structure: to draw such a conclusion is to confuse use with mention. If *realize* expresses a relationship between a person and not a proposition but a way of expressing a proposition, then a sentence with *realize* mentions the words involved in that mode of expression, much as the sentences (15) mention the words *Angus* and *dandelion*:

(15) (a) My cousin is called Angus.
      (b) This kind of flower is called a dandelion.

Saying that a semantic structure contains the words that are MENTIONED in the sentence in question implies nothing about the insertion of the lexical items that are USED in it.

3.2

Chomsky's discussion of (12–13) leads him into the second half of DS^4I. After asking such questions as 'Is it possible for someone to realize that John is believed to be incompetent by everyone without realizing that everyone believes John to be incompetent, or to realize that Bill saw John but not that John was seen by Bill?' (p. 88), he notes that an affirmative answer would imply that the standard theory is defective, since it would imply that sentences that according to the standard theory must have identical deep structures would differ in meaning and thus would have meanings that were not predictable from their deep structures. Chomsky devotes the rest of DS^4I to the examination of a number of putative cases 'in which semantic interpretation seems to relate more directly to surface structure than to deep structure' and to the modification of the standard theory which he holds to be necessary in order to account for these cases.

3.2.1

Before taking up the various points which Chomsky raises, it will be worthwhile for me to try to clarify the expressions 'preserve meaning' and 'change meaning'. I think the following explication of 'change of meaning' accords fairly well with Chomsky's references to 'aspect of meaning being determined by surface structure': a derivation

$(P_1, \ldots, P_n)$ involves 'change of meaning' if there is some characteristic of the meaning of the sentence which is predictable from P_i but not from P_{i-1}, for some i. Saying that a grammar allows 'change of meaning' is not equivalent (as had been suggested by G. Lakoff) to saying that it involves global rules: a grammar can involve global rules without involving derivations that 'change meaning' (for example, if a grammar contains a global rule that excludes derivations in which one quantifier 'has precedence over'[42] another at one stage and the latter has precedence over the former at the next stage, derivations in which quantifier scope 'changes' are excluded). One equivocation in my explication of 'change of meaning' should be pointed out here, namely an equivocation involving the word 'predict'. Depending on how one interprets 'predict', one could either assert or deny that a grammar involving predicate-first word order and negatives and quantifiers as higher predicates must involve 'change of meaning': in a derivation beginning with the logical structure 'Some$_x$ (Not (Like x bananas)))', one could either say that the scopes are predictable from the intermediate stage 'Not$_v$ someone$_{NP}$ (like bananas)$_S$' on the basis of a statement that 'a quantifier in the first NP of a clause has highest scope; otherwise quantifiers and negatives have higher scope than what follows them in the same clause' or only allow 'predictions' on the basis of a uniform rule and thus claim that quantifier scope is not 'predictable' from that intermediate stage. Chomsky's statements about the relationship between surface structure and semantic structure are not explicit enough to allow me to decide which interpretation of 'predict' fits his position better.

3.2.2

The first class of examples that Chomsky discusses crucially involve details of stress, particularly contrastive stress. What implications these examples have for the question of whether 'transformations preserve meaning' depends on what implications, if any, the other assumptions of the standard theory have for the relationship of stress to deep structure. For example, whether one considers the difference in presupposition between (16a) and (16b) to show that certain aspects of meaning can only be predicted from stages of a derivation after where passive applies will depend on whether one regards the passive of (17a) to be (17b) or to be (17c) or regards (17a) to be ambiguous, with (17b) and (17c) each corresponding to one of its senses (in which case (17b) would be ambiguous between a sense which is the passive of the 'neutral' sense of (17a) and one which is the passive of (17d)):

(16)   (a)   Did Booth murder Líncoln?

          (b)   Was Lincoln murdered by Bóoth?

(17)   (a)   Booth murdered Líncoln.

          (b)   Lincoln was murdered by Bóoth.

          (c)   Líncoln was murdered by Booth.

          (d)   Bóoth murdered Lincoln.

Chomsky himself recognizes that it is not clear how the full gamut of stress assignment works:

> The concept 'normal intonation' is far from clear, but I will not try to explicate it here. I am assuming that the phonological component of the grammar contains rules that assign an intonation contour in terms of surface structure, along the lines discussed in Chomsky and Halle (1968). Special grammatical processes of a poorly understood sort may apply in the generation of sentences, marking certain items (perhaps even syllables or lexical items) as bearing specific expressive or contrastive features that will shift the intonation center . . . (p. 89).

Chomsky considers the question of what presuppositions the following sentences can have and how a grammar might relate them to their presuppositions:

(18)   (a)   Was it an ex-convict with a red shírt that he was warned to look out for?

          (b)   Was it a red shirted ex-cónvict that he was warned to look out for?

          (c)   Was it an ex-convict with a shirt that was réd that he was warned to look out for?

He notes that while there are certain answers that would be appropriate to any of the three questions, for example, (19), there are other answers that would be appropriate to only one of the questions, for example, (20a) would be an appropriate answer to (18a) but not to (18b) or (18c), etc:

(19)   No, he was warned to look out for an áutomobile salesman.

(20)   (a)   No, he was warned to look out for an ex-convict with a red tíe.

          (b)   No, he was warned to look out for a red-shirted áutomobile salesman.

    (c)   No, he was warned to look out for an ex-convict with
             a shirt that is gréen.

He states that it is impossible 'without great artificiality' to give deep
structures for (18a–c) from which their presuppositions (as reflected
in the possible answers) are predictable. He concludes that the presuppositions are determined on the basis of surface structure rather
than deep structure, according to the rule that the 'focus' can be any
surface constituent containing the primary stress and the 'presupposition'
is what one obtains by replacing the focus by an indefinite pronoun or
something such. For example, the focus of (18a) can be any of (21),
with the corresponding presuppositions as in (22):

    (21)   (a)   shirt
             (b)   a red shirt
             (c)   with a red shirt
             (d)   an ex-convict with a red shirt
    (22)   (a)   *He was warned to look out for an ex-convict with a
                     red something.
             (b)   He was warned to look out for an ex-convict with
                     something.
             (c)   He was warned to look out for an ex-convict of some
                     type. (?)
             (d)   He was warned to look out for someone/something.

    There are two major defects in this part of DS^4I. First, Chomsky has
not formulated, even informally, any SIR for relating sentences like
(18) to their semantic structures. Indeed, he gives no clue as to how
'focus' and 'presupposition' fit into semantic structure, saying only
that the semantic representation of a sentence 'must indicate, in some
manner' what its focus and presupposition are. This leaves open an
enormous range of possibilities for semantic structure, and each possibility allows a range of possible SIRs. I conjecture that Chomsky has in
mind a system of semantic representation in which 'focus' and 'presupposition' are represented 'directly' as relations between nodes of the
deep structure (that is, a mode of representation formalizable as an
'annotated deep structure' in the sense of McCawley (1973a)). However,
nothing he has said would rule out the possibility of 'focus' and 'presupposition' not appearing as such in the semantic representation but
being reducible to some other characteristic of semantic representation;
for example, one might propose setting up semantic structures in such a

way that the 'focused' material is simply the non-matching part of one of two 'almost identical' constituents of semantic structure, for example, the semantic structure corresponding to one of the senses of (16a) might be along the lines of 'I request that you tell me whether Booth murdered Lincoln or Booth murdered someone other than Lincoln'. What conception one adopts of the semantic structure of the sentences in question will obviously influence whether one finds reason to distinguish between SIRs and transformations. For example, under the latter conception of the semantic structure of (16a), the rules needed to relate semantic structure to surface structure appear to be a rule stressing non-matching parts of parallel structures and a rule deleting a 'redundant' conjunct, neither of which is a distinctly 'semantic' as opposed to 'syntactic' rule.

Second, Chomsky treats sentences as homophonous which in fact differ in secondary stress, at least in slow speech.[43] To take a simplified version of one of Chomsky's examples, the focus of (23a) ought to be any of (23b–e):

(23) (a) Was John warned to expect objéctions?
      (b) objections
      (c) (to) expect objections
      (d) warned to expect objections
      (e) John was warned to expect objections

However, depending on which of (b–e) is the focus, the stress on the various words of (23a) differs:

(24) (b) Was Jŏhn wărned to ĕxpect objéctions?
      (c) Was Jŏhn wărned to êxpect objéctions?
      (d) Was Jŏhn wârned to êxpect objéctions?
      (e) Was Jôhn wârned to êxpect objéctions?

Such stress contrasts are useful in evaluating Chomsky's claims about what can be the focus of what. For example, his statement that either *win* or *certain to win* can be the focus of *John is certain to win* is made doubtful by the relative unacceptability of (25a–b):[44]

(25) (a) *Is Jŏhn cĕrtain to wín?
      (b) ?Is John cêrtain to wín?
      (c) Is Jôhn cêrtain to wín?

By contrast, sentences with *eager for adventure*, which according to Chomsky's treatment should work like *certain to win*, are fine:

(26)   (a)   Is Jŏhn ĕager for advénture?
       (b)   Is Jŏhn êager for advénture?
       (c)   Is Jôhn êager for advénture?

The one concrete argument that Chomsky gives for his claim that one cannot 'without great artificiality' set up deep structures from which the presuppositions of the sentences in question can be predicted is actually an argument that one specific such proposal involves 'great artificiality', namely the proposal that the sentences have underlying structures containing a cleft sentence 'It is/was X that Y', where X is the focus and Y (in essence) the presupposition. He notes that when the focus is as indicated below by capitalization, the corresponding cleft sentences are at best marginal:

(27)   (a)   Is John believed to be A HOMICIDAL MANIAC?
       (a′)   ?It is a homicidal maniac that John is believed to be.
       (b)   Is John believed to be CERTAIN TO WIN?
       (b′)   *?It is certain to win that John is believed to be.
       (c)   Was he warned to look out for an ex-convict with a red SHIRT?
       (c′)   **It is shirt that he was warned to look out for an ex-convict with a red.

This is not much of an argument for Chomsky's conclusion since (i) there is at least one fairly obvious alternative approach which does not involve cleft sentences and is not as vulnerable to this line of objection, namely underlying structures with 'parallel clauses', such as 'Is John believed to be a homicidal maniac or is John believed to be something else?' in the case of (27a) or 'John doesn't write X in the outhouse; rather, John writes poems in the outhouse' (with 'X' chosen to fit the context) in the case of *John writes póems in the outhouse*; (ii) it is not even a real argument against the cleft sentence proposal, since the oddity of (a′–c′) can probably be ascribed to the movement or deletion that takes place in cleft sentences, and Chomsky has not demonstrated that the movement or deletion would have to have already taken place at the point in the derivation where the 'stress from cleft' proposal would require the deletion of the cleft super-structure to take place; and (iii) he has not demonstrated that his alternative allows one to get away with any less 'artificiality' in representing the meanings of the sentences in question.

Two major failings of Chomsky's focus assignment principle should be noted. First, in a sentence which is not 'neutrally stressed', there are always constituents which contain the primary stress but cannot serve as focus; for example, only the first of the following examples can be answered 'No, Sammy Davis did a soft shoe dance':[45]

(28)   (a)   Did Frank Sinatra sing 'Yellow polka-dot bikíni'?
        (b)   Did Frank Sinátra sing 'Yellow polka-dot bikini'?

This fact, of course, is no problem for an analysis in which there is an underlying conjoined structure ('Did Frank Sinatra sing "Yellow polka-dot bikini" or did someone else sing "Yellow polka-dot bikini"?'): the only way that main stress could get onto *Frank Sinatra* would be for the following material to be 'shared' by the two conjuncts. Secondly, as noted by Ross, there are cases where the focus is not a constituent in surface structure, for example, *look . . . over* in [46]

(29)   Did he look the plans over?

Strictly speaking, in most of Chomsky's examples the focus is not a surface constituent, since the tense in them is part of the 'presupposition', for example, in (30) the largest possible focus is not *The Red Sox played the Tigers* (past tense) but *The Red Sox play the Tigers* (tenseless): a retort to (30) will have to involve not only a past tense but one with the same time reference as in (30).

(30)   The Red Sox didn't play the Tigers.

3.2.3

Chomsky concludes the discussion of focus by taking up the relation of his proposed analysis of focus to the 'standard theory'. Since he has concluded that he needs a rule which predicts focus from structures in which various movement transformations (and the 'poorly understood' stress assignment processes) have applied, he has to give up the important claim of the standard theory that deep structure determines semantic representation. He notes, however, that

> these considerations do not touch on one aspect of the standard theory, namely the hypothesis that the grammatical relations that enter into semantic representation are those represented in deep

structure. In fact, it seems to me that insofar as the standard theory is plausible in its approach to semantic interpretation, it is with respect to this specific hypothesis. (p. 102)

This passage gives a capsule summary of the EXTENDED STANDARD THEORY, which forms the framework for the rest of DS^4I and for Chomsky's subsequent work: it is identical to the 'standard theory' except that the hypothesis that there is a system of rules which determine the semantic representation of a sentence from its deep structure is replaced by the hypothesis that there is a system of rules which determine the semantic representation of a sentence from the lexical items and grammatical relations of its deep structure and from information of other types about surface structure.

To understand this, it is necessary to understand Chomsky's conception of 'grammatical relation', which I confess I do not. The best I can do in explicating the above hypothesis is probably to circumvent the term 'grammatical relation': I conjecture that Chomsky intends that all deep structure occurrences of any 'predicate' element should be such that for any argument of that predicate, the NP which expresses that argument should be in the same location relative to that predicate. If this conjecture is correct, then Chomsky's discussion of *V-able* adjectives in 'Nominalization' conflicts with a basic claim of the extended standard theory: while *this book* fills the same argument slot of *read* in (31b) as in (31a), Chomsky explicitly rules out a deep structure for (31b) in which *this book* is in 'object position' relative to *read*:

(31) (a) Bill hasn't read this book.
      (b) This book is very readable.

Until Chomsky clarifies his notion of 'grammatical relation' and its relationship to semantic structure, it will not be possible to say for sure whether his analyses are consistent with the extended standard theory.[47]

3.2.4.1

Most of the rest of DS^4I is devoted to various analyses involving SIRs that refer to derived syntactic structure, though Chomsky gives little reason why such rules would be necessary. The first phenomenon is a supposed restriction that there can only be one occurrence of *even* or of *only* per clause. Chomsky, following Kuroda (1965, 1969) maintains that

(32)   (a)   Only John reads books on politics.
        (b)   John only reads books on politics.
        (c)   John reads only books on politics.

all have the same deep structure, and that *only* is moved into its surface position by a (necessarily meaning-changing) transformation. The facts, however, are not as Chomsky states them. There is no obstacle to two *even*s in the same clause if appropriate 'negative' elements are present (see Fraser 1971), and many persons (myself included) find sentences with two *only*s impeccable:

(33)   (a)   Not even half his claims are even plausible.
        (b)   You're lucky if even half his claims are even plausible.
        (c)   Only Jack loves only himself.

Anderson (1972) has shown that the oddity of those sentences in which two *even*s are odd can be explained without resorting to any restriction to one *even* per clause. Furthermore, even if the facts were as Chomsky says they are, his claim that 'constraints of this sort are transformational rather than "phrase-structural" in character' (p. 103) makes no sense. First, transformations and phrase-structure rules are not the only sources of restrictions on cooccurrence (for example, there are also such things as output constraints and the panderivational constraint against conjoining identical items), and second, there are no well-established transformations which do what the transformation proposed by Chomsky and Kuroda does: to adjoin an element to whatever one's fancy dictates that it be adjoined to; it is not even clear that the *Aspects* theory allows the formulation of such a rule.

3.2.4.2

Chomsky next turns to Jackendoff's analysis of the scope of quantifiers and negatives. He states that (34a–b) 'suggest that scope of negation is determined by surface structure unless we were [*sic*] to permit *not* to appear in deep structure in association with the phrase that constitutes its "scope" — a conclusion that violates the standard theory when applied to [(34c) and some other examples]' (p. 104):

(34)   (a)   Not many arrows hit the target.
        (b)   Many arrows didn't hit the target.
        (c)   The target wasn't hit by many arrows.

The passage quoted has an unfortunate ambiguity: does 'a conclusion' refer to 'that scope of negation is determined . . .' or to 'we . . . permit *not* to appear . . .'? If the former, then the statement that the conclusion violates the standard theory is trivial (since any analysis involving SIRs that refer to derived syntactic structures 'violates the standard theory'); if the latter, then Chomsky has not made clear what kind of analysis he is saying violates the standard theory and why it does. Assuming the latter interpretation (which is the only one under which the reference to (34c) would make any sense), I can think of two ways to 'permit *not* to appear in deep structure in association with the phrase that constitutes its scope' which Chomsky might be referring to. One is an analysis in which *hit by many arrows* would appear as such as a constituent of deep structure; this would presumably violate the standard theory by virtue of its allowing *many arrows* to have a different grammatical relation to *hit* in (34b) than in (34c). The other is an analysis (such as is discussed in Lakoff (1970a) and McCawley (1972)) in which quantifiers and negatives are predicates of superordinate clauses and (34a) and (34b) differ as to whether the *many*-clause is embedded in the *not*-clause or vice versa. Analyses of the latter type in fact 'violate the standard theory' since they require something that the standard theory does not admit, namely a global constraint ruling out derivations in which a quantifier and a negative 'cross', thus allowing derivations which lead from (35a) to (34a) or (34c), or from (35b) to (34b), while ruling out derivations which lead from (35a) to (34b) or from (35b) to (34a) or (34c):

(35)   (a)   (b)

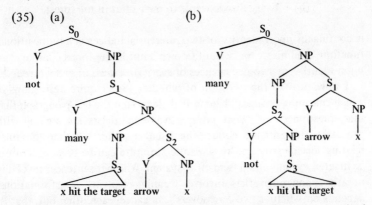

The examples (34) thus provide reason for giving up the standard theory, but they allow several possibilities for what it is given up in favor of. The principal difference between Chomsky and Jackendoff's treatment of (34) and Lakoff's is whether Quantifier-lowering (or whatever rule associates structures that indicate the scopes of quantifiers to structures in which the quantifiers are simply the clauses in which they appear in surface structures) is precyclic or in the cycle. The Chomsky–Jackendoff approach amounts to taking as an approximate semantic structure an *Aspects*-type deep structure (thus, one in which all quantifiers are inside their NPs) and making successive corrections on this approximate semantic structure on the basis of conditions in surface structure (for example, moving quantifiers and negatives up the tree into positions where their 'precedence' relations match the precedence relations of the corresponding nodes of surface structure). If the condition that precedence relations in semantic structure must match those in surface structure is factored out, the two approaches involve the same global constraint on precedence relations and roughly the same quantifier lowering rule (that is, the rules would differ only in so far as the two approaches are combined with different conceptions of how the scope of quantifiers and negatives is represented in semantic structure) and differ principally in whether quantifiers and negations are inside their clauses when Passivization and other cyclic rules apply to the clauses in question.[48] The available evidence as to whether quantifiers are in their clauses when rules of the cycle apply indicates that they are not; for example, the application of Reflexivization and Equi-NP-deletion in

(36)   (a)   Every American admires himself.
       (b)   Every Swede wants to own a hut in the forest.

is contingent upon identity of two referential indices in a propositional function 'x admire x' or 'x want (x own a hut in the forest)' rather than upon identity of two occurrences of *every American* or *every Swede*.[49]

I now turn to the question of whether (34) require derivations in which 'meaning changes'; I hope it is clear from the last paragraph that that question is not what interpretive semanticists are arguing with generative semanticists about: the issue is rather whether the rules relating surface structure to semantic structure can be organized into a 'syntactic' system and a 'semantic' system. Whether sentences involving negatives and quantifiers involve 'meaning-changing transformations' depends on whether two 'crossovers' can cancel each other out, that is, whether derivations have to be admitted in which the precedence relation of one quantifier to another (or to a negative) is reversed twice. It has been argued by Schiebe (1970) on the basis of German analogues to examples in Jackendoff (1969) that crossovers can cancel each other out, even assuming that quantifiers are higher predicates; for example, if adverb preposing is postcyclic, as has been assumed generally, then the derivation of (37) would involve an intermediate stage in which *never* was to the left of *any, not*, and *one* (since the operations that put them into their surface positions are in the cycle), and the derivation involves two crossovers that cancel each other out.

(37)   Never before had any of his friends not come to one of his parties.

I would feel more confident in asserting that crossovers can cancel each other out if I had a solid argument that the adverb preposing of (37) must be postcyclic.[50]

3.2.4.3

Chomsky next takes up his best putative example of derivations in which 'meaning changes': (38a-b), which (according to the most popular analysis) are simply different options as to what NP is moved into subject position by 'Tough-movement', differ in meaning:

(38)   (a)   The sonata is easy to play on this violin.
       (b)   This violin is easy to play the sonata on.

Chomsky ought to have pointed out that there has to be a movement rule in the derivation of (38a-b), since the surface subject can be part of an idiom, the rest of which is in the infinitive phrase:

(39)   (a)   Bernie's leg is hard to pull.
       (b)   Mark's hand won't be easy to force.
       (c)   Jerry's goat is easy to get.

Since I have not been able to state coherently what the difference in meaning between (38a-b) is, I am unable to determine what significance they have for the syntax/semantics dichotomy. Chomsky, of course, is in the same position.

3.2.4.4

There next follow some phenomena involving modal auxiliary verbs. Chomsky states that 'If we assume that the sentences of [(40)] are related as are those derived by replacing *shall* by *will*, or by perfect

aspect, etc., then the standard theory in its strongest form is refuted'
(p. 107):

(40)   (a)   I shall go downtown.
        (b)   Shall I go downtown?
        (c)   I asked/wonder whether I shall go downtown.

To say that these sentences 'are related as are those derived by replacing
shall by *will* . . .' is a roundabout way of saying that all three involve
the same *shall* and that they involve 'ordinary' interrogation. Both of
those propositions are highly dubious. Since most American speakers
use *shall* only in sentences like (40b), it is quite reasonable to say that
there are both a future *shall* and a 'request for orders' *shall* and that the
presence of one in a particular dialect does not entail the presence of
the other. Since (40b) can not be answered *Yes, you shall/will* or *No,
you shan't/won't*, (40b) evidently is not the interrogative counterpart
of (40a). I am at a loss to see why Chomsky finds that (40) would
provide any refutation of the standard theory: even if there is only
a single *shall* and its interpretation must be assigned by a rule, the
difference in meaning of the various occurrences of *shall* appears to be
as easily predictable from an *Aspects*-type deep structure as from surface
structure.

Chomsky also claims that Langendoen's (1970) analysis of sentences
like (41), according to which *can* and *not* originate in the complement
of *seem* and are raised into the main clause by a transformation, involves
'an otherwise unmotivated complication' which is not present in two
alternative analyses involving SIRs that refer to derived structures:

(41)   John can't seem to get his homework done on time.

Specifically, 'raised *can't*' is possible only in sentences where *can* means
'able', not in sentences where it means 'possible':

(42)   *The war can't seem to be ended by these means.
        (cf. It seems as if the war can't be ended by these means).

The 'unmotivated complication' to which Chomsky refers is that Langendoen's *can't*-raising rule must be sensitive to the difference between
can 'able' and *can* 'possible' and apply only to the former. He finds
this 'complication' absent from the alternative which has a *can't*-raising
rule which is not sensitive to the meaning of *can* and has a surface SIR

to assign the proper meaning to *can* and the alternative in which there is no *can't*-raising rule and there is a SIR which is identical to Langendoen's transformation except for having the head on the other end of the arrow.[51] Since all three alternatives draw a distinction between two senses of *can*, it cannot be simply the drawing of the distinction that Chomsky is calling an 'unmotivated complication'; evidently he finds it an 'unmotivated complication' only if it appears in a syntactic rule. Here once again Chomsky violates his own admonition that 'We have no *a priori* insight into the "trading relation" between the various parts [of a grammar]' (p. 13) and takes it as an '*a priori* insight' that certain things which are 'complications' in a transformation are not 'complications' in a SIR.

Chomsky appends to the above discussion a passage which is of significance in connection with subsequent developments in his and his recent students' work. He states that 'Thus a decision that *can* in [(41)] appears at the deep structure level in association with *seem* would not be refuted by the observation that [(42)] is deviant; rather, the deviance ... would be attributed to the filtering function of a principle of semantic interpretation applying at the surface structure level' (p. 109). Chomsky's choice of the word 'deviant' rather than 'ungrammatical' here is intentional: he is adopting the position that there are deviant grammatical sentences whose deviance corresponds either to the failure of the SIRs to assign a semantic interpretation to them or to the ill-formedness of the semantic representation that the SIRs assign to them.[52] This implies that for Chomsky there is no longer any empirical test for 'grammaticality': whether a particular deviant sentence is grammatical or not will depend only on whether the 'most highly valued' grammar provides a deep structure for it, and that can be determined only by finding out what the 'most highly valued' grammar will be like in the relevant respects. Chomsky has thus adopted a position according to which there are no longer any 'grammaticality facts' and thus the choice as to what is the 'most highly valued' grammar cannot be based on 'grammaticality facts': only by choosing among alternative systems of rules that relate meanings to surface structures will one be able to determine which one is 'most highly valued', and correspondingly, which deviant sentences are ungrammatical and which ones grammatical but 'uninterpretable'. DS^4I and subsequent works by Chomsky are confusing because they are inconsistent in their adoption of this policy: they treat it now as known, now as unknown, what facts are within the domain of 'syntax'. Consistency would require Chomsky to reject all arguments with premises of the form 'X is ungrammatical' (as opposed to just 'deviant') and to refrain from assuming the existence of, say, a passive transformation until it has been demonstrated that the examples that are used in justifying a passive transformation (**John is played by golf*, etc.) are really ungrammatical and not just 'uninterpretable'. The policy that Chomsky adopts here implies that there can be no such thing as 'syntactic motivation' and that it hence makes no sense to object to a rule (as Chomsky often does) on the grounds that it is 'syntactically unmotivated'.

3.2.4.5

Chomsky next turns to some phenomena involving anaphoric devices. Discussion of anaphoric devices has often failed to separate three distinct issues: (i) what underlies the anaphoric device? (ii) are specifications of purported reference or purported coreference present throughout the entire derivation? (iii) how is the choice among alternative anaphoric devices of the same type made (for example, *he* vs. *she* vs. *they*)? Practically all logically possible combinations of answers to these questions are attested in the literature; for example:

	All personal pronouns derived from copies of antecedents?	(Co)reference specifications present throughout the whole derivation?
Ross (1967a)	yes	yes
Lees and Klima (1963)	yes	no
Lakoff (1968b)	no	yes
Jackendoff (1972)	no	no

Chomsky quotes Akmajian and Jackendoff (1970) to the effect that 'stress plays a role in determining how the reference of pronouns is to be interpreted' and cites the example (43), in which *him* must refer to Bill if it is unstressed and to either John or some fourth person if it is stressed:

(43)   John hit Bill and then George hit him.

Akmajian and Jackendoff choose to predict coreferentiality from stress rather than vice versa, as a result of their negative answer to question (ii). However, they (likewise, Jackendoff (1972)) present no arguments against the claim that reference specifications are present throughout the derivation but rather argue against 'current theory' (by which they mean the analysis of Ross (1967a)) as a whole. While there are many good arguments against Ross's answer to question (i), [53] I know of no good objections to his answer to question (ii), that is, I know of no consideration that would require NPs to be unspecified as to reference prior to some stage of derivations. Indeed, purported reference appears to be relevant to the operation of all rules that require identity between two constituents that CAN CONTAIN something with a purported referent; for example, deletion of the repeated *cat that once belonged to Steve* in (44) is possible only if both occurrences of *Steve* purport to refer to the same individual: [54]

(44)   Tom owns a cat that once belonged to Steve, and Mark owns one too.

While it is possible that an adequate analysis of examples like (43) may require rules that the 'standard theory' does not countenance (though this is not obvious, since whether that is the case depends on the largely open question of where the stresses come from), it has not been demonstrated that (43) requires a derivation in which some step 'changes meaning'.

Chomsky's next illustration of a supposed 'principle of surface structure interpretation' involving stress and reference is

(45)   (a)   John washed the car; I was afraid someone élse would do it.

        (b)   John washed the car; I was afráid someone else would do it.

His statement that in (45a) '*someone else* refers to someone other than John, whereas [in (45b)] it refers to John himself' is misleading. The anaphoric device in (45) is not *someone else* but *else*. In (45a), *else* means 'other than John', and in (45b) it means 'other than *x*', where *x* is some person that the speaker wanted to have wash the car. (45b) involves destressing of the complement of *afraid* not on the basis of the reference of *someone else* or of *else* but on the basis of *someone else do it* referring to the information conveyed by the earlier clause *John wash the car*; the same phenomenon is manifested in the infinite range of sentences of the form 'S_1; I was afráid that S_2' for which, by virtue of knowledge shared by speaker and addressee, S_2 can be a reference to the information conveyed by S_1, for example:

(46) (a) John washed the car; I was afráid some innocent bystander would set off the bomb by accident.
      (b) John washed the car; I was afráid our plan to get Willie to commit suicide would fail.

I conjecture that in light of the above discussion Chomsky would reject his treatment of (45b) as mistaken and instead propose that there is a different 'principle of surface structure interpretation' which marks an unstressed complement as referring to the information conveyed by an appropriately placed clause elsewhere in the discourse. Such a rule, however, could not be a principle of SURFACE structure interpretation, since the antecedent clause need not be a constituent of surface structure: [55]

(47) John has been proven to have washed the car; I was afráid someone else would do it. (antecedent = 'John washed the car')

While such a rule is rather similar to the kind of treatment that generative semanticists would favor, namely a transderivational rule of destressing, which destresses a factive clause which is deducible from the beliefs which the speaker believes the addressee to share with him, it differs in one important way, namely that the SIR would require an additional rule to destress the clause in question, whereas the transderivational destressing rule accomplishes the destressing and the 'interpretation' of the destressed clause in a single rule.

Chomsky's final example of a supposed surface SIR involving anaphoric devices involves such sentences as

(48) (a) Each of the men hates his brothers.
      (b) The men each hate his brothers.

He states that 'Dougherty gives considerable evidence to support the view that [(48b)] is derived from a structure such as [(48a)] by a rule that moves *each* to one of several positions in a sentence. But clearly [(b)] and [(a)] differ in the range of possible interpretations for the reference of the pronoun *he*' (p. 110). The view to which Chomsky refers involves two claims: that *each* in preverbal position originates as part of the subject NP, and that the form of the pronouns (that is *his* rather than *their*) is selected in deep structure (as opposed to, for example, pronouns in deep structure being unspecified as to person and number). The 'considerable evidence' presented by Dougherty relates entirely to the first of these two claims;[56] however, Chomsky's argument relates to the second claim. If the sense of (48a) in which *his* refers to *each* has the same deep structure as not (48b) but (49), the difference in meaning between (48a) and (48b) is irrelevant to the question of whether surface SIRs are needed.[57]

(49)   The men each hate their brothers.

3.2.4.6

The final phenomenon which Chomsky takes up in DS^4I is the presupposition that is carried by certain present perfects. He notes that (50a) is appropriate only if one believes that Einstein is alive, whereas (50b) is appropriate regardless of whether one believes Einstein to be alive:

(50)   (a)   !Einstein has visited Princeton. [! indicates counter-factual presupposition]
        (b)   Princeton has been visited by Einstein.

He concludes on the basis of these and similar examples that 'the semantic interpretation of perfect aspect would appear to depend on certain properties of surface structure' (p. 112). While Chomsky does not attempt a formulation of a SIR, his references to 'surface subject' on p. 112 suggest that he intends a rule which adds to the semantic structure of certain clauses in the present perfect the presupposition that the person to whom the surface subject refers is alive.[58] In this part of DS^4I, Chomsky repeats the error of considering only 'neutral stress' in judging what is the passive of what. His observations apply to versions of (50) in which primary stress is on the final word; with stress on the surface subject, the situation is reversed:

(51)   (a)   !Einstein has visited Prínceton.
        (b)   Éinstein has visited Princeton.
        (c)   Princeton has been visited by Éinstein.
        (d)   !Prínceton has been visited by Einstein.

These examples suggest that a rule relating this presupposition to syntactic form ought to be sensitive not to surface subject but to TOPIC, that is, the examples which commit the speaker to the false assumption that Einstein is alive are those in which *Einstein* is topic. As I have argued (1971b), the phenomenon under discussion is broader in scope than Chomsky indicates and does not directly involve the proposition that the individual in question is alive. Specifically, the phenomenon is restricted to existential present perfects (that is, present perfects expressing the proposition that there exist past events of the type in question; three other uses of the present perfect can be distinguished) and corresponds to a presupposition that the domain of the quantified time variable includes the present, subject to the general constraint that variables are only allowed to have 'relevant' domains. What this amounts to is that an existential present perfect carries with it a presupposition that events of the type in question can still occur. In (51a, d), where *Einstein* is 'old information', the events in question are events of Einstein visiting some place (if *Princeton* is 'new information') or of Einstein visiting Princeton; since only a living person can visit a place, they would thus commit the speaker to the proposition that Einstein is alive. In (51b, c), where *Einstein* is 'new information', the events in question are events of someone visiting Princeton, and the speaker is only committed to the proposition that it is possible for people to visit Princeton, which does not require that Einstein be alive. In most cases, the possibility of the event occurring will not depend merely on the relevant person being alive. For example, for (52) to be appropriate, it is necessary (Leech 1969: 156) that the exhibition still be running and in addition (McCawley 1971b: 107) that the addressee be physically capable of getting to the exhibition before it closes (for example, it would be inappropriate if said to a person who is in prison or in the hospital and is to remain there until long after the exhibition has closed):

(52)   Have you visited the Monet exhibition?

It thus appears that the presupposition involved in Chomsky's discussion has no particular connection with surface structure.

While Chomsky's discussion of present perfects fails to establish his conclusion, it is filled with fascinating examples which have been of great value to subsequent authors (such as myself) who have written on tense and aspect. It is regrettable that Chomsky subordinated his discussion to the goal of finding a surface SIR; he appears to have led himself on a wild goose chase around a pond filled with juicy ducks that were waiting to be shot.

3.3

$DS^4 I$ ends with a four-page section that is partly a summary and partly a program. He gives a rough sketch of the 'extended standard theory' which the considerations of the second half of DS^4I have led him to regard as better justified than the standard theory:

base: $(P_1, \ldots, P_i)$ (P_1 the K-initial, P_i the post-lexical (deep) structure of the syntactic structure which is a member of K)

transformations: $(P_i, \ldots, P_n)$ (P_n the surface structure; $(P_1, \ldots, P_n)$ $\in$ K)

phonology: $P_n \rightarrow$ phonetic representation

semantics: $(P_i, P_n) \rightarrow$ semantic representation (the grammatical relations being those of P_i, that is, those represented in P_1). (pp. 113-4)

The notation used here is not very clear in one important respect. The parallelism in notation between the last two items suggests that Chomsky intends the relationship of a paired deep structure and surface structure to semantic representation to be similar to that of a surface structure to phonetic representation. However, that could hardly be the case, since for Chomsky the phonological rules act sequentially, converting a surface structure by successive steps into the corresponding phonetic representation, with each rule taking the preceding step as input, whereas SIRs do not convert a pair of trees into a semantic representation in such a fashion. Chomsky's informal descriptions of SIRs suggest that each SIR makes a 'correction' on an approximate semantic structure, the exact nature of which can depend on where the corresponding nodes in surface structure are, rather than converting a pair of trees into a pair of trees. The relationship between surface structure and semantic structure in Chomsky's theory can then be discussed in terms of a derivation $(P_{-m}, \ldots, P_{-1}, P_0, P_1, \ldots, P_n)$, where P_{-m} is semantic structure, P_0 is deep structure, and P_n is surface structure.[59] The general form of a surface SIR would then be 'if P_{-j} meets condition X and P_n meets condition Y, then $P_{-(j+1)}$ differs from P_{-j} in such-and-such respect', that is, a surface SIR would be a global derivational constraint which mentions an approximation to semantic structure, a surface structure, and a correction to the approximate semantic structure. Two points should be added to this. First, to apply such rules, it is necessary to know not only what trees appear as P_{-j} and P_n but also what nodes in the one tree correspond to what nodes of the other (see below, § 4.5); for example, the scope-assignment rules of Jackendoff which Chomsky alludes to cannot apply correctly unless one knows which surface occurrence of a quantifier corresponds to which occurrence of it in deep structure. Second, work by Jackendoff and others has extended the 'extended standard theory' even further than Chomsky's sketch indicates, by allowing SIRs which refer to derived syntactic structures other than surface structure.

Chomsky next turns to an observation which is of interest in connection with the history of linguistic thought. He points out that in the conceptions of 'projection rule' found in Katz and Fodor (1963) and Katz and Postal (1964), there is a projection rule corresponding to each 'choice' that the grammar affords.

> Since surface structure is fully determined by base rules and transformational rules, it seems natural to suppose that properties of surface structure, not being a matter of 'choice', could not contribute to semantic interpretation. Underlying this assumption one might perhaps discern the remnants of the 'Saussurian' view that a sentence is constructed by a series of successive choices and that each of these may be related to semantic considerations of some sort. (p. 115)

Chomsky finds this use of the word 'choice' 'loose and metaphoric' and thinks that when it is dropped, 'we see that there is no reason why properties of surface structure should not play a role in determining semantic interpretation'. I agree with Chomsky that the word 'choice' has been used loosely and metaphorically, and I would add that the word 'determine' has also. Speaking involves constructing a surface structure and a semantic structure which 'match' according to the rules of the language, and the use of the word 'determine' with either term as subject misleadingly suggests that it has some kind of priority over the other.

$DS^4 I$ closes with a brief summary of recent developments relating to output constraints and structure-preserving transformations (in the sense of Emonds (1970)), which he says suggest modifying the extended standard theory by incorporating into grammars 'a set of context-free rules [that] generates structures that become surface structures by application of last-cycle transformational rules, and a related set (perhaps a subset of these) [that] serves as the categorial component of the base' (p. 117). He says that if this highly tentative proposal is warranted, it 'would be an interesting and suggestive supplement to the proposal that properties of surface structure play a distinctive role in semantic representation', but he gives no clue as to what connection he sees between these two proposals; the only connection I can see is that both proposals could be described as implying that surface structure is where the action is.

4

4.1

The last paper in this volume, 'Some empirical issues in the theory of grammar' (pp. 120–202; henceforth 'Empirical issues') coincides in its goals and overlaps to a fair extent in its contents with DS^4I, from which it differs principally in that it is more concerned with rebutting real arguments by generative semanticists and less with discussion of imaginary theoretical positions.

The first section of 'Empirical issues' begins with the observation that in the works that have been produced by generative grammarians since *Aspects*

There is an appearance of considerable diversity of points of view — and to some extent, the appearance is correct. However, I think that . . . it is now perhaps possible to identify a number of real, empirically significant theoretical questions that have been raised. I also think much of the apparent controversy is notational and terminological — including many issues that appear to be fundamental and have been the subject of heated, even acrimonious dispute. (p. 120)

Chomsky gives as examples of apparently fundamental controversies that are really notational and terminological the issues raised in the papers by George Lakoff and Ross that appear in the first number of the *Journal of philosophical linguistics*. Lakoff (1969b) argues that it makes no sense to speak of the grammaticality of a sentence in itself but only its grammaticality relative to a set of presuppositions; Ross (1969a) argues that auxiliary verbs are not the totally idiosyncratic entities that they appear to be in the analyses of *Syntactic structures* and *Aspects* but belong to the category 'Verb' and appear in the same kinds of deep-structure configurations as do such ordinary verbs as *seem* and *try*. Chomsky cites exactly one of Lakoff's examples, namely (1), which Lakoff says is grammatical not in itself but only relative to a belief by the speaker that it is an insult to call someone a Republican:

(1)   John called Mary a Republican and then shé insúlted hím.

Chomsky notes that it is not the speaker's beliefs but John's and Mary's that are relevant to whether an occurrence of (1) is felt as normal: 'even someone sharing Lakoff's beliefs couldn't insult Barry Goldwater by calling him a Republican'. With this amendment, Chomsky finds Lakoff's observations about (1) correct but holds that 'very little' follows from them:

> 'Well-formedness' is a theoretical term. We are free to define it so that it takes its place within a sensible theory. One terminological proposal — the one I would advocate as the most natural — would be this: (I) define 'well-formed' so (1) is well-formed independently of the beliefs of John, Mary, or the speaker; (II) assign to the semantic component of the grammar the task of stipulating that (1) expresses the presupposition that for John to call Mary a Republican is to insult her. (p. 121)

If (1) and similar sentences were the only examples that Lakoff treated, then it would be quite proper to conclude, as Chomsky does, that it is a matter of taste whether one speaks of the well-formedness of (Sentence, Presupposition) pairs, or of well-formedness of sentences, where rules associate presuppositions to (well-formed) sentences. However, Lakoff discussed a number of additional examples which cast doubt on the notion of presupposition-free grammaticality. For example, he noted that the stressing of the pronouns (and destressing of the verb) in (1) is parallel to that in

> (2) $John_i$ insulted $Mary_j$ and then $shé_j$ insúlted $hím_i$.
> (cf. * . . . $shĕ_j$ insúlted $hĭm_i$).

Under the assumptions that were generally accepted when Lakoff (1969b) was written, in particular, the assumption that coreferentiality relations are present throughout derivations, some process of stress assignment would have to apply obligatorily in the derivation of (2), stressing *she* and *him* and destressing *insult*. Lakoff's observation thus presented the advocate of 'autonomous syntax' with the following three-horned dilemma: either there is a single obligatory process of stress assignment applying in both (1) and (2) and its application is sensitive to presuppositions, or different rules of stress assignment apply in (1) and (2), or a single optional rule of stress assignment applies in both (1) and (2) and sentences such as the following must be considered grammatical but either uninterpretable or semantically anomalous:

(3) (a) *John insulted Mary and then shĕ insúlted hĭm.
  (b) *John showed Mary a portrait of Queen Victoria and then shé insúlted hím.
  (c) *Frank_i slapped Charlie_j and then hé_j stăbbed hím_j.

Lakoff also observed that the choice between *who* and *which* as a relative pronoun is not made on the basis of any syntactic property of the antecedent but rather on the basis of whether the speaker believes the individual(s) referred to have minds, for example, one's choice between (4a) and (4b) depends on whether one believes that cats have minds.

(4) (a) the cat which was tormenting me
  (b) the cat who was tormenting me

Again there is a dilemma for the advocate of autonomous syntax: either the rule choosing between *who* and *which* is obligatory and is sensitive to presuppositions, or the choice between them is free and the following sentences are grammatical but commit one to counterfactual presuppositions:

(5) (a) *I can't find the pencil who I just sharpened.
  (b) *The man which loves Geraldine is in jail for draft evasion.

Lakoff's point was that the conception of grammaticality which a strict position of autonomy of syntax would lead to, in which (3) and (5) are called grammatical, involves relegating to semantics rules that are generally regarded as syntactic, and that it is not obvious that that conception of grammaticality has any theoretical significance.

Regarding Ross (1969a), Chomsky states that

> [In *Aspects*], the symbol *V* was used for such words as *read*, *eat*, etc. and the feature *v* was proposed characterising *V*s as well as *be*, *have*, and the modals. Thus Ross' proposal is to replace *v* by [+V] and *V* by [+V, −Aux]. So far, at least, nothing is at stake except the use of the term 'verb': shall we use it to refer to *V* or to *v*; i.e. in the new notation, to to [+V, −Aux] or to [+V]? (pp. 122-3)

Before commenting on Chomsky's evaluation or Ross's proposal, I will briefly castigate Ross for his promiscuous use of feature notation, which obscures the point of his paper. The only place in Ross (1969a)

where the feature notation serves any function is where he proposes
that the ubiquitous expression (6a) be replaced by (6b) in the formulations of transformations such as Negative-placement:

(6)   (a)   Tense $\left(\left\{ \begin{matrix} \text{Modal} \\ \textit{have} \\ \textit{be} \end{matrix} \right\} \right)$

      (b) $\left[\begin{matrix} +\text{V} \\ +\text{Aux} \end{matrix} \right]$

However, given the way that Ross is using features, in particular that
tenses appear as features of verbs, (6b) and (6a) are not equivalent:
in a sentence such as *Birds eat*, 'Pres' matches the formula (6a), but
nothing would match the formula (6b), since '[+Pres]' would be only
a feature of *eat*, which is '[−Aux]'. For the rules in question to work
right, tenses must be separate constituents rather than features of verbs.
It would have made much more sense for Ross to treat not only *have*,
be, and modals but also 'Pres' and 'Past' as verbs (which, in view of the
alternation between Past and *have* discussed in Hofmann (1966), is no
more counterintuitive than calling the auxiliary verb *have* a verb) and to
supplement the grammar with a rule of 'Attraction to tense' which
adjoins *be*, a Modal, or certain uses of *have* to an immediately preceding
Pres or Past, as was proposed in Hofmann (1966). The various transformations would then have to mention neither (6a) nor (6b) but could
instead mention simply *V*: the only *V* that would be in the position in
question would be a tense plus whatever auxiliary verb (if any) has been
adjoined to it by Attraction to tense. '[+Aux]' would then amount to
a rule-exceptionality feature: the verbs marked '[+Aux]' in Ross (1969a)
would be simply those which undergo Attraction to tense.[60]

    Most of Ross's arguments for labeling auxiliary verbs 'V' have the
same structure as those given in Rosenbaum (1967) for labeling various
embedded sentences 'NP': auxiliary verbs act like *V*s with respect to
transformations that refer to *V*, and they can be analyzed as occurring
in the same deep structure configurations as do *V*s. Chomsky dismisses
these arguments as 'unconvincing' but only takes up one of them
explicitly, one which I (and probably also Ross) would concede is pretty
weak. However, Ross gives other arguments that are more deserving of
comment, particularly his observation that the sentences (7) show that
Tom might have been popping pills has a derived constituent structure
[. . . might [have [been [popping pills]]]] ; since *which* and *that* can
have as antecedent any of *popping pills*, *been popping pills*, and *have*

been popping pills, each of those expressions is a constituent (indeed, an NP), which they are in the surface structures implied by Ross's analysis but not in those implied by Chomsky's.

(7) (a) They said that Tom might have been popping pills, which he might.

(b) They said that Tom might have been popping pills, which he might have.

(c) They said that Tom might have been popping pills, which he might have been.

(d) They said that Tom might have been popping pills, and that he might.

(e) They said that Tom might have been popping pills, and that he might have.

(f) They said that Tom might have been popping pills, and that he might have been.

It is surprising that Chomsky treats the 'auxiliaries as main verbs' proposal as 'largely a notational issue', since Ross's paper and another paper listed in Chomsky's bibliography (McCawley 1971b) use that proposal as the basis of arguments that Chomsky's celebrated rule (8) yields the wrong derived constituent structure (argued by Ross) and that no such rule as (8) is needed to get auxiliary verbs to occur in the right order:

(8) Aux → Tense (Modal) (have -en) (be -ing)

Those conclusions are hardly mere matters of notation.

Ross also gives two arguments based on cross-linguistic data. These Chomsky dismisses as involving 'some general assumptions about translatability of rules that seem to me unwarranted'. Ross is not explicit as to what his assumptions are nor is Chomsky explicit as to what assumptions he is attributing to Ross. What I would attribute to Ross is the claim that adequate analyses of languages must make explicit what the differences between them are and that an analysis of a language must be rejected if it makes the language look more different from other languages than it really is. Ross's arguments are that (1) German auxiliary verbs are verbs because they undergo the same 'Verb final' movement transformation that main verbs do,[61] and (2) auxiliary verbs in general are verbs because, with practically no exceptions, auxiliary verbs in the various languages of the world appear in the same position as ordinary verbs do relative to their complements and objects. My impression is that Chomsky is observing a double standard by refusing to grant syntactic categories the same universal status that he assigns to phonological features. The proposal that auxiliary verbs can only occur in the deep structure configurations where ordinary verbs can occur imposes a significant limitation on the class of possible grammars and thus (according to the methodological discussion which Chomsky presents in his § 2.2) is 'a theoretical advance ... if it could be shown that no linguistically significant generalizations are lost by placing this additional condition on grammar'.

4.2.

Section 2 of 'Empirical issues' deals mainly with 'excessive power': 'The gravest defect of the theory of transformational grammar is its enormous latitude and descriptive power. Virtually anything can be described as a phrase marker. Virtually any imaginable rule can be described in transformational terms. Therefore a critical problem in making transformational grammar a substantive theory with explanatory force is to restrict the category of admissible phrase markers, admissible transformations, and admissible derivations . . .' (p. 125). If by 'described in transformational terms' Chomsky means 'expressed as a transformation of the *Aspects* theory', this is simply false. The output constraints discussed in Ross (1967b) and Perlmutter (1970) are not 'describable in transformational terms', nor is the Greek case agreement rule discussed in Andrews (1971) and Lakoff (1970b).[62] The *Aspects* theory is both too powerful and too weak: it both allows for a wide range of rules that are impossible in natural languages and fails to allow for a wide range of rules that are parts of real languages. There is, incidentally, a striking gap in Chomsky's list of things that must be restricted: he does not mention placing any restriction on the category of 'admissible semantic interpretation rules'. In view of the fact noted above that Chomsky's present assumptions leave one with no way of determining in advance what the factual domains of 'syntax' and of 'semantics' are, any restriction on 'syntax' can be met simply by calling rules that violate it 'semantic', if 'semantic' rules are left unconstrained. Restrictions on 'syntax' which are not coupled with restrictions on 'semantics' no more affect the descriptive power of grammars than a law limiting political contributions made by check or money order but not contributions made in cash would affect the economics of political campaigns.

Apparently alluding to the arguments of Postal (1972), which had been read at the same conference as an earlier version of 'Empirical issues', Chomsky states that

> it is often a step forward, then, when linguistic theory becomes more complex, more articulated and refined . . . For example, it is a step forward when we complicate linguistic theory by distinguishing among all imaginable rules the two categories of 'transformational rules' and 'phonological rules' WITH THEIR SPECIFIC PROPERTIES, and formulate conditions on their application and interrelation . . .
> Thus it is misleading to say that a better theory is one with a more limited conceptual structure, and that we prefer the minimal conceptual elaboration, the least theoretical apparatus. (pp. 126-7, emphasis added).

The distinction which Postal was referring to, that between 'transformation' and 'semantic interpretation rule' is nowhere near as clear as that between 'transformation' and 'phonological rule'. While various works of Chomsky's contain precise characterizations of what a transformation is and what a phonological rule is and these characterizations imply that the two classes are disjoint, Chomsky has never even attempted a characterization of the class of possible SIRs, and there are indeed many examples of transformations in earlier works by Chomsky whose function is performed by SIRs in later works. The phrase 'with their specific properties' in the above quotation is the key to understanding how Chomsky and Postal are both correct. Chomsky is saying (following Karl Popper) that a theory that claims more is more vulnerable to refutation and thus more interesting; Postal is saying (following William of Occam) that unless a supposed distinction between entities or types of entities embodies claims with empirical consequences, it is self-deception to draw such a distinction. Postal holds that Chomsky's theory does not in fact claim more than one which does not posit a distinction between transformation and SIR, since it provides no way of telling whether something is a SIR or not.

Chomsky compares the claim that there is a stage of all derivations which fits the definition of 'taxonomic phonemic representation' and the claim that there is a stage which fits the definition of 'deep structure'. He finds that both claims severely constrain the class of possible grammars and that theories embodying them are thus *ceteris paribus* 'better' than other theories. To determine whether these claims should be accepted, one must in each case ask the questions, 'is the hypothesis correct in the case of particular grammars?; is the class of grammars restricted in a way that facilitates the choice of grammars?; are there further conditions on derivations that can be expressed in terms of the level of representation [in question]?' (p. 128). He maintains that while the status of deep structure is 'conceptually somewhat on a par with that of autonomous phonemics', it 'differs in a fundamental way in that, in the case of deep structure, the questions just asked receive positive answers, whereas in the case of autonomous phonemics, they do not' (pp. 128-9). Some of the details of Chomsky's answers to these questions can be dug out of the following sections, though I can find no answer to the second question; I will take them up as they arise.

4.3

Section 3 (pp. 130-6) is devoted to a brief sketch of 'standard theory', 'extended standard theory', and 'generative semantics'. The version of 'standard theory' given in 'Empirical issues' is considerably less constrained than that given in DS^4I. Here Chomsky explicitly allows for 'output conditions' in standard theory, mentions an output condition to the effect that 'a designated symbol $\#$ ... cannot appear internally to a well-formed surface structure', and explicitly allows rules to insert $\#$ into structures that are ill-formed in some way. He also suggests that when a general constraint on the action of transformations is violated (for example, when something is moved out of a coordinate structure), a $\#$ is inserted into the offending constituent. He justifies this proposal by saying that one can thereby explain why (9b) is better than (9a) without resorting to the global derivational constraint that Ross (1969b: 276) had proposed.

(9)   (a)   *Irv and someone were dancing together, but I don't
               know who Irv and were dancing together.
       (b)   ?Irv and someone were dancing together, but I don't
               know who.

According to Chomsky, (9a) and (9b) both involve a violation of the coordinate structure constraint, with concomitant insertion of $\#$, but in (9b) the constituent containing $\#$ is deleted, so that in surface structure only (9a) contains the stigma. However, Chomsky's treatment wipes out the distinction noted by Ross between fully grammatical sentences which involve no violation of the movement constraints, and mildly deviant sentences such as (9b), in which a violation of a movement constraint has been rendered less patent through deletion; Chomsky in fact treats (9b) as fully grammatical. I am baffled by Chomsky's claim (footnote 13) that this distinction is 'not relevant' to the issues under discussion. When he says that 'What is at issue is only whether in determining (degree) of deviance, we refer to presence of # only in the surface structure or, alternatively, to its presence anywhere in the derivation . . .' (p. 132), he is allowing for precisely the global rule that Ross stated.[63] He is also inconsistent when he says that 'Thus the issue is one that belongs to the theory of interpretation of deviant structures', since according to his assumptions, (9b) should not be deviant at all.

Chomsky's sketch of generative semantics begins with an in-joke, his statement that 'Comparison of the alternatives is facilitated by the fact that [Lakoff (1969a, 1971a)] adopt, with only a few changes, the general framework and terminology of $[DS^4 I,]$, so that differences between EST and generative semantics, as so conceived, can be identified with relative ease' (p. 134). Much of Lakoff (1969a, 1971a) was a conscious parody of $DS^4 I$, replete with interpretation of all known grammatical theories in terms of a 'basic theory', the words 'basic theory' being chosen 'simply for convenience and with no intention of suggesting that there is anything ontologically, psychologically, or conceptually, "basic" about this theory' (1971a: 119). It is precisely because of the generality of the 'basic theory' that it fails to 'facilitate comparison of the alternatives'. In particular, Lakoff took 'semantic representation' within the 'basic theory' to be so broad as to cover Chomsky's apparent conception: 'Semantic representation = $(P_1, PR, Top, F, . . .)$, where PR is a conjunction [*sic*] of presuppositions, Top is an indication of the 'topic' of the sentences, F is the [*sic*] indication of the focus, and . . . indicates other elements of semantic representation that might be needed.' Chomsky accuses Lakoff of inconsistency for claiming that a semantic representation is a phrase-marker but defining the term in such a way that 'a semantic representation is not a phrase-marker at all, and hence not part of a derivation' (p. 135). What Lakoff is guilty of is failure to distinguish adequately between what he would seriously propose as a correct theory of language and what he offered (partly in jest) as a general framework for the discussion of theories both correct and incorrect. He ought to have stated that it is an empirical issue whether any of the items following P_1 is actually needed in semantic representation; in the event that they are not, then a semantic representation is a phrase-marker.

4.4

In the one short paragraph that constitutes section 4, Chomsky states his conclusions about the standard theory and the two descendants of it that he has just sketched:

> In my opinion, the standard theory is inadequate and must be modified. The evidence now available seems to me to indicate that it must be modified to the extended standard theory (EST). Furthermore, when some vagueness and faulty formulations are eliminated, I think we can show that generative semantics converges with EST in most respects... The clearest and probably most important difference between EST and generative semantics has to do with the ordering of lexical and nonlexical transformations. This, in fact, seems to me perhaps the only fairly clear issue with empirical import that distinguishes these theories. My feeling is that present evidence supports the narrower and more restrictive assumption of the (extended) standard theory that nonlexical transformations follow all lexical transformations, so that 'deep structure' is a well-defined notion, and so that the conditions on deep structure given by base rules narrowly constrain K (the class of derivations). (p. 136)

4.5

The remainder of 'Empirical issues' is devoted to a comparison of EST and generative semantics, with some criticism of case grammar thrown in for good measure. Chomsky devotes section 5 to miscellaneous apparent differences between EST and generative semantics which he holds not to be empirical issues but rather to be 'terminological or in an area of indeterminacy and vagueness'.

He holds Lakoff's claim that semantic representations and syntactic phrase-markers are formal objects of the same kind to be without empirical content:

> virtually any proposal that has been made concerning semantic representation can ... be reformulated so as to use phrase markers for semantic representation. In particular, this is surely true of Katz's semantic representations. It is difficult to imagine any coherent characterization of semantic content that cannot be translated into some 'canonical notation' modeled on familiar logics, which can in turn be represented with properly bracketed expressions where the brackets are labeled (phrase-markers). (p. 137)

Chomsky is correct that the claim that content can be represented by labeled trees[64] is trivial; however, generative semanticists have generally made a much stronger claim than that: that for a linguist's purposes (and also a logician's: see McCawley (1972)), content MUST be represented as a labeled tree, that the labels appropriate to non-terminal nodes in semantic representations correspond to the three categories 'Sentence', 'Predicate', and 'Argument', and that those categories can be identified with the syntactic categories S, V, and NP in the sense that those are the categories which they will be realized as in surface structure unless something happens in the course of a derivation to make things turn out otherwise.[65] Chomsky is quite right to say that 'The real question is whether phrase-markers provide the most "natural" or the most "illuminating" way to represent semantic content'; and there are in fact several papers which argue that they do (McCawley 1970a, 1972; Lakoff 1971b). When he goes on to say that 'I cannot really believe that anyone would be willing to take a stand on this issue with any conviction, given the present state of descriptive semantics' (p. 137), he is merely reporting an idiosyncratic personal view of 'the present state of descriptive semantics'.

Objecting to Lakoff's statement (1969a: 120) that instead of saying that 'certain aspects of semantic structure are determined by surface structure' one should use 'the more neutral locution "semantic representation and surface structure are related by a system of rules"', Chomsky replies that the EST makes a stronger claim than that 'more neutral locution' would attribute to it: 'that the relation between surface structure and these specific aspects of semantic representation is independent of other terms in the derivation' (p. 140). While Chomsky is correct that he was claiming something stronger than what is embodied in Lakoff's 'more neutral locution', Lakoff appears to have been applying that locution not to what Chomsky had claimed but to what Chomsky had justification for claiming. Lakoff's point was that Chomsky's examples of a systematic relation between surface structure and semantic structure do not imply anything about how those relationships are most appropriately embodied in a grammar. In admonishing Chomsky to use a 'more neutral locution', Lakoff was criticizing Chomsky for treating as an empirically verified conclusion something that consisted of a factual observation plus a statement of how Chomsky has chosen to incorporate such observations into his theory. To draw conclusions about what stages of a derivation quantifier scope can be predicted from, one needs to know what stages the derivation has, and Chomsky's conclusions were based on many gratuitous assumptions about what stages the derivations of the relevant examples have, for example, the assumption that quantifiers are inside their NPs from the beginning of the operation of the cycle.

Chomsky grossly exaggerates when he indicates that the EST involves a narrow departure from standard theory:

> Then the standard theory asserts that the rules include transformations, the base rules, and the output condition noted [the condition that a surface structure may not contain # or Δ], along with the rules that map deep structures onto semantic representations. EST identifies certain aspects of semantic representation that are determined by deep structure, others that are determined by surface structure, but otherwise permits no new sorts of rules. (p. 141)[66]

His use of 'otherwise' brings to my mind the line 'Aside from that unfortunate incident, how did you enjoy your evening at the theater, Mrs Lincoln?' To state how surface SIRs and deep SIRs interact with each other, it is necessary to supplement the 'standard theory' with a radically new theory of rule interaction. The application of Chomsky's SIRs in specific derivations would have to be sensitive to the identity between surface structure nodes and corresponding deep-structure nodes, for example, in describing the meaning of *Many men aren't admired by many men*, one cannot just say that there are two *many*s, each with scope such-and-such, but must indicate which *many* binds the x and which one the y of the propositional function 'x admires y' that is presumably part of the deep structure's contribution to the meaning.[67] Also, whereas the SIRs of Katz and Postal (1964) were 'local', that is referred to an 'input' and an 'output' which were consecutive stages in a chain leading from deep structure to semantic structure and made no reference to any other stage, Chomsky's surface SIRs will have to be global and refer to three stages of a derivation: besides an 'input' (an approximate semantic structure) and an 'output' (a 'corrected' version of that approximation, say, a representation in which some indication of quantifier scope has been either added or changed), the rule makes reference to corresponding nodes in surface structure and whatever property of surface structure determines what 'correction' is to be made in the evolving semantic structure. It is ironic that Chomsky's statement that EST 'otherwise permits no new sorts of rules' appears only a few lines below a passage where he ridicules Lakoff's theory of derivational constraints on such grounds as 'As this theory is presented, it is not even required that derivational constraints be pairwise constraints'. Lakoff's theory of derivational constraints is the only theoretical framework thus far advanced which allows one to express in precise terms how SIRs such as Chomsky envisions would interact with each other; to make sense out of Chomsky's programmatic theory, it is necessary to invoke precisely the thing that Chomsky finds absurd, rules that refer to more than two stages of a derivation at a time.

4.6.1

Section 6 begins with criticisms of the generative semantic position on lexical insertion, which Chomsky takes to be the most important area of difference between generative semantics and interpretive semantics. He objects that the generative semantic position requires otherwise unmotivated rules:

> Generative semantics holds that a lexical transformation replaces a subphrase-marker Q by an item I . . . Furthermore, it has been proposed . . . that Q must be a constituent of the phrase marker. This is almost never the case, it would appear. For example, we must presumably insert *uncle* in place of the subphrase-marker *brother of* (*mother or father*), but the latter is no constituent. Rather, underlying the phrase *uncle of Bill,* we would presumably have (*brother of* [(*mother or father*) OF BILL]), where the italicized item is what is replaced by *uncle*. Of course the italicized item could be made a constituent by a new and otherwise unmotivated rule of 'collapsing'. This is the approach taken by McCawley in the case of words such as *kill* = 'cause to die' . . . the unit that is replaced by *kill* is not a constituent, but it becomes one by the otherwise quite unnecessary rule of predicate raising. Such a device will always be available, so that the hypothesis that Q is a constituent has little empirical content. (pp. 142–3)

Rather than having 'little empirical content', the hypothesis is extremely rich in consequences and provides the area where generative semantics is most vulnerable to empirical refutation. First, it is not a foregone conclusion that the necessary prelexical rules 'will always be available': it is in fact easy to imagine non-existent lexical items which would require rules that violate otherwise valid generalizations about what a grammar may do; for example, a word meaning 'exchange one's motorcycle and', as in sentences such as (10) would require a rule that broke up the conjoined object of *exchange* and thus would violate the co-ordinate structure constraint of Ross (1967b):

(10)   *Sam snarped 10 Beatle records for a nude photo of Tricia Nixon. 'Sam exchanged his motorcycle and 10 Beatle records for a nude photo of Tricia Nixon'.

The hypothesis that lexical items are inserted in place of constituents that arise through prelexical movement rules implies that no such lexical item as *snarp* can exist and would be falsified by a demonstration that such a lexical item exists or could exist in a natural language. Furthermore, the prelexical rules that are postulated as applying in the derivation of some lexical item could perfectly well apply in the derivations of other lexical items; if the 'functional composition' rule that Chomsky alluded to in connection with *uncle* were only applicable in the derivation of that word and other hypothetical lexical items requiring it were uniformly judged as un-English, the hypothesis would have implications as to what is a possible lexical item that would suffice to refute it. All generative semantic treatments of lexical insertion have placed so much emphasis on the question of 'possible lexical items' that I find it surprising that Chomsky should ignore it almost entirely.[68]

Regarding Predicate-raising, as long as *x kill y* is taken to have a semantic representation in which *y* is the subject of an embedded clause (. . . BECOME (NOT (ALIVE *y*))), a grammar must contain at least a special case of Predicate-raising, that is, some mechanism which relates a representation in which *y* is object of a semantically complex verb to a semantic structure in which *y* is subject of one of the 'components' of that verb. The position taken in generative semantics is that the mechanism involved is a highly general rule which applies in the derivations of hundreds of lexical items. There are also cases of postlexical Predicate-raising, for example, in the productive verb derivation processes of Japanese, Swahili, and many other languages, as well as in the derivation of such structures as French *L'automne* FAIT JAUNIR *le feuillage* 'Autumn makes the foliage turn yellow' (Querido (1971), Seuren (1972)) and English *Fred* MADE CLEAR *his intentions*.[69]

Before going on, it should be noted that throughout this section Chomsky bases arguments on paraphrases which, while they may be lifted bodily from a reliable dictionary, have not been subjected to at all rigorous demonstrations that they really are paraphrases, let alone that one of them (or rather, what you would get from one of them by replacing its words by corresponding semantic units) is the semantic representation of the other. This deficiency is not restricted to work by interpretive semanticists: it also constitutes a major fault of such generative semantic works as Postal (1969). I have argued

(1973b) that what underlies *uncle of* is not 'brother of mother or father' but 'male and equivalent to a sibling of a parent of', where 'equivalent' refers to the culture-specific equivalence of kinship links described in such works as Lounsbury (1964). Among my reasons for drawing this conclusion were that postulating underlying structures with *or* would imply the possibility of various (within English) impossible kinship terms (for example, a word **schmuncle* that covered only three of the four relationships that *uncle* covers) and that there are languages in which a morphemically complex kinship term contains the morphemes describing some 'basic' genealogical relationship but covers other relationships that are 'equivalent' to it (for example, Swedish *morbror* covers not only 'brother of mother' but also 'husband of sister of mother'; similarly with *moster*, *farbror*, and *faster*); only by bringing in 'equivalence' can the morphemes of *morbror* be related to semantic constituents of that word.

Chomsky's next example is in fact one for which the traditional definition which he quotes is demonstrably wrong. One can 'kill X by unlawful means and with malice aforethought, where X is human, reasonably important, . . .' without assassinating X. To assassinate a person one must kill him in order to remove him from political influence (for example, you wouldn't be assassinating Richard Nixon if you killed him solely to revenge yourself for his having cuckolded you). If this observation is incorporated into the definition, then 'where X is human, reasonably important, . . .' becomes superfluous: you can only remove from political influence a person who has some. It is also doubtful that 'by unlawful means' belongs there: even if there were a law making killings legal when carried out on the third Tuesday of the month, killing Nixon so as to stop him from making peace with China would be just as much an assassination on the third Tuesday as on the fourth Wednesday.[70] We now have a possible source for *assassinate* which allows one to say that it replaces a constituent that is derived through a fairly widespread prelexical rule of adverb incorporation, which adjoins 'in order to remove from political influence' and 'with malice aforethought' (if it is not rendered superfluous by the motive clause) to CAUSE-BECOME-NOT-ALIVE. A similar incorporated adverb is found in the idiom *kick upstairs* 'promote in order to eliminate the influence of'.

Chomsky adds some observations that are of great relevance to formulating correct dictionary entries but do not create any more of a problem for generative semantics than for any alternative theory: that a 'tone of sinister intent . . . is associated with *cohort* or *henchman* as compared with *colleague*[71] and that *dissuade* 'presupposes some sort of intention on the part of the person dissuaded', whereas *persuade not* does not. The observation about *dissuade* indicates a deficiency in Lakoff's (1969a) proposal of an underlying structure CAUSE BECOME INTEND NOT but provides support for the alternative CAUSE BECOME NOT INTEND. Since something can become the case only if it was not previously the case, the latter analysis implies that *X dissuaded Y from Z* is appropriate only in case 'Y not intend Z' was false, that is 'Y intend Z' was true, prior to the event in question; under Lakoff's proposal, the presupposition contributed by BECOME would be that prior to the event in question Y did not intend not to Z, which does not imply that Y intended to Z. Chomsky's observation thus fits easily into the mode of analysis which generative semantics affords.

As a possible way out of the difficulties that Chomsky sees in having lexical items replace constituents, he considers the possibility that part of the dictionary entry could be presuppositions which are not replaced by the lexical item but are rather part of the environment for inserting it. He finds this proposal beset with insuperable problems having to do with which presupposition goes with which lexical item. He correctly objects to Lakoff's assumption that presuppositions are lumped together in a huge conjunction that is associated with the whole sentence, pointing out that presuppositions associated with a lexical item need not be presuppositions of the whole sentence.[72] A remedy to this defect was proposed by Morgan (1969b) in the volume containing the paper of Lakoff's which Chomsky is criticizing: to take presuppositions as associated with specific clauses of semantic structure. The example which Chomsky gives to show the incoherency of the proposal he is discussing rests on a false claim, namely Fillmore's (1971b) claim that '*x* accuse *y* of *z*' means '*x* say (*y* did *z*)' and presupposes '*z* bad'. I have pointed out (1975a) that saying that a person did something may fail to be an accusation, depending on the speaker's motive in saying it, for example, the utterance *While you were drunk last night you raped and killed your mother* is an accusation if uttered by a policeman who will arrest you unless you come up with an alibi fast or by your mother's lover, who is out for revenge, but not if said by a friend who (while he regards your actions as reprehensible) is merely informing you of the facts in order to help you escape arrest or vendetta. To accuse a person of something is not just to say that he did it but to thereby create a situation of 'jeopardy', which requires that the person successfully defend himself against the charge or suffer undesirable consequences. Thus, while Chomsky is correct that the following three sentences differ in meaning:

(11) (a) For John to accuse Bill of lying is worse than for John to state that Bill lied.

(b) For John to state that Bill lied is worse than for John to accuse Bill of lying.

(c) For John to state that Bill lied is worse than for John to state that Bill lied.

he is incorrect in stating that they would have the same underlying structure under the version of generative semantics in which pre-suppositions of lexical items are conditions on their insertion. Rather, given a correct analysis of *accuse*, the motive expression would be part of the semantic structure of the first clause in (a), of the second clause in (b), and of neither clause in (c).

Chomsky now takes up several arguments that have been advanced for abandoning the hypothesis that 'all nonlexical transformations follow all lexical transformations'. After briefly mentioning two argu-ments that he had already discussed in DS^4I and dismissing Lakoff's argument for decomposition of *dissuade* into *persuade*+NOT, on the grounds that it is not clear that the facts are as Lakoff records them (here I agree with Chomsky), he takes up Morgan's (1969a) argument that (12) is three-ways ambiguous as to the scope of *almost* and thus provides evidence for an underlying structure for (12) that contains at least three Ss, one for each of the possible scopes of *almost:*

(12) I almost killed John.

Morgan proposed to describe this range of interpretation of (12) by postulating a rule which raises *almost* (and perhaps some other items) up over certain predicates. This adverb-raising rule, when applied to (13a) or (13b) would wipe out the difference between it and (13c).[73] If it and Predicate-raising are both in the cycle, then all three trees in (13) can give rise to a single derived structure in which *kill* can be inserted (14).

In his exposition of Morgan's argument Chomsky glosses over the important question of what exactly serves as the scope of *almost*. Morgan took *almost* as having a different S for its scope in each of the three senses of (12), but Chomsky states that Morgan 'observes that [12] has two senses when *almost* takes *kill* as scope (and a third, which we can disregard, when it takes *kill John* as scope)' (p. 149). Morgan assumed (justifiably, in absence of evidence to the contrary that a uniform statement of what can be a possible scope of *almost*

(13)

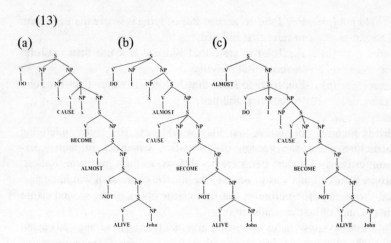

(14)

is possible. The fact that in two readings of (12) *almost* modifies something which does not appear in the syntactic structures of those who distinguish between syntax and semantics implies that to maintain such a distinction one must either relegate specifying what *almost* modifies to semantics or give up a uniform statement of what *almost* may modify.

Chomsky presents as a 'difficulty' for Morgan's analysis the fact that 'The range of meaning he perceives seems to be characteristic of many, perhaps all verbs that specify a process that can reach a terminal point: for example, *I almost solved the problem. I almost persuaded Bill to leave. The planes almost destroyed the city*' (p. 150). Of the last example, he says that 'there is little sense to the idea of an internal analysis and surely no causative analysis'. I do not see what Chomsky finds counterintuitive about taking *destroy* to be a causative; 'cause to cease to exist' sounds plausible enough as a paraphrase. He mentions briefly arguments by Fodor (1970) and Bresnan (1971) which he says support Jackendoff's 'extended lexical hypothesis': the thesis that 'the only changes transformations can make to lexical items are to add inflectional affixes such as number, gender, case, person, and tense'.[74] This strictly speaking is not relevant to a discussion of the proposed derivation of *kill*, since no one has claimed that it involves 'changing' any lexical items (that is no one has proposed that the word *die* is inserted for 'BECOME NOT ALIVE' in the course of the derivation of *kill*).[75] Fodor's paper, rather than providing a clear case for choosing an interpretivist account of *kill* over a generative semantic account shows the situation to be one that is not attractive to either camp: some sentences with causative verbs allow adverbs that modify pieces of their semantic structures and some do not, for example, while (15a), with an adverb that modifies the 'BECOME NOT ALIVE' part of *kill*, is bad, (15b) is most normally interpreted with *slowly* modifying the embedded structure 'the meat cook':

(15) (a) *John killed Bill on Sunday by stabbing him on Saturday.
       (b) John cooked the meat slowly.

Either Chomsky's theory or generative semantics would receive strong confirmation if it were shown that it but not the other theory could be supplemented by some simple principle that would explain WHICH adverbs could appear modifying part of the meaning of a word that appears in surface structure; no such explanation has as yet emerged. Bresnan's conclusion that the Nuclear Stress Rule is in the syntactic cycle not only is based on questionable arguments (see Lakoff (1972b), Berman and Szamosi (1972)) but indeed implies nothing about the 'extended lexical hypothesis' or the existence of deep structure: her conclusion is perfectly consistent with the idea that lexical insertion is in the cycle (which I have claimed anyway; see

McCawley (1973b)), a position which precludes the existence of a level
of deep structure.

4.6.2

Chomsky's discussion of the celebrated case of *remind* suggests to me
that he has missed the point of Postal's (1970a) paper, which was that
remind exhibits a large number of syntactic restrictions that would
simply have to be put into a gigantic dictionary entry if the syntax/
semantics dichotomy of *Aspects* is accepted but turn out to be not at
all idiosyncratic if that dichotomy is given up and the rules relating the
semantic structure of clauses with *remind* to their surface structures
are taken to be a homogeneous system. For example, Postal argued
that the restriction against coreferentiality between the subject and
object of *remind* is paralleled by a similar restriction with *strike*:

(16) (a) *John reminds himself of a gorilla.
      (b) *John strikes himself as similar to a gorilla.

and that both restrictions can be explained as violations of a constraint
against moving an NP across a coreferential NP, provided that a *remind*
sentence such as (17a) and a *strike* sentence such as (17b) have a
common semantic structure such as (17c):

(17) (a) John reminds me of a gorilla.
      (b) John strikes me as being like a gorilla.
      (c) PERCEIVE (I, SIMILAR (John, a gorilla)).

Chomsky gives no clue as to how he would account for the peculiarities
of *remind* that Postal described. Instead he castigates Postal for adopting
a position that would require radically different sources for sentences
involving agentive and non-agentive *remind*:

(18) (a) John reminds me of a gorilla.
      (b) John's presence reminds me of an appointment I missed.
      (c) John reminded me of an appointment I missed.

'It is merely an accident, from this point of view, that they share the
same surface form' (p. 153). As far as I can determine, Chomsky's
position is that to account for the fact that *remind* in each case cooccurs
with NP *of* NP, one must postulate that there is a single verb *remind*
and that it has the strict subcategorization feature [+__NP *of* NP].

However, the various uses of *remind* are in fact not identical with regard to 'strict subcategorization':

> (19)　(a)　John cautiously reminded me of my appointment with the dentist.
>
> 　　　(a')　*John cautiously reminded me of a gorilla.
>
> 　　　(b)　John reminded me of a gorilla in that he was big and hairy.
>
> 　　　(b')　*John reminded me of my appointment in that he told me that the dentist expected me at 3.00.

I am fairly convinced that we have to do here with neither fortuitous homonymy nor a single lexical item that covers a wide range of cases but with 'distinct but related' lexical items. Either position would receive strong support if one could show that it but not the other allowed one to pinpoint the differences between the uses of *remind* in such a way as to explain both how they act alike and how they differ. Chomsky is justified in objecting to Postal's ignoring the similarities, but by ignoring the differences Chomsky is open to objections that are more serious to the extent that the known differences exceed the similarities.

I should make clear that my criticism of Chomsky's statement about *remind* does not constitute an endorsement of Postal's analysis. I regard Postal's analysis as a first approximation to the truth, but inadequate in some important respects pointed out particularly by Bolinger (1971), who among other things provides many convincing examples of discourses in which *remind* conveys no notion of similarity. Bolinger demonstrates that generally *make think* and *bring to mind* are closer paraphrases of *remind* than is Postal's *strike like*, which suggests that some kind of causative analysis of *remind* may give a closer approximation to the truth than does Postal's proposal.

I have intentionally employed the hedge 'some kind of': there are a wide range of possible 'causative analyses', differing as regards what kind of 'causation' is involved and what else besides the 'causation' is involved, and all but at most one of those analyses will be wrong. Note that the subject of *remind* is generally something that either could not serve as subject of any of the standard senses of *cause* (for example, *John's mustache*) or can only serve as the subject of an irrelevant sense (for example, *John*, which can serve as subject only of the agentive sense of *cause*, for example, *John caused me to get fired*). Chomsky, quoting a personal communication from Jackendoff, suggests a promising approach: that *John reminds me of a gorilla* 'can be regarded as a special case of' sentences with subjects such as *John's presence* which refer to a 'specific characteristic' of the subject of the 'simpler' sentence (pp. 154–5). To put this suggestion into a form which I am sure would not be acceptable to Chomsky, the subject of *John reminds me of a gorilla* might be derived through deletions from a structure that could serve as the subject of a relevant sense of *cause*, for example, 'My perception of John's appearance causes me to think of a gorilla' might underlie *John reminds me of a gorilla*.

Chomsky takes up explicitly only one argument for Postal's analysis, namely that based on the deletion found in (20), which Lakoff (1971a) claims only applies 'when the clause where the deletion takes place is a complement of a verb of saying or thinking and when the NPs to be deleted are coreferential to the subject of that verb of saying or thinking'.

(20)   Bill says/thinks that shaving himself is like torturing himself.

If that generalization were correct, then (21) would have to involve a verb of saying or thinking whose subject was *John*, just as in Postal's analysis:

(21)   Shaving himself reminds John of torturing himself.

However, Chomsky claims that the generalization is incorrect, citing the following examples:

(22)   (a)   Shaving himself seems to John like torturing himself.
        (b)   Shaving himself makes John think of torturing himself.
        (c)   Shaving himself brings to John's mind the idea of torturing himself.
        (d)   Shaving himself appears to John to be as pointless as torturing himself.

Chomsky is right that the controller of the deletion need not be the subject of its clause and the verb of the higher clause need not be a verb of saying or thinking, though he could have chosen better examples on which to base that claim: (22a, d) are open to an analysis in which *John* is subject and 'Psych-movement' takes place, and *seem* and *appear* could reasonably be called 'verbs of thinking'. (22b, c) are more to the point, though they are hardly enough to establish that the deletion 'can apply quite freely to such structures', by which Chomsky appears to mean that the rule is applicable to structures of approximately the same constituent structure as (20) and (22), regardless of what words they contain. He could have made a stronger case by adding examples such as

(23) (a) Shaving himself prevented John from torturing himself.
　　　(b) Shaving himself makes John regret having tortured himself.

Chomsky appends to his discussion a footnote that is of interest mainly because of what it reveals about where he is willing to draw his line between syntax and semantics. He rejects Perlmutter's claim that the Spanish example (24a) must have an underlying structure like that of (24b) and that *mis padres* can replace *mi madre y mi padre* after a generalized conjunction reduction that introduces *respectivamente*, on the grounds that *respectively* and its analogues cannot be derived by a conjunction-reduction transformation, since there are examples 'involving an infinite set or a finite set of unknown size' such as (25).[76]

(24) (a) Mis padres son respectivamente alta y bajo. 'My parents are respectively tall (fem.) and short (masc.)'
　　　(b) Mi madre y mi padre son respectivamente alta y bajo. 'My mother and my father are respectively tall and short'
(25) The successive descendants of my fruit fly will be heavier, respectively, than the successive descendants of yours.

He concludes that 'If [Perlmutter's] empirical observations are accurate, it would appear that gender agreement may be a matter of surface interpretation, perhaps similar to determination of coreference' (p. 155).[77] Chomsky is thus willing to regard gender agreement (and presumably also person, case, and number agreement?) as outside the domain of syntax proper and thus to regard the following as grammatical but either semantically anomalous or uninterpretable:

(26) (a) *Le plume de mon tante sont sur le table de mes oncle.
　　　(b) *Omnibus Gallia sum in tria partes divisum.

However much violence this may do to commonly held conceptions of 'grammaticality', it does even more to commonly held conceptions of 'semantic interpretation rule'; the SIR to which Chomsky alludes could hardly be anything other than a rule marking as inadmissible those derivations in which a word fails to agree with what it is supposed to agree with; this is not something that I would normally describe as predicting some aspect of meaning on the basis of surface structure.

Much the same can be said of a later digression (pp. 185-7) dealing with an objection by Lakoff to Chomsky's claim that surface structure is the only level of derived structure to which the SIRs of Chomsky's theory would need to make reference. Lakoff noted that in (27), the *many* of the deleted part of the second conjunct must be assigned a scope, and hence the scope assignment rule must make reference to stages of the derivation that precede the application of the VP-deletion transformation:[78]

(27)   Jane isn't liked by many men, and Sally isn't either.

Chomsky replies to Lakoff by expressing doubts that such a transformation as VP-deletion exists. He notes that while *Bill has been here for a month* unambiguously means 'Bill has been here throughout the last month', (28) is ambiguous between the senses 'it is not the case that John has been here throughout the last month, but Bill has been here throughout the last month' and 'John has not been here at any time during the last month, but Bill has been here at some time during the last month'.

(28)   John hasn't been here for a month, but Bill has.

The latter sense is not possible for the sentence of which (28) is supposedly a truncated form:

(29)   John hasn't been here for a month, but Bill has been here for a month.

Chomsky rejects the analysis according to which there are two senses of *for a month*, one of which is a negative polarity item subject to the output constraint that in surface structure it must be commanded by the negative that 'triggers' it.[79] He holds rather that it is 'more natural' to conclude that there is no VP-deletion rule and that '"compositional semantics" must be abandoned (or at least restricted), with the semantic interpretation in such cases as [(28)] constructed along lines that have been explored by Jackendoff (1969) and Akmajian (1969)'. I will not comment on the SIRs that Chomsky hints at here, since his hint is not sufficient to make clear to me what he has in mind. I wish merely to emphasize that this means that Chomsky must set up his base component in such a way that it will derive the following sentences from deep structures that are virtually the same as their surface structures (Affix-hopping and *do*-support are the only transformations that would apply in their derivations):

(30) (a) John did.
 (b) Marilyn has.
 (c) There was.
 (d) Bill may.

It is not clear how Chomsky would get the right combinations of auxiliary verbs and affixes to turn up here; if he excludes VP-deletion, would he allow a rule that deleted auxiliary elements in a V-less structure, so as to derive (31a) from (31b)?

(31) (a) Bill has been drinking and Mark has too.
 (b) Bill Pres have -en be -ing drink and Mark Pres have -en be -ing too.

If not, then his phrase structure rule for 'Aux' will be a maze of paren-theses, since the affixes that normally accompany *have* and *be* would have to be kept out of the deep structures of (30); if so, then the work of the old VP-deletion rule is divided between a syntactic auxiliary-deletion rule and a SIR for the interpretation of V-less clauses, and the division of rules into 'syntactic' and 'semantic' is open to an argument like Halle's argument against the phoneme. Moreover, if there is no VP-deletion rule, there can be no *there*-insertion rule either (since the conditions for *there*-insertion in *There was* are met in the deleted part), and sentences like (32) would demand deep structures in which *Frank's* is a possible subject NP:[80]

(32) Bill's leg has been pulled many times, and Frank's (*leg) has too.

The following sentences would be 'grammatical' but 'uninterpretable' by virtue of failure of the SIR to provide a coherent interpretation of the missing material:

(33) (a) *Tom loved to swim, but there wasn't.
 (b) *Harry is drunk, and Bernie's will too.

Such deep structures, incidentally, appear to conflict with Chomsky's claims about how 'grammatical relations' are connected with semantic structure: in *Bill was mugged but Dave wasn't*, the deep structure would have *Dave* in subject position, though semantically it is the object of *mug*. See Grinder and Postal (1971) and Hankamer (1973) for further arguments against Chomsky's position on zero VPs.

4.6.3

Chomsky claims that there are syntactic generalizations which are 'not formulable unless deep structure exists as a well-defined level of derivation'. He observes that the subject of (34a) can only be interpreted as generic, that of (34b–c) only as 'specific', and that of (34d) as either generic or specific:

(34) (a)   A beaver builds dams.
      (b)   That beaver builds dams.
      (c)   A beaver is building a dam.
      (d)   The fattest beaver is the builder.

He states that

> Clearly, the possibility of generic or specific interpretation is not determined simply by the choice of subject or the choice of predicate, but in part by an interaction between the two. At the level of deep structure, there is a very simple generalization governing such sentences as [(34)] : any noun phrase can be followed by any verb phrase. (p.157)

At this point there appears a footnote which begins with an apparent retraction of this patently absurd statement ('Obviously, this is only a first approximation and further refinements are necessary. Thus certain phrases, for example, *any beaver with teeth*, can appear only with one interpretation') and ends with an apparent reaffirmation of it. ('If we choose to preserve the simplest syntax, with free choice of subject and predicate, the deviance of *Any beaver with teeth is building a dam* (etc.) would be attributed to the filtering effect of the semantic rules.') The only sense that I can make out of this is that Chomsky may have meant that any determiner can appear in deep NPs in combination with any auxiliary verbs; determiners and auxiliaries at any rate are the only items whose distributions seem to be relevant to what he is saying.[81] Chomsky's remarks later on the same page suggest that he intends this as part of a broader generalization: that there is more homogeneity in the class of deep structures that his theory would set up than there is in the class of semantic representations that can correspond to utterances of English. He notes that if derivations of (34a–d) 'begin' with semantic representations, (34d)

> will have two quite different initial phrase-markers in its two derivations, one of them similar to the initial phrase-marker of [(34a)] and the other similar to the initial phrase-marker of [(34b–c)]. By accident, later transformations happen to give the forms satisfying the simple regularity illustrated by [(34)]. In addition, it is necessary to ensure that [(34a)] does not have an initial phrase-marker similar to those of [34b–c)]. (p. 157)

Chomsky's use of the expression 'by accident' is presumably supposed to suggest that his treatment explains some generalization that other treatments fail to explain. To see whether such is the case, it is necessary first to see what there is to be explained, and as far as I can see, the one thing to be explained is that the words manifesting quantifiers (the existential quantifier on *beaver* in (c)), 'genericness', and 'identification' (the demonstrative in (d)) appear in the same position, namely 'determiner position'. (The absence of a 'specific' interpretation for the subject of (34a) is not relevant here, since as far as I can see, all existing theories have equally much of a problem of inhibiting an otherwise general rule that allows $a(n)$ as the expression of an existential quantifier). To the extent that 'genericness' can be identified with a quantifier[82] and it is 'natural' to have a rule that attaches a quantifier to an occurrence of the index that it binds, a theory which dispenses with deep structure and has semantic representations in which quantifiers are predicated of (something containing) their scopes makes it 'no accident' that the sentences in question have similar surface structures: they have the same innermost clause in semantic structure and differ only with respect to external material which must be adjoined to particular indices in that clause in the course of the derivation.

4.6.4

Chomsky next responds to the three arguments against the lexicalist hypothesis which had appeared in print at the time 'Empirical issues' was written. His objection to the first argument hinges on an easily correctible error in Ross (1969b). Ross stated that (35) requires an application of 'Sluicing', which throws away the parts which a clause shares with an 'almost identical' preceding clause, and hence that the first part of (35) must contain something that is 'almost identical to' *He plans to do away with whom* in the second part.

(35)   Bill mentioned his plans to do away with someone, but he didn't mention who.

He stated that this 'provides evidence against any theory of grammar in which *his plans to do away with someone* is not IDENTICAL, at some stage, to *He plans to do away with someone*' (1969b: 276, emphasis added). Chomsky rightly objects that if that conclusion followed, then it would also follow that the sentences in (36) must at some stage of their derivations be identical to *He plans to do away with someone* and hence to each other:

(36) $\left\{ \begin{array}{l} \text{His plan} \\ \text{Those plans of his} \\ \text{His several weird plans} \end{array} \right\}$ to do away with someone

Ross made the mistake of assuming that the lexicalist/transformationalist controversy is about whether a nominalization has an underlying structure IDENTICAL to a corresponding clause, when it is in fact about whether a nominalization has an underlying structure CONTAINING something that underlies a corresponding clause (and generally containing other material as well). Ross's premises yield only the conclusion that *his plans to do away with someone* CONTAINS a constituent that underlies *He plans to do away with someone*; however, that weaker conclusion is exactly what he needs to argue that the lexicalist hypothesis wrongly implies that Sluicing should not be applicable in (35).

The second argument that Chomsky takes up, from Ross (1970: 267), deals with a matter that is sufficiently unclear that Chomsky is justified in saying that it shows nothing. Ross proposed that to account for the correspondence of many intransitive verbs such as *shrug, roar,* and *smile* to transitive clauses such as (37a) and nominalizations such as (37b) it is necessary to set up an underlying structure for (37a) along the lines of (38):

(37)   (a)   He shrugged his/*ϕ displeasure.
        (b)   His shrug of (*his) displeasure.
(38)   He show (he be displeased) by (he shrug).

Ross claims that an underlying structure such as (38) would explain which verbs and what objects appear in structures like (37a–b). Chomsky finds Ross's derivation implausible on the grounds that (39) then ought to mean the same as *He manifested his displeasure by manifesting his annoyance by shrugging*, 'but this seems to give the wrong meaning: he didn't manifest his displeasure by manifesting some emotion, but by a shrug' (p. 164):

(39)   He manifested his displeasure by a shrug of annoyance.

I am not convinced that this is a real difference in meaning and thus am not convinced that there is anything semantically wrong with Ross's proposed derivation. On the other hand, Ross's proposal is quite fragmentary and programmatic and does not really explain the fact which Ross laid special emphasis on (and Chomsky ignored): that the possessive is obligatory in (37a) but inadmissible in (37b).

Finally, Chomsky takes up Postal's (1969: 219–24) discussion of examples like

(40)   (a)   America's attempt to attack Cuba
        (b)   The American attempt to attack Cuba

Postal claimed that unless these NPs contain the sentence [*America attempt* [*America attack Cuba*]], 'no general account of which NP controls complement subject deletion will be possible'. Chomsky replies that

Postal's counter-argument is based on a misunderstanding. He overlooks the essential claim of the lexicalist hypothesis, namely, that grammatical relations must be generalized in such a way that the subject-verb relation holds of (*America, attempt*) in [(40a)], and perhaps even of the same pair in [(40b)]. (p. 165)

As I noted above, this 'generalization of grammatical relations' and of transformations reduces to zero any implications that the lexicalist position might have about what transformations apply in what nominalizations. Without this 'generalization' the lexicalist hypothesis implies that too few transformations are applicable in nominalizations, and without some equally arbitrary way of ruling out certain transformational applications in nominalizations, 'transformationalist' treatments imply that too many are. There is, however, one important point relating to examples like (40b) which may resolve this apparent standoff. Chomsky evidently takes the position that *American* in (40b) and in such examples as *American wheat, the American flag, an American soprano* is simply a prenominal adjective in deep structure, and elsewhere has taken the position that 'grammatical relations' must be determined by deep structure configurations. This means that *America(n)* is equally much the subject of *attempt* in (40b) as it is in:

(41)   The American desire for America to declare itself a monarchy.

American desire, however, is ambiguous between 'desire by America' and 'desire by Americans', and only when it means 'desire by America' can Equi-NP-deletion apply to yield:

(42)   The American desire to declare itself a monarchy.

It would thus appear that Chomsky's notion of 'grammatical relation' cannot be generalized so as to cover the relation between *America* and *attempt* in (40b) unless different occurrences of *American* are distinguished as to whether they are derived from *America* or *Americans*, which is for all practical purposes equivalent to saying that the underlying subject of *desire* in (42) IS *America* or *Americans*, as the case may be. This means that to get Chomsky's generalized notion of grammatical relation to work, it is necessary to adopt what is in effect Postal's 'Proper-pseudo-adjective (PPA) formation' rule. Or rather, I should say Postal's rule with one important error corrected. Postal stated (1969: 219) that (40b) is derived FROM (40a), whereas he should have said that it is derived from the structure that underlies (40a), in which a sentence *America attempt* (*America attack Cuba*) is embedded in a larger structure that contains whatever underlies the article *the*. The rule that replaces *the* by the subject of the nominalization has applied in the case of (40a) but not (40b). When the underlying subject is *Americans* ((43c), due to Chomsky, is an especially clear case where *Americans* and not *America* is the subject), there is no corresponding form like (40a) since (as has been observed by Zwicky) genitive plurals are virtually excluded in English.

(43)   (a)   *Americans' offers to join a cane-cutting brigade
       (b)   Offers by Americans to join a cane-cutting brigade
       (c)   American offers to join a cane-cutting brigade

This corrected version of Postal's proposal is immune to Chomsky's objection (p. 167) that Postal has no way of deriving:

(44) (a) An American attempt to attack Cuba has been expected for years.
     (b) Lots of American attempts to attack Cuba have failed.

Postal (MS) also points out that prenominal adjectives may stand in relations other than 'subject' to the nominalization, for example:

(45) (a) the Martian expedition ('goal')
     (b) (the Association for) Asian Studies ('object')
     (c) arboreal mammals ('location').

This fact implies that 'grammatical relations' are not predictable from deep structure topological relationships unless the various adjectives are derived from NPs that appear in the appropriate positions in clauses.[83]

Some additional examples cited by Chomsky only show that things which look like PPAs sometimes are really something else. For example, while (46a) allows the interpretation (46b) (as observed by Postal), it is more commonly used (as observed by Chomsky) with the interpretation (46c):

(46) (a) the Markovian solution of that problem
     (b) the solution by Markoff of that problem
     (c) the solution of that problem along lines associated with Markoff

Since Postal is no more committed to having a single source for *Markovian*, etc. than Chomsky is committed to having a single source for genitives, the existence of the interpretation (46c) is no objection to Postal's analysis.

Chomsky takes his criticism of Postal's analysis of PPAs as knocking down the strongest arguments for Postal's ANAPHORIC ISLAND PRINCIPLE, which excludes anaphoric relations between material under a 'lexical' node (that is material which is part of a noun, verb, or adjective) and something not under that node, as in:

(47) (a) *An orphan generally misses them. [= . . . his parents]
     (b) *There's a lot of meat on the it-rack. [= . . . meat-rack]

Postal argues that PPAs are anaphoric islands but can arise through a transformation, prior to which the underlying NP can play a role in the application of such transformations as Equi-NP-deletion:

> (48)   (a)   Her enemies were pleased by America's invasion of Vietnam.
>
>   (b)   *Her enemies were pleased by the American invasion of Vietnam.

There consequently must be some principle making PPAs anaphoric islands in the course of the derivation, and the above principle accomplished precisely that. But then the ungrammaticality of (47) creates no problem for an analysis which would derive *orphan* and *meat-rack* from the same sources as *person whose parents have died* and *rack for meat*: they are excluded by the same principle which excludes (48b), a principle which Postal has shown to be necessary to explain the interaction of Equi-NP-deletion and PPA-formation. Chomsky suggests an alternative to Postal's principle: 'The correct generalization seems to be that items that have a lexical entry are "anaphoric islands"'. However, Chomsky shows no way in which this conclusion is any more 'correct' than Postal's, and all cases where the two conclusions have different implications, that is, all cases of productive derivation or compounding involving NPs, seem to support Postal's conclusion and disconfirm Chomsky's:

> (49)   (a)   *Artichoke-eaters buy a lot of them. [= artichokes]
>
>   (b)   *Hegelian philosophers write huge books about him. [= about Hegel]
>
>   (c)   *Let's go to the taco stand and buy some. [= some tacos]

Thus, Chomsky agrees with Postal that an anaphoric island principle is necessary but proposes one which fits the facts less well than does Postal's.

Subsequent work (for example, Shibatani (1972)) has shown the determination of what is an anaphoric island to be far from as simple as Postal indicated. There are also interesting differences in the degree of acceptability of supposed violations of the principle. For example, while (50a) may be produced spontaneously and not felt as odd, (50b) is outrageous:

(50)   (a)   (?) I won't answer your objections, since they don't require one. [= an answer]

      (b)   *Marty hates to cook, so he's hired one. [= a cook]

These examples show the inadequacy of the proposal in Lakoff and Ross (1972) that the anaphoric island constraint may be violated in the case of anaphoric relations involving morphologically related items.[84]

4.7.1

Section 7 is devoted to discussion of some phenomena for which analyses have been proposed that involve derivational constraints. Chomsky argues in each case for an alternative analysis that does without the derivational constraint in question but instead has some SIR(s), generally SIRs involving surface structure. Since surface SIRs can be given a coherent interpretation only as a kind of global derivational constraint (see § 3.3, 4.5 above), Chomsky is in each case arguing that one kind of derivational constraint should be replaced by another. I do not find the reasons he gives for his preferences very convincing.

(51)   (a)   Many men read few books.

      (b)   Few books are read by many men.

(52)   (a)   (b)

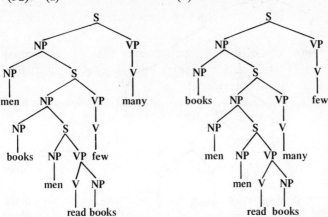

He first contrasts Jackendoff's (1969) treatment of quantifier scope, according to which (51a–b) have essentially the same deep structure and the scopes of the quantifiers are predicted from surface structure by a SIR, with Lakoff's (1970a) treatment, according to which (51a–b)

have the respective underlying structures (52a–b), there is a rule of Quantifier-lowering which attaches the quantifier to the corresponding NP of the embedded clause (and also deletes the other occurrence of that NP?), and a global derivational constraint excludes derivations in which the 'precedence' relations (see note 42) of quantifiers are reversed.

Before commenting on Chomsky's discussion, I wish to denounce (52a–b) as a half-assed attempt at generative semantics. They do not represent the meanings of (51a–b), since *Men read books* is not a constituent of the meanings of those sentences. The innermost constituent of the semantic structure should rather be the propositional function x *read* y, where x is the variable bound by *many* and y the variable bound by *few*. The indices are necessary at the very least to indicate which quantifier goes with which NP (cf. *Few men hate many men*), and the plurality of the nouns is clearly predictable from the quantifiers. In addition, quantifiers cannot be taken as predicated of NPs like *men who read few books*, as in Lakoff's proposal; see McCawley (1972) for an argument that a quantifier is predicated of an NP that denotes a set of propositions, for example, the semantic structure of (51a) would have *many* predicated of the set of propositions x *reads few books* for which x is a man:[85]

(53)

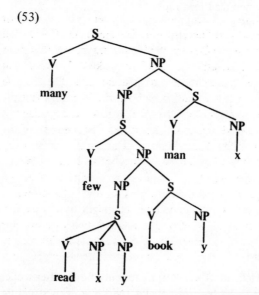

Chomsky's first objection to Lakoff's treatment is an objection to half-assed generative semantics but not to real generative semantics:

Given [Lakoff's proposal], we can say that deep structure . . . relates directly to 'logical form'. Thus we could convert [(52a)] directly to a pseudo-quantificational form such as

[(54)]   for many x ∈ Men, for few y ∈ Books, x read y.

Exactly the same is true if we drop the rule of quantifier lowering from the grammar, eliminate the derivational constraint, and take the deep structure of [(49a)] and [(49b)] to be (approximately)

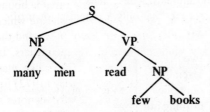

. . . There is a trivial algorithm which, applied to the surface structures, gives the pseudo-quantificational forms such as [(54)]. (p. 182)

The deepest level of derivations in real generative semantics is not just 'related to' but is identical to 'logical form'. See McCawley (1972) and Lakoff (1971b) (now also McCawley 1981c) for arguments that both linguistic and logical considerations demand trees like (53) rather than strings like (54) as the representation of content and that a single representation of content is adequate from both the logician's and the linguist's points of views. Chomsky's 'trivial algorithm' is anything but trivial, since to get it to work one must identify ALL occurrences of the variable which the quantifier binds, some of which may not be manifested at all in surface structure, and since the scope of a quantifier can perfectly well be a clause which does not appear in surface structure (for example, the scope of *two* in the most obvious sense of *John wants two children* is 'John have x', the underlying complement of *want*);[86] the analogue to this not so trivial algorithm is quantifier lowering plus a large number of rules of grammar plus the global constraint against quantifier crossover, all of which must be incorporated in some form into Chomsky's algorithm.

Chomsky claims that (55a) would require the bizarre underlying structure (55b) under Lakoff's proposal and thus presents insuperable difficulties for it:

(55)   (a)   Che's strategy of many Vietnams will succeed.
       (b)   [Vietnams [Che's strategy of Vietnams will succeed]$_s$]$_{NP}$
             many.

However, (55b) does not even come close to representing what (55a) means: (55a) does not assert that there are many of anything but rather that a certain strategy will succeed, where *many* is part of a description of that strategy. To represent the content of (55a), one must set up an embedded sentence 'there be many Vietnams' (that is, Che's strategy of there being many Vietnams, or of causing there to be many Vietnams) to serve as the scope of *many* and postulate a deletion of 'there be'. Such a proposal is supported by the fact that only 'existential' quantifiers are possible in sentences like (55a):

(56)   Che's strategy of $\left\{\begin{array}{l}\text{two}\\\text{several}\\\text{only one}\\\text{nothing but}\\\text{no}\end{array}\right\}$ Vietnam(s) will succeed.

(57)   *Che's strategy of $\left\{\begin{array}{l}\text{all}\\\text{most}\\\text{every}\end{array}\right\}$ Vietnam(s) will succeed.

A similar analysis is suggested by Jespersen (1937: 42) for sentences such as *Too many cooks spoils the broth* and *No news is good news.*

Chomsky suggests that Quantifier-lowering may be an 'impossible rule' because it violates a constraint he has proposed which excludes derivations in which a rule 'introduces an item into a phrase of an embedded sentence from outside of this sentence' (p. 184).[87] He presumably intends this constraint as applying to the purely 'syntactic' part of derivations and not to affect the action of SIRs, since the SIR which associated (54) to his surface structure would violate the constraint. To accept the constraint one must take all rules which do not conform to it to be SIRs rather than transformations; this would include sequence of tense rules, rules putting the complements of certain verbs into the subjunctive, and also conjunction reduction, which can apply 'into a lower clause' in examples such as:

(58)   (a)   Harry claimed first that Kepler and then that Newton
             had discovered Neptune.
       (b)   Chomsky and Hockett believe that word boundaries
             are phonological and semantic respectively.

I know no independent reason for this particular way of dividing rules into 'semantic' and 'syntactic'.

The examples Chomsky gives of applications of this constraint are highly dubious. He claims that it may explain the restriction on Reflexivization that the antecedent and the reflexive must be clause-mates. However, (i) it is possible to a limited extent to reflexivize into subordinate clauses in English, for example, (example from Jackendoff (1972)):

(59) That there is a picture of himself in the post office bothers Harry.

(ii) in Japanese, reflexivization goes quite freely into subordinate clauses (see Kuroda (1965), N. McCawley (1972)), and (iii) this explanation is inconsistent with the position taken elsewhere by Chomsky that reflexive pronouns are not derived by transformations but are generated as such in deep structures, their antecedents being determined by SIRs.[88] Chomsky also claims that it may explain why the copying that has been proposed in items such as (*John is*) *out of his mind* is restricted to application within the clause. However, there is in fact no such restriction, and even if there were such a restriction, it would not suffice to get the copying to work right. The contrast between *John gave Mary a piece of his/*her mind* and *John gave Mary her/*his due* shows that the idioms in question would have to be supplied with an indication of which NP gets copied. If an idiom can only require copying of an NP that is required to be present, as I will assume to be the case, then copying of an NP of a higher clause could only take place in idioms that require a higher clause of a specific shape. There are relatively few idioms that have such a restriction, but among them there indeed are a couple where copying from a higher clause takes place: *X tell Y to kiss X's/*Y's ass* and *X put X's money where X's mouth is*. Finally, Dougherty's claim, quoted by Chomsky, that Chomsky's constraint explains the ungrammaticality of (60) is based on a dubious analysis.

(60) *The robbers expected Officer O'Rourke to catch each other.

Dougherty argues that *each other* clauses have deep structures containing *each* and *the other(s)* and that *each* may be detached from its NP (61b) and then combined with *the other(s)* (61c):

(61)   (a)   Each of the men saw the others.
       (b)   The men each saw the others.
       (c)   The men saw each other.

Fiengo and Lasnik (1973) have pointed out that this would require such sentences as (62a, b) to have underlying structures with impossible combinations of quantifiers:

(62)   (a)   All of the men were hitting each other.
       (a′)   *Each of all of the men was hitting the others.
       (b)   Several of the boys were glaring at each other.
       (b′)   *Each of several of the boys was glaring at the others.

4.7.2.

Chomsky appends to his discussion of quantifier and negation scope a discussion of presupposition which contains some worthwhile observations but is too short to really get anywhere. He observes that *not many* carries with it a presupposition of non-emptiness and thus that sentences with *not many* are not simple negations of sentences with *many*, that is, (63a) is appropriate in the case where no arrows hit the target, but (63b) is not:

(63)   (a)   It is not true that many arrows hit the target.
       (b)   Not many arrows hit the target.

He draws a distinction between presuppositions that it is reasonable to 'incorporate into grammar' in some way and presuppositions that are only a matter of 'conversational implicature' in the sense of Grice's work, and maintains that in (64) the proposition that I have five children is a presupposition of the first kind and the proposition that the rest of my children are not in elementary school is a presupposition of the second kind.

(64)   Two of my five children are in elementary school.

Chomsky is inconsistent in applying the one criterion that he gives for distinguishing between these two kinds of presupposition, namely that in the 'conversationally implied' case there are 'conditions under which [the] assumption would be withdrawn'. This criterion is met not only by the presupposition that my other children are not in elementary school in (64) but also by the non-emptiness presupposition in (63b):[89]

- (65) (a) Two of my five children, if not more, are in elementary school.
  - (b) Not many arrows, if any, hit the target.
- (66) You get a 10% discount if you leave at least two children in elementary school; are two of your five children in elementary school? A: Yes, indeed they all are.

Chomsky maintains that a presupposition is involved in all of the cases which Jackendoff calls 'constituent negation'. While Chomsky is correct that *John and Bill are arguing about nothing*, when used in the sense in question, 'presupposes that John and Bill are arguing and asserts that there is no substance to their argument', *John and Bill often argue about nothing* does not seem to me to require any presupposition that John and Bill argue. Chomsky's discussion does not make clear whether he intends the notion 'constituent negation' to play a role in semantic representation as well as in syntax, but I get the feeling that he does. If that is in fact his intention, I hope he will provide some time an exposition of how 'constituent negation' fits into semantic representation and how it is related to the question of determining the truth value of a complex proposition. I frankly doubt that truth values could be assigned to propositions involving 'constituent negation' without in effect reinterpreting 'constituent negation' in terms of sentence negation. Chomsky dismisses an argument by Lakoff and Ross that all known examples of 'constituent negation' can be analysed as involving sentence negation:

> The argument has no force. By the same logic, we could show that sentence negation is an unnecessary notion, since there is always a paraphrase in terms of constituent negation (i.e. *not*-S can always be paraphrased as *it is false that S* or *it is not the case that S*, where we interpret *not the case* as 'constituent negation'). (p. 191)

That conclusion does not conflict with Lakoff and Ross's point, that is that there is no need to distinguish between two kinds of negation. However, as Ross (personal communication) has pointed out, it yields an inhomogeneous notion of constituent negation, since *not the N* does not otherwise function as a constituent:

- (67) Not a/*the person did I see.

4.7.3

Chomsky discusses briefly two examples involving modal auxiliary verbs. He describes the use of *may* in requests such as *May I (please) have the ashtray?* as 'another case which illustrates fairly clearly what I believe to be the typical situation' with regard to the general applicability and worthwhileness of the extended standard theory. The controversy which now rages about the status of such sentences makes it amusing that Chomsky should have used the words 'clear' and 'typical' in connection with them. 'Whimperatives' (as Sadock (1970) has christened them) have the word order (and often also the intonation) of questions but in some other respects behave syntactically like imperatives and unlike questions:

(68)   (a)   Would you please hand me the ashtray?
         (a′)   *Would you please marry a black girl if you loved her?
         (b)   Would you help me, somebody?
         (b′)   *Would you buy a used car from Nixon, somebody?
         (c)   May I have another drink, and then I'll leave.
         (c′)   *May Johnie play in your yard, and then I'll leave.

Sadock has accordingly proposed an underlying structure that involves both interrogative and imperative elements. Gordon and Lakoff (1971), on the other hand, propose that the relation between 'whimperatives' and the requests that they convey is one of conversational implicature: that one implies a request when one asserts a speaker-based felicity condition for the request (for example, the condition that the speaker desire that the action be performed: *I'd like you to please open the window*) or questions an addressee-based felicity condition (for example, the condition that the addressee be capable of performing the action: *Can you please open the window?*). In their framework, the rule inserting *please* is sensitive not to the meaning *per se* but to what is conveyed by the sentence. The treatment sketched by Chomsky may turn out not to be materially different from Gordon and Lakoff's when its details are worked out. While Chomsky proposes that *May I please have the ashtray?* is interpreted as a request by a surface SIR, he could probably equally well have chosen to have a surface SIR assign to *may* one of its 'normal' interpretations, for example, interpret *may* in (69) as meaning 'you permit me S' and '*you permit you S' respectively (which would exhibit the source of the anomaly of (69b)), and have an analogue to Gordon and Lakoff's 'conversational postulate' that would apply to the output of the latter SIR:

(69)　(a)　　May I please examine you, Dr Schwartz?
　　　　(b)　　*May you please be examined by me, Dr Schwartz?

Whether such a treatment would really require a SURFACE SIR depends on whether the interpretation of *may* as '*x* permit *y* S', with correct choice of *x* and *y*, requires one.

4.7.4

In the final example in section 7, Chomsky further extends the class of sentences that he is willing to call 'grammatical but semantically anomalous'. Labov has noted that in certain dialects of English, subject-auxiliary inversion takes place not only in independent questions, but in dependent questions which describe information which the whole sentence requests:

(70)　(a)　　I want to know were you here on Sunday.
　　　　(a′)　　*Bill knows were you here on Sunday.
　　　　(b)　　Tell me why did you do it.
　　　　(b′)　　*I told him why did you do it.

Lakoff proposes that in these dialects subject-auxiliary inversion is a global rule making reference to information in semantic structure which specifies what information, if any, the sentence requests. Chomsky replies that 'equivalently, we can say that the rule applies freely, and the result must be interpreted as such a request – it will be excluded as semantically anomalous if for some reason this interpretation is impossible' (p. 195). Chomsky does not make clear what he means by 'freely' here; I conjecture that he means the rule to be restricted to clauses which Bresnan (1970) treats as having the complementizer Q and to be optional. It is not completely clear that a simple SIR based on surface structure is possible: there are sentences in which the effect of subject-auxiliary inversion either is vacuous or is cancelled out by other rules (for example, *Who hit you?*), and the subject-auxiliary inversion in sentences with preposed negative expressions and in exclamatory sentences gives rise to surface structures that differ but little from those of questions:

(71)　(a)　　At no time has he felt better.
　　　　(a′)　　At any time has he felt better?
　　　　(b)　　Boy, do I feel tired!
　　　　(b′)　　Do you feel tired?

As in many previous cases, Chomsky's failure to state the relevant SIR leaves one unable to discuss his analysis in any detail.

4.8

Chomsky begins the brief final section (pp. 195–9) by summing up the arguments of the preceding sections and stating that 'It seems to me that in the few areas of substantive difference, generative semantics has been taking the wrong course. But to a certain extent, the differences between these two approaches are hardly more than notational, hence of no serious concern' (p. 197).

In the final two pages of 'Empirical issues', Chomsky states explicitly some premises which can be seen lurking beneath some of the discussions in its earlier sections. He takes the following position on how transformations work:

> Such sentences as *John received the book, John read the book, John expected the book to be good, John gave Bill the book,* and so on, undergo the passive transformation in exactly the same way. The transformation applies blindly to any phrase marker of the proper form, caring nothing about meanings or grammatical relations. This situation is typical; I know of no exceptions, and no counterarguments that amount to more than terminological revision. (p. 197)[90]

Chomsky's reference to 'terminological revision' misleadingly suggests that his conception of 'blindly applying' transformations had achieved the status of a paradigm. Actually, 'terminological revision' is an equally good description of the alternative that Chomsky suggests in cases where transformations have been proposed that do not apply 'blindly', that is, his suggestion that what is at work is a blind transformation acting jointly with a seeing-eye SIR. His claim that all transformations are 'blind' has the same status as the claim that all human beings are blind but that their heads contain two parasitic organisms which are connected to the brain in an intricate fashion and provide sensory data: while there is no obvious way to refute the claim, there is also no apparent point in making it. What little justification Chomsky attempts for his claim is contained in the following passage:[91]

> A central idea in much of structural linguistics was that the formal devices of language should be studied INDEPENDENTLY OF THEIR USE. The earliest work in transformational-generative grammar took over a version of this thesis, as a working hypothesis. I think it has

been a fruitful hypothesis. It seems that grammars contain a substructure of PERFECTLY FORMAL RULES operating on phrase
markers in narrowly circumscribed ways. Not only are these rules
INDEPENDENT OF MEANING OR SOUND in their function, but it
may also be that the choice of these devices by a language-learner
. . . may be INDEPENDENT, TO A SIGNIFICANT EXTENT, OF CON-
DITIONS OF MEANING AND USE. (p. 198, emphasis added)

I see no justification for Chomsky's judgement that the 'blindness'
hypothesis has been fruitful. Early transformational grammar generally
steered clear of areas that would provide any test of the efficacy of
that hypothesis, and even so, in many cases the then current conception
of grammaticality ought to have led to the conclusion that some of
the rules are not so blind, for example, 'Tag-formation', as it has
generally been formulated, implies that (72) are grammatical and indeed
Passive is not really blind either, as is illustrated by Postal's examples
(73):

(72) *Someone is waiting outside, isn't he?
      *The best pitcher in the National League is Steve Carlton,
      isn't he?
      *Tabs are being kept on Harry, aren't they?
      *Tom may not be in Pittsburgh yet, may he?
(73) *Seven gorillas are slept by this cage.
      *Nixon was seen in the White House by 1969. (cf. *1969
      saw Nixon in the White House*)
      *Our consideration is merited by his suggestion.

Chomsky's observations about passives do not imply that transformations
are blind — only that they sometimes keep their eyes closed.
   The passage just quoted suggests that Chomsky's belief in the blindness of transformations rests ultimately on his belief that language
acquisition consists to a significant extent in 'accounting for' a corpus
of 'purely linguistic' data (that is, utterances isolated from their meanings
or conditions of use). I find such a picture of language acquisition highly
counterintuitive, but I have nothing better to pit against Chomsky's
gut feelings about language acquisition than my own gut feelings:
Chomsky's guts tell him that rules which apply 'blindly' have a special
status in grammar and in language acquisition, and mine tell me that
they do not.[92] It should be emphasized, however, that an awful lot of
what Chomsky subscribes to rests ultimately on this gut feeling about

the 'blindness' of transformations: his position that grammaticality is something which one determines with his eyes closed, that 'syntax' is a coherent domain, autonomous from 'semantics', and that 'syntax' is of more central concern than 'semantics', in particular, that being explicit as regards what the SIRs of a particular language are, what in general is a possible SIR, and what semantic representations are possible for the particular language and in general, can properly be neglected by the linguist in favor of the problem of making explicit what the transformations of the particular language are, what is a possible transformation in general, and what deep structures and surface structures are possible both in the particular language and in general.

In general, I find this book disappointing, as a result of Chomsky's failure to grapple with important questions which are intimately connected with the proposed or implied revisions in his grammatical theory in which this book abounds. Only by considerable exercise of the imagination can one fit the pieces together and fill in the lacunae and come up with some picture of what Chomsky currently considers to be a possible grammar of a human language. Until Chomsky does this filling in of gaps and working out of details himself, he does not have a linguistic theory but only a program of a theory. While there now exists a work (Jackendoff 1972) which gives a fairly systematic exposition of a linguistic theory resembling what Chomsky appears to be advocating in this book, Chomsky has not made clear whether he subscribes to Jackendoff's specific conception of semantic structure and of how rules of a grammar interact. Chomsky owes it to the linguistic profession to publish a formulation of his current conception of a grammar that is explicit enough to allow a reader to determine answers to the many questions which I have been forced in this review to answer only on the basis of conjectures about Chomsky's intentions or to leave unanswered altogether.[93]

Notes

*I am grateful to Noam A. Chomsky, Donald Frantz, Robert Freidin, Georgia Green, R. A. Hudson, S.-Y. Kuroda, Susan Schmerling, and the anonymous referee of an anonymous journal, and especially to George Lakoff, Paul Postal, and Haj Ross, for valuable criticism of all or part of an earlier draft of this review. This review embodies a fair amount of plagiarism of ideas expressed by Lakoff and Ross in letters written in 1967-70; I express my gratitude to them for not prosecuting me.

1.   I use the word 'reprint' loosely: *SSGG* appeared six months before the volume in which its third paper 'originally appeared', and what is reprinted is

not the published versions of the papers but the prepublication versions that circulated in mimeographed and dittoed form. The few discrepancies between the two versions are mainly in the bibliographies, which in *SSGG* are out of date and mutually inconsistent; papers published as long ago as 1968 are cited as unpublished, and the same paper is sometimes cited under different titles and dates.

2. Throughout this review, I will use the term 'nominalization' in a narrower sense than Chomsky does. Where Chomsky speaks of a 'gerundive nominalization' (for example, the bold-face part of *I am amazed at **Bill's killing his wife***), I will speak of a 'Poss-ing complement'.

3. [As evidence against a derivation of *John felt sad* from a deep structure with a sentential complement, Chomsky cites several differences between *John felt sad* and *John felt that he was sad*. However, the behavior of *feel* with a *that* complement is not characteristic of its behavior with complements in general; indeed, *feel* with an *as if* complement behaves like *John felt sad* in all respects in which Chomsky shows *feel* with a *that* complement to behave differently, e.g. it allows a progressive form:

John was feeling sad.
John was feeling as if he was sad.
*John was feeling that he was sad.]

4. Whatever treatment of selectional restrictions one might have provided in the *Syntactic structures* framework could be supplemented by rules like (1) which referred to more restrictive categories than 'V' and 'NP'.

5. An observation very close to this is made in Lakoff (1965: § A–6): 'The underlying subject-object relation is unchanged in nominalization'. Chomsky's observation differs from Lakoff's in referring to all transformations rather than only to those which change 'grammatical relations' (for example, create a new subject). Later in this section I will show that Lakoff's observation fits the facts better than does Chomsky's.

Postal (1974, ch. 10) argues that Subject-raising does in fact take place in certain nominalizations, for example, *John's tendency to be rude*. Chomsky (personal communication) holds these to involve not Subject-raising but Relative-clause-reduction, from a relative clause based on *John has a tendency to be rude*. This issue revolves about the question of whether the latter structure is 'basic' (Chomsky) or 'derived' (Postal).

6. [Newmeyer (1976: 156–61) argues that a nominalization transformation would have to be precyclic, from which he concludes that the rules of word-formation are separate from transformations in a narrow sense, even if they are regarded as involving the same sorts of operations as transformations in the narrow sense. Since Newmeyer's arguments all relate to failure of MOVEMENT transformations (indeed, of relation-changing transformations such as *there*-insertion) to apply prior to word-formation rules, they are consistent with the alternative generalization by Lakoff (1965) referred to in note 5; for further discussion of this point, see note 8 to Chapter 4.]

7. [Subsequent to the appearance of *SSGG*, interpretive semanticists have unanimously rejected a transformation of Equi-NP-deletion in favor of analyses involving either non-finite Ss with empty subjects (Jackendoff 1972: 178–228) or subjectless VPs (Bresnan 1971: 263–9, Brame 1976: 73–86). Regardless of whether the relationship between understood subjects and their controllers is expressed in terms of a deletion transformation or a SIR, Chomsky's treatment of nominalizations will require not only Ss but also NPs to be admitted as domain of application of the rule(s) in question. Similar comments apply to reflexivization, discussed below. The arguments that have been offered against an Equi-NP-deletion transformation have been concerned entirely with the 'classical' version of that transformation, in which not merely coreference but also lexical identity between

the controller and the deleted NP is required. Little attention appears to have been given to an alternative version of Equi-NP-deletion in which what is deleted is a personal pronoun coreferential with the controller. The choice between this version of Equi-NP-deletion and the 'interpretive' accounts of Jackendoff, Bresnan, and Brame rests on rather subtle distinctions: for example, the 'empty' subject NP in Jackendoff's account functions as a pronoun (as it must, if it is to be taken in under Jackendoff's general anaphora rule), and thus the difference between Jackendoff's account and the alternative suggested in the last sentence rests largely on the distinction between a pronoun that is phonologically zero throughout a derivation and a pronoun that becomes phonologically zero in the course of a derivation.]

8.   Ross (personal communication) points out that there is at least one deletion rule which does not 'generalize' to NPs:

The roast is ready to carve.

*The roast's readiness to carve

(cf. John's readiness to carve the roast)

Lakoff (personal communication) has pointed out that while *easy, difficult*, etc. do not allow nominalizations such as **John's easiness/ease to please*, they do allow *Our ease in deceiving John, Bill's difficulty in writing clearly*, etc. According to Chomsky's hypothesis, the nominalizations reflect base structures and *easy*, etc., ought thus to have the 'experiencer' as deep subject. Chomsky's hypothesis thus appears to imply that *To please John is easy for us* should be derived from *We be easy in* [*we please John*] by the transformation that has been variously called Flip, Psych-movement, etc.

9.   [In Chomsky's subsequent treatments of passivization (for example, 1976), there is no passive transformation as such but only a transformation formulated as 'move NP' or even 'move α', that applies twice in the derivation both of passives and of passive-like NPs such as *the city's destruction by the enemy*. Chomsky assumes Emonds's (1970, 1976) typology of movement transformations, according to which this rule must be 'structure-preserving' and thus can only move NPs into positions where NPs are in some sense 'allowed'. Under the specific version of structure-preservation that Emonds argues for, in which the constraint on movement transformations is that the items affected must replace constituents (possible empty ones) of the same syntactic category, there is no ready explanation of the oddity of (7a'–b') or the difference in acceptability between:

(i)   the destruction by the enemy

(ii)   *was destroyed by the enemy.

This is because Emonds's structure-preserving constraint constrains only the structure into which the moved item is inserted and says nothing about what is left behind in the structure from which it is extracted; similarly, it imposes no constraint on deletion transformations. Thus, in Emonds's framework, the base rules yield restrictions on what is allowed in surface structure but not on what is required: transformations are prevented from inserting items into positions in which their occurrence would be anomalous but are not prevented from removing them from positions in which their absence is anomalous. (This last point is made in Abbott (1979)). There is an alternative to Emonds's version of structure-preservation in which 'base rules' can serve not only to constrain what may occur in surface structure but to make certain constituents obligatory in surface structure, namely that in which the 'base rules' are treated AS combinatoric restrictions on surface structure, that is only those surface structures are permitted that conform to those rules. Such an approach is developed in McCawley (1981a) and below in Chapter 4, where I argue that the evidence offered by Emonds for a principle of 'structure-preservation' is really only evidence that languages have combinatoric restrictions on surface structure and is neutral as to whether anything is 'preserved' in the course of the derivation (that is, his evidence is neutral as to whether deep structures are subject to the same constraints).

Adherents of Chomsky's 'move α' treatment of passives have given remarkably little attention to the question of how to insure that passive auxiliary verbs (*be* and *get*) occur if and only if the appropriate NP movements take place; to my knowledge the only discussion of this question is in Fiengo 1974: 60–3. The point that has been largely lost in the discussion of NP-movement is that movement of NPs into NP positions is constrained not only by general principles about movements and traces but by language-particular rules that require particular constructions to be marked in specific ways.

10.   [Much of the published discussion of nominalization transformations speaks of them as involving change of category (for example, the index of Jackendoff (1972) includes an entry 'Nominalization transformations (V → N)'). There actually are two notions of 'change of category' that must be distinguished: change of the category to which a particular linguistic unit belongs and change of the category that appears in a given position of a construction. Proposed nominalization transformations generally do not involve the former sort of change of category, for the trivial reason that they give rise to such derived structures as [N [V kill] -er] , in which *kill* remains as much a verb as when it is an independent word (cf. Chomsky and Halle (1968), ch. 3, where such structures are regularly assumed). Different transformational treatments of nominalization differ with regard to whether they involve the second kind of category change. The 'updated Lees' treatment of the last paragraph does not, since the derived noun (for example, *killer*) is in a position that had been filled by an N (here, *-er* or an abstract agent nominalization marker); indeed, one could trivially make that treatment conform to Emonds's 'structure-preserving' principle by setting up deep structures involving [N [V Δ] -er], etc. By contrast, an alternative discussed in note 17, in which nominalization involves not extraction of the predicate element of an embedded S but insertion of a nominalization marker into the S, does involve the second kind of change of category, since it leaves an N in a position previously occupied by a V or an A (or occupied by something that underlies a V or an A, to choose a locution that does not prejudice the issue of whether lexical insertion has already applied to the predicate of the embedded S).

11.   [For a thorough discussion of the syntax and semantics of 'complex nominals', of which nominalizations are only a very special case, see now Levi (1978). Levi derives complex nominals from relative clause and N-complement constructions via steps that include formation of prenominal modifiers, deletion of a limited set of semantically primitive predicates, and conversion of certain dependent nouns into adjectival form, for example, *musical clock* is derived from a structure that also underlies *clock that makes music* via intermediate stages that correspond to *music-making clock* and *?music clock*. She argues that aside from idioms such as *honeymoon* and *Dutch oven*, which provide no more reason for one to treat the syntax and semantics of complex nominals as irregular than *kick the bucket* forces one to treat [V̄ V NP] combinations as irregular, it is morphology rather than syntax and semantics that is the locus of irregularity in complex nominals, that is, it is unpredictable whether a given verb, adjective, or noun has particular derived forms at all and what their morphemic composition is.]

12.   Such a deletion is necessary since, for example, from (13b) and the proposition that Susan is going to marry Tiny Tim one can infer that you will never believe that Susan is going to marry Tiny Tim, but not that you will never believe Tiny Tim.

13.   I note parenthetically that generative semanticists have had very little to say about articles and generally, lacking any concrete proposal for the derivation of articles, have omitted them from their proposed derivations, trusting that

whatever analysis of them is right could be combined with the proposed analyses of complements, relative clauses, etc. without their having to be changed materially. In many cases the resulting trees have misleadingly suggested that the underlying structure of a nominalization is the same as that of a complement; so misleadingly, indeed, as ocasionally to mislead the respective authors into speaking as if that were the case (I cite an example of this in § 4.6.4).

14.   Most of the use of features in *Aspects* had to do with strict subcategorization and selection. Strict subcategorization features amount to environments in the various dictionary entries (taking a dictionary entry to be a rule 'insert lexical item X in environment Y_Z'), selectional features represent presuppositions, whose fulfillment depends on the semantic structure of the sentence and the speaker's knowledge of the world, and 'inherent' features are either properties of the entities referred to or morphological properties of words. I regard these kinds of features as an artifact of the approach to the base component which Chomsky adopted, except for the morphological features, which, while not artifacts of the approach, are really not SYNTACTIC features. The one respect in which the influence of *Aspects* has been really pernicious is that it has touched off a wave of promiscuous employment of syntactic features, a fault which mars such otherwise admirable works as Ross (1967b).

[In note 16 I take up one part of Chomsky's feature representation that I now endorse, namely his separating out the lexical category of the head as one factor in a constituent's syntactic behavior. See McCawley (1981d) for elaboration of the point that 'in transformational grammar you can get away with anything if you formulate it in a feature notation'. One of the rare occasions on which transformational grammarians have objected to a use of features is Chomsky's (1966) denunciation of Harman's (1963) use of features to encode dependencies among constituents, by which Harman claimed to be able to eliminate the need for transformations. A more sophisticated version of Harman's approach has subsequently been developed by Gazdar (1981, in press), who appears not to have thereby antagonized many transformational grammarians.]

15.   [See Chapter 3 for the further point that relatively few languages conform to the supposedly possible rule $\overline{\overline{X}} \to \overline{X}$ [Spec, $\overline{X}$].]

16.   [In this paragraph I failed to recognize a very important advance that Chomsky's X-bar notation made, namely that of identifying the lexical category of the head of a constituent as an independent factor in the constituent's syntactic behavior. In my recent work on syntactic categories (for example, Chapter 4), I have argued that it is not syntactic categories as such but simply a number of distinct factors (one of them being the lexical category of the head) that determine the applicability of syntactic rules. The main fault that I now find with X-bar syntax as practised by Chomsky, Jackendoff, and others is that it gives an undeserved priority to base rules rather than to the syntactic factors themselves; for example, both Chomsky and Jackendoff require that a surface PP node correspond to a deep structure PP node and thus do not treat transformationally derived P + NP combinations (as in *the arrival* OF THE GUESTS) as PPs.]

17.   [In this passage I made the same error as Chomsky did, namely that of granting linear order an importance that it does not deserve. The following examples, discussed in Levi (1978: 200), provide evidence that nominalizations have a constituent structure like [*the* [[*criticisms of Chomsky*] *by Quine*]], in which the subject of the nominalization is outside the constituent composed of the nominalization and its object:

    (i)   the criticisms of Chomsky by Quine and those by Hockett
    (ii)   the criticisms by Quine of Chomsky (*and those of Russell)

This shows that parallelism in deep constituent structure between the nominalization and the corresponding sentence is a more reasonable demand than parallelism in deep word order, a point that becomes even clearer if one brings in the full range of forms that nominalizations can take (Levi 1978: ch. 5), that is, not only (iii) but also (iv)–(vi):

(iii)   abuse of children by parents
(iv)   child abuse by parents
(v)   parental abuse of children
(vi)   parental child abuse

A demand that one but not all of these expressions have a deep structure parallel to that of a corresponding S would seem to me to be completely capricious.]

It should also be noted that the point made about (i)–(ii) also presents a serious problem for the nominalization transformation that I defend in this review: if nominalization involves extraction of the predicate element of an embedded S and amalgamation of it with an element outside that S, then the nominalized predicate will be one level higher in the constituent structure than the facts about (i)–(ii) argued it to be. The closest analogue to the nominalization transformation proposed above that is consistent with the facts about (i)–(ii) may be one in which the abstract head noun that I posited is adjoined to the predicate of the embedded S, rather than vice versa.]

18.   In his criticism of Lakoff's 'abstract verb' proposal, Chomsky makes an admonition which he could well have applied here: 'This requires devices of great descriptive power which should, correspondingly, be very "costly" in terms of a reasonable evaluation measure' (p. 31).

19.   [For ways of doing X-bar syntax so as to make S and NP parallel, see Jackendoff (1977) and Koster (1978), which in turn are criticized in Verkuyl (1981).]

20.   Chomsky gives no attention to the possibility of multiple sources for *V-able* adjectives, which a generative semantic treatment would have to admit in view of the fact (observed by Chomsky) that there is a wide range of relationships that the meaning of *V-able* can have to the meaning of *V*. Indeed, *readable* is ambiguous between a sense 'easy to read' and a sense 'can be read', as illustrated by the fact that the presence of a *by*-phrase precludes the presence of *very*:

This book is (*very) readable by a 10-year-old.

I have not examined *V-able* adjectives in enough detail to have a clear feeling as to whether they represent a fairly small number of ways of combining semantic material into a word.

21.   Note that the underlying subject of *avoid* serves as controller for deletion of the subject of *change*.

22.   [+ cause] is evidently supposed to be a verb. Chomsky does not make clear whether it is intentional on his part that the embedded verb has a tense but [+ cause] does not. He indicates (p. 15) that he writes [+ cause] instead of *cause* since the hypothetical verb has a different meaning from the English verb. Distinctions would have to be drawn even among the things that he calls [+ cause] : the hypothetical verb of (25b) obviously does not mean the same as the one which he hypothesizes in *The stories amused him.*

23.   [See now Dowty (1978) and Wasow (1977) for detailed proposals regarding the role of redundancy rules in grammar. Wasow (1977: 333–8) gives an account of *V-able* adjectives in which he is able to explain the oddity of **John is believable to have left* without assuming a 'Raising to object' transformation (which Chomsky rejected subsequently to the writing of 'Nominalization'; for both Chomsky and Wasow, *Bill believes John to have left* has a deep AND surface structure in which *John to have left* is a surface S). Wasow maintains (1977: 331) that lexical rules can 'involve only NPs bearing grammatical relations to items in question'. Since, under the analysis he assumes, *John* bears no grammatical relation to *believe* in *Bill believes John to have left,* it cannot serve as subject of *believable* in Wasow's lexical rule for *V-able*.]

24.   Chomsky's analogical rule is inadequate to account for a number of the examples of adverbs inside nominalizations given in Ikeuchi (1972), for example:

> I am indebted to many students whose reactions and ideas when this material has been presented have led to quite substantial modifications (*Aspects*, p. vii).

> The decline of property values in an area after a new racial group enters it.

25.   [I realize now that I likewise did not appreciate what the real issues were. I now place a very different interpretation on the arguments that Chomsky criticized here. Lakoff, Bach, and I were able to take our arguments as establishing that the categories of syntax were identical to those of logic only because we made certain gratuitous assumptions that Lakoff and I at least have subsequently repudiated, namely the assumptions that 'base rules' must refer to the deepest level of derivations and that the syntactic categories at that level are all the syntactic categories that there are. I now interpret our arguments as having at most shown that the logical category of an item plays a role in its syntactic behavior; they showed absolutely nothing about whether any other factors also influenced the way that items behave syntactically.]

26.   Becker and Arms (1969) provide arguments for treating predicate prepositions (for example, *John is in the woodshed*) as belonging to the same underlying category as verbs. The prepositions of such sentences as *He hammered the dent out of the fender* are discussed in McCawley (1971a), where it is proposed that they involve Predicate-raising (yielding BECOME-NOT-IN in this case) followed by whatever process adjoins prepositions to their objects. It is the latter rule which explains the lack of 'intransitive prepositions': a 1-place predicate can not meet the conditions for the rule that distinguishes prepositions from adjectives. No generative semanticist has yet attempted a general survey of prepositions; I have no general feeling as regards how broad a range of prepositions can be taken as corresponding to predicates in semantic structure.

[I now follow Jespersen, Jackendoff, and Emonds in treating 'particles', as in *He looked the plans over*, as intransitive prepositions and thus now deny the 'fact' to which I referred in this note. On the superficiality of the distinctions among preposition, particle, and subordinating conjunction, see Jespersen (1924: 88). I disagree, however, with Jackendoff's and Emonds's judgement that one-word PPs are necessarily prepositions without objects; I regard *home* in *He ran home* as an object with understood or incorporated preposition.]

27.   He evidently had not yet read Bach (1968), which was written at roughly the same time as 'Nominalization'.

28.   [The matter I brought up in this passage is an extraneous issue: if Chomsky wants to make the deep structures of nominalizations parallel to, but not identical to, those of corresponding sentences, he can undoubtedly build aspectual features into the structures in some way or other without setting up embedded sentences. I should have pointed out here that Lakoff and Chomsky were simply talking about different topics: Lakoff's analysis requires that the nouns in question be treated as underlying predicates but does not require that 'predicate' be identified with 'verb', notwithstanding the use by both me and Lakoff of 'V' as a symbol for 'predicate' in our underlying structures. Treating *author* or *assistant vice-chancellor* as involving a predicate need not obscure one's perception of the fact that the words in question belong to the lexical category 'noun' and can thus appear only in the surface configurations in which items of that category are permitted.]

29.   Chomsky included a fourth example here, *the plan for John to leave*. However, since it is open to an obvious analysis as a nominalization of the verb *plan* (cf. *Our plan for John to leave* and *We planned for John to leave*), there is no particular reason to try to analyze it as involving a reduced relative.

30.   See, however, Gruber (1976: 34) for a more cogent argument against the Lakoff-Fillmore treatment of *of*.

31.   I was wrong in assuming that indices are 'features' at all. In later work I have represented an index as a daughter of an NP node, since it constitutes a whole NP in semantic structure, is realized as a personal pronoun if the NP is not otherwise supplied with lexical material, and can reasonably be taken as underlying the article (if any) of the corresponding NP of surface structure.

[See the introduction to this volume and Chapter 2 for remarks on the subsequent status of referential indices in work in (revised) extended standard theory. The point I make about (34) remains valid in an approach that avoids transformations of Reflexivization and Equi-NP-deletion in favor of SIRs specifying possible coreference relations, with the indices then being part of a semantic structure rather than of syntactic structures. See note 54 for the point that the identity involved in (33) is actually identity neither of NPs nor of Ns but of N̄s.]

32.   However, he withholds an unqualified endorsement of Emonds's specific way of incorporating that generalization into linguistic theory, which is to allow deep structures containing 'empty nodes' (for example, an NP node which dominates no nodes) and to constrain rules of the cycle so that they can only put material under an already existing node of the same type. Emonds does not totally avoid the problem of arbitrary labeling, since his conception of a possible base component is so unconstrained that virtually any desired derived structure and labeling could be admitted by allowing the desired nodes to appear in base structures as 'empty nodes'. [Emonds (1976) and Jackendoff (1977) formulate a number of constraints on 'possible base component' that greatly reduce one's freedom in writing these 'base rules'.]

33.   [I cringe at reading 'what comes "first" in some sense or other' as my informal paraphrase of 'directionality'. Until I began preparing the revision of this review for this volume, I labored under the blissful misconception that I had never used 'first' in that way in print. I reject everything that 'first' in such a sentence connotes, including (i) the idea that in speech production the construction of sentences on one particular level (such as semantic structure) temporally precedes their construction on other levels; (ii) the idea that there is one 'basic' linguistic level, such that linguistic structures on all other levels are derived from structure on that level; and (iii) the idea that there is a linguistic level such that well-formedness on that level is a precondition to the question of well-formedness on other levels even arising. See McCawley (1981a) for discussion of (ii) and (iii), which are two versions of what I dub there 'combinatory Platonism'.

I included the parenthesized plural marker in 'stage(s)' to indicate that there need not be only one stage of derivations for which a grammar contains a system of well-formedness constraints, and if there is more than one, one need not assign any particular priority to one of them. I accordingly reject as absurd the idea that it is desirable 'not to generate' the 'garbage' that output constraints 'dispose of'; that supposed objection to output constraints makes the, to me, unintelligible supposition that the surface structures in derivations that conform to all rules of the grammar except for the output constraints 'are generated' whereas those in which the deep structure does not conform to the base rules but everything otherwise conforms to the grammar are 'not generated'. It was partly as a result of the gratuitous assumptions alluded to in note 25 that I regarded rules of wellformedness for semantic structures as a closer analogue than a system of output constraints to Chomsky's 'base component'. In addition, I shared the then widespread belief that output constraints did not make up a 'complete' set of wellformedness conditions (for example, there were surface configurations like [S NP VP] whose well-formedness I did not at that time think had to be expressed in an output constraint) whereas the set of well-formedness conditions on logical structures WAS supposed to be as 'complete' as Chomskyan 'base rules' were supposed to be.]

34.   I have assumed that by 'substructure' Chomsky meant 'subtree', that is, a node and whatever nodes it dominates.

35.   Fillmore (1971a: 54) has since rejected this particular aspect of his analyses and now holds that node labels are not an appropriate way to represent 'functions' or 'relations'.

36.   Fillmore actually did not take case representations to be unordered but left it open whether they are ordered or not. Chomsky gives the question of the orderedness of elements far more emphasis than Fillmore did and far more than it deserves. While it is obviously easier to do without deep constituent order in a system with labeled relations than would otherwise be the case, the question of whether deep structures (or semantic representations) should be taken as ordered is logically independent of the question of whether they should involve labeled relations, and all logically conceivable combinations of answers to these two questions are attested in the literature; in particular, the assumption that deep structures are ordered has been contested in Staal (1967) and Sanders (1971) from viewpoints that are otherwise close to the standard theory. I conjecture that the reason why Chomsky finds unordered underlying structures such a departure from the standard theory is that he subscribes to the position that strings rather than trees are basic in syntax and wishes to reduce trees to classes of strings, and operations on trees to operations on classes of strings. This is to a certain extent possible if all structures are ordered, but is completely out of the question if unordered trees are admitted. [In McCawley 1981a: 177, I maintain that 'the proposition that at least some underlying structures in at least some languages involve at least some left-to-right ordering' is 'a weakly supported empirical proposition'. On the status of left-to-right order and constituent structure, see also Matthews (1967), an unduly neglected gem whose significance is discussed in Pullum (1980b), and McCawley (to appear a), where I argue that surface structures involving discontinuous constituents are necessary, for example, an extraposed clause remains a constituent of its NP even though it is not adjacent to the rest of the NP.]

37.   My proposal was that the underlying structure of (2a) was 'All $x \in \{\text{Tom}, \text{Dick}\}$, x love $f(x)$' plus an *ad hoc* definition of the function f: $f(\text{Tom}) = \text{Mary}$, $f(\text{Dick}) = \text{Alice}$.

38.   Chomsky's misinterpretation of my proposal is not totally outlandish, since in one case where he falsely attributed the conjunction-reduction treatment to me, that treatment is more plausible than what I was actually proposing, and since some of my later remarks in McCawley (1968b) suggested that I still accepted the conjunction-reduction treatment of *respectively*.

39.   Chomsky's juxtaposition of the terms 'semantically based grammar' and 'generative semantics', is misleading, coming as it does at the end of an argument which began with an almost verbatim repetition of the passage quoted above in which 'semantically based' is identified with 'semantic structures are chosen "first"'.

40.   I will ignore the fact that strictly speaking they need not have any semantic representation, since the expression 'semantic representation of X' makes sense only in cases where X is a sentence. [This is incorrect: the use of the lambda-operator that is made in Montague grammar in fact enables one to assign semantic representations to constituents other than sentences.] Chomsky can be interpreted as having meant that (12a–c) 'make the same contribution to semantic representation'.

41.   Discussing the inferences that can be made from (13a–c) is made awkward by the fact that (13a) is at least three ways ambiguous: the embedded sentence can be interpreted as either involving a definite description or not (in the

latter case the embedded sentence can be paraphrased as 'The bank robber is uncle to John', which does not presuppose that John has one and only one uncle, whereas the 'definite description' sense does), and the definite description could have either the embedded clause or the whole sentence for its scope; (13b–c) are each at least two-ways ambiguous, having an ambiguity as to the scope of the definite description operator. Chomsky evidently refers throughout the discussion to senses of (13a–c) which have a definite description with the embedded clause as scope. The haphazard choice of articles in (12b–c) makes the argument harder to follow than it might otherwise be; Chomsky's intentions would probably be served better by replacing *the* by *a* before all the nouns except *person*.

42.   In his discussion of quantifiers, Lakoff (1969a) defines 'precedence' as follows: X has precedence over Y if either X and Y are clause mates and X is to the left of Y or X and Y are not clause mates and X commands Y.

43.   My remarks here owe much to Schmerling (1971). [See now Schmerling (1976).]

44.   (25a–b) are acceptable if used as questions about choice of words, for example, in a rehearsal of an appearance in court, where the witness is asking the lawyer if he has the story correct. In this case the words are mentioned and not just used.

45.   Chomsky recognizes this problem and remarks (pp. 98–9) that it 'suggests that when expressive or contrastive stress shifts intonation center, the same principle applies as in normal cases for determining focus and presupposition, but with the additional proviso that naturalness declines far more sharply as larger and larger phrases containing the intonation center are considered as a possible focus'. However, size of the focused constituent is surely irrelevant: any NP, no matter how complicated (for example, *the celebrated singer and actor who is a frequent golfing partner of the former Vice President*), could serve as focus in place of *Frank Sinatra* in (28b), but *Sinatra sing* could not serve as focus in *Did Sinátra sing yesterday*?

46.   [This objection rests on the widely accepted assumption that all constituent structure is continuous. According to the position for which I argue in McCawley (to appear a), in which transformations that, like Particle separation, serve only to change word order have no effect on constituent structure and thus yield discontinuous structures when non-sisters are permuted, *look over* is a surface constituent in (29) and thus Ross's objection evaporates.]

47.   [In Chomsky's subsequent work, for example, in the Specified Subject Constraint of Chomsky (1973), grammatical relations sometimes play a role in general principles of rule application, though not in the formulation of particular syntactic rules. Since the writing of this review, an approach to syntax has been developed in which the bulk of syntactic rules are formulated directly in terms of grammatical relations, namely relational grammar, of which Johnson and Postal (1980) and Perlmutter (in press) provide detailed presentations. A precursor of relational grammar can be seen in Jespersen (1937), in which a syntactic analysis is a single structure in which items are represented as having underlying and superficial grammatical relations to other items.]

48.   [The well-known disagreements among linguists over the proper analysis of quantifier scope are remarkable for the disputants' near-unanimous acceptance of a statement of the facts that is well known to be incorrect. Kuno (1971: 351–70) and Ioup (1974) are among the few linguists that have grappled seriously with factors other than precedence and command that affect possible scope relations, for example, the identity of the quantifiers (in *Two secretaries assist each executive*, the second quantifier and not the first has higher scope) and the 'derivational history' of the relevant NPs (Kuno argues that rightward movement does not

reverse scope relations, as in *Welcoming kisses were given many boys by every girl*, in which *every* has higher scope than *many*.) The advocates of the better known analyses of quantified NPs have for undetermined reasons accorded higher priority to giving an elegant statement of a popular misrepresentation of the facts than to exploiting their approaches in providing an accurate account of the facts.]

49.   Chomsky's statement that (34c) would be related not to (34a), of which it is a paraphrase, but to (34b), of which it is not, 'by the simplest form of the passive operation' presupposes that passivization applies to structures in which quantifiers are within their NPs and negatives are within the clauses which they negate. Strictly speaking, the 'simplest form of the passive operation' is that which the contrary assumption, in conjunction with the assumption that auxiliaries are main verbs, allows: the formulation in that case need not mention auxiliary verbs and an optional *not*.

50.   [Jacobson and Neubauer (1976) argue that Adverb-preposing is in the cycle, on the basis of its interactions with Super-Equi-NP-deletion.]

51.   Chomsky makes clear that he prefers this alternative. He states that a deep structure having *can* in the complement of *seem* 'appears implausible in that in general *to*-VP constructions, as in [(41)], exclude modals'. I have argued (1971b) that the absence of modals in '*to*-VP constructions' and many other environments is a fact of morphology rather than syntax (namely that modals in English have at most a present and a past form) and that the absence of sentences such as **John seems to can't get his homework done on time* follows from the universal output constraint that a sentence may not contain a non-existent form (in this case, the non-existent infinitive of *can*) and implies nothing about the existence of such a structure at earlier stages of derivations. [Jespersen (1924: 286) also noticed the *can't seem* construction and speculated that it exists as a means of avoiding the non-existent infinitive of *can*. See, however, Boertien (1979) for discussion of dialects of English in which some modals have infinitive forms; it appears, though, that *to can* does not exist in any of them.]

52.   Chomsky, to my knowledge, has never explicitly distinguished between these two sources of deviance, though I conjecture that he would have to in order to work out the details of his proposal. Jackendoff (1972: 17) explicitly makes such a distinction.

Under Chomsky's assumptions, all the deviant sentences relevant to the analysis of *can't seem* may be grammatical. For example, since in his preferred analysis the deep structure of (41) has *John gets his homework done on time* as complement of *seem*, the result of applying extraposition to that structure, namely **It can't seem that John gets his homework done on time* will also be grammatical.

53.   Since the question in the first column above involves the word *all*, a negative answer to it does not imply that *no* personal pronouns are derived from copies of their antecedents. Lakoff (1968b) in fact presents solid arguments for taking sentential *it* as derived from a copy of its antecedent: saying that sentential *it* is derived from a copy of its antecedent but 'ordinary' personal pronouns are not allows an explanation of the fact that only the latter can form 'Bach–Peters sentences':

The boy$_i$ who loved her$_j$ kissed the girl$_j$ who admired him$_i$.
    *(That Bill predicted it$_i$)$_j$ suggests that (Tom denied it$_j$)$_i$.

54.   [Jackendoff (1977: 58) points out that *one* stands not for a noun but for an $\bar{\text{N}}$, that is, the constituent consisting of a noun plus its strictly subcategorized adjuncts:

The students of physics did better than the students/*ones of chemistry.
The students of physics who took the oral exam did better than the ones who took the written exam.]

55. [Under Chomsky's current conception of movement rules, in which a moved item leaves in its place a phonologically zero 'trace', the surface structure of (47) DOES contain a constituent that corresponds to 'John washed the car', namely '*t* washed the car'.]

56. See Fiengo and Lasnik (1973) for arguments against the first claim, given within a theoretical framework apparently identical to Dougherty's. [See Dougherty (1974) for a reply to Fiengo and Lasnik.]

57. One important distinction which has been overlooked in discussions of sentences such as (48-9) is that (48a) is more specific as to how many brothers each man has than is (49): (49) is appropriate in the case where each man has only one brother, but (48a) is not. Since (49) is clearly unspecified rather than ambiguous as to whether each man has only one brother, (49) and (48a) could not have exactly the same semantic structure but would have to differ at least to the extent of *brother* in (49) but not in (48a) being unspecified as to number. I made essentially the same point in my discussion (1968b) of *the (respective) string quartets of Eierkopf and Misthaufen*, which is unspecified as to how many quartets each composer wrote, whereas in *the string quartet(s) of Eierkopf and the string quartet(s) of Misthaufen*, each conjunct must be specified as singular or plural. [See now McCawley (1976b) for arguments that underlying structures must be admitted in which items can be indeterminate with regard to such features as person, number, and gender.]

Partee (1971: 662) has argued on the basis of the following examples that *each*-movement would not preserve grammaticality unless the form of pronouns were determined by a later rule:

(a)   Each of the men shaved himself.
(b)   *The men each shaved himself.
(c)   *Each of the men shaved themselves.
(d)   The men each shaved themselves.

and that Chomsky's position would thus require an analysis according to which (48a) was related to (49) rather than to (48b). I conjecture that Chomsky would consider (b-c) to be grammatical (though 'uninterpretable') and would thus not regard (a-d) as providing any evidence against the second part of Dougherty's claim.

58. Chomsky points out that there are many cases where a present perfect is not accompanied by such a presupposition, for example, *Aristotle has demonstrated that S* and the use of *Einstein has (just) died* to report 'hot news'. His reference to 'interpretation of perfect aspect' in the passage quoted is evidently a mistake, since he gives examples where the same phenomenon appears in a simple present tense and makes clear that it does not appear in the past perfect. If the presupposition is to be 'tied' to any one syntactic constituent, that would have to be the present tense morpheme.

Ross (personal communication) has pointed out that even in 'neutrally stressed' examples like (50), it is not the surface subject but the CYLIC SUBJECT (that is the NP that is subject of the clause in question at the end of the application of the cycle to that clause) which is required to refer to something that still exists, since the raising of *who* into a higher clause in

!Einstein, who many people realize has visited Princeton, is widely admired.
does not affect the presupposition. Thus Chomsky's SIR gives incorrect results if it is taken to be a SURFACE SIR. [As in the case taken up in note 55, the surface structure of the last example WOULD contain a constituent corresponding to the cyclic subject according to Chomsky's present views, namely the trace left behind by WH-movement. For more on the question of how many distinct senses the English present perfect has, see now Inoue (1979) and McCawley (1981e).]

59.   I have ignored the steps from 'P_i' to 'P_{j-i}' in Chomsky's exposition of (extended) standard theory, since the incomplete trees that appear as those stages of his derivations play no role in any issues of any importance.

60.   [Akmajian, Steele, and Wasow (1979) offer an analysis of auxiliary verbs that combines characteristics of both Chomsky's and Ross's analyses. They treat auxiliary verbs other than modals as verbs that head what are roughly VPs but are divided into distinct categories V^3, V^2, and V^1, with auxiliary *have* heading a V^3, progressive *be* a V^2, and 'main' verbs a V^1; they in addition have a constituent labeled 'AUX', which, unlike Chomsky's 'AUX', consists in deep structure only of a tense and an optional modal auxiliary. (The superficial resemblance between ASW's superscripts and the multiple bars of X-bar syntax is misleading, since the V which serves as head of a V^1 is its daughter and not its i-th order descendant, for example, *have* and not *play*(*ing*) is the head of the V^3 *have been playing cards*). It is unclear to me why Akmajian *et al.* treat modal auxiliaries as *sui generis*, in that their framework provides all the machinery required in order to treat modal auxiliaries as verbs; this is one of a number of criticisms of Akmajian *et al.*'s approach presented in Gazdar, Pullum, and Sag (to appear). See also Pullum and Wilson (1977) for arguments that auxiliary verbs must be treated as verbs even under the assumptions of extended standard theory.]

61.   [While this remark presupposes that German verbs in subordinate clauses are moved into final position from an underlying first or second position, Ross's point is equally valid under any other analysis in which main and subordinate clauses have the same underlying constituent order. See Koster (1974, 1975) for solid arguments, largely applicable also to German, that it is main clauses in Dutch rather than subordinate clauses that undergo movement of the verb. In Chapter 3, I sketch an alternative analysis, not greatly different from Koster's, in which instead of the deep SOV constituent order that Koster argues for, there is no underlying constituent order at all.]

62.   Lakoff (1972a) has observed that Baker and Brame's (1972) supposed reformulation of this rule within the *Aspects* framework requires an infinite stock of syntactic features and an indexing mechanism that the *Aspects* theory does not provide. [Baker and Brame's reanalysis of Greek agreement does not avoid global rules but simply provides a formalism for a particular kind of global rules: their indices simply encode what predicates given NPs used to be the subjects of, thus allowing their agreement rule to make reference to precisely the information about earlier stages of derivations that Lakoff and Andrews argued that the agreement was sensitive to.]

63.   There is one obvious error in Chomsky's formulation: marking sentences which have # 'anywhere in the derivation' as deviant would mean that all structures with an embedded sentence are deviant. Chomsky's (1965) proposal that all embedded sentences originate with #s around them and that the #s are removed when a transformation of some kind applies to it suffers from the defect (pointed out by Lakoff (1965), Perlmutter (1971), and Kuroda (1971)) that the ill-formedness of the sorts of examples that Chomsky had in mind cannot always be attributed to failure of transformations to apply, for example, the oddity of *the man such that China is industrializing rapidly* is due to the violation of a deep structure constraint and not to the failure of Relative clause formation to apply to it.

[Chomsky's insertion of # differs only subtly from the blatant confusion of language and metalanguage in his suggestion (Chomsky 1973: 94) that 'the feature *' be assigned to sentences possessing certain defects. Stigmata such as * and ? express judgements about linguistic structures and are not parts of the structures themselves.]

64.   I refer to labeled trees where Chomsky refers to labeled bracketed strings, since in every case syntactic rules are sensive to topological relations

between nodes in a tree rather than to adjacency relations between brackets and terminal symbols in a bracketed string. [Only continuous trees are equivalent to bracketed strings. See McCawley (to appear a) for arguments that a certain class of transformations (including parenthetical placement and extraposition of relative clauses) change word order without altering constituent structure and thus give rise to discontinuous trees, thus to structures not representable by labeled bracketings.]

65.   [See note 25. The one respect in which my statement here is misleading is my identification of 'predicate' with 'V'. There are Vs that do not correspond to predicates, namely those which are inserted by transformations (for example, passive *be*) and those which are parts of complex expressions that express a single predicate (for example, the *give* of *give up*.]

66.   [Chomsky in fact DID introduce other kinds of rules in 'Nominalization', notably lexical redundancy rules (see above § 2.3.2) and analogical rules (§ 2.4.1), though he may regard the latter as technically not part of the grammar.]

67.   Note that the two different scopes correspond to different truth conditions: if admirers are more widely distributed than admirees, it is possible for (many: man x) (many: man y) (x admire y) to be true and (many: man y) (many: man x) (x admire y) to be false at the same time.

68.   He mentions it only on p. 143, where he contests Morgan's (1969a) claim that the impossibility of a certain hypothetical lexical item follows from the complex NP constraint. Chomsky correctly points out that even if Morgan's example is adjusted so as to remove the violation of the CNPC, it is still not a possible lexical item, which implies that Morgan has not shown that the CNPC is responsible for the impossibility of the item in question. [Morreall (1979) argues that my putative 'impossible lexical items' are impossible not because of violation of any constraints on linguistic rules but because of the lack of any easily imaginable need for such items. He proceeds to sketch a science-fiction story set in a world in which there is a need for my *flimp 'kiss a girl who is allergic to' (which I had claimed would violate the Complex NP constraint), namely one in which mutations have made it possible to transmit allergies through physical contact, with allergies so transmitted being particularly serious in males. Of course, one can respond that Morreall's *flimp* does not mean the same as mine but rather 'become allergic to by kissing someone'; however, that way out of the difficulty raises a new difficulty that has been pointed out by Dowty (1979: 237–8), namely that it is extremely hard to identify any putative counterexample to my supposed universal constraints on possible lexical items, since for any supposed counterexample one can generally make up a paraphrase that has roughly the same truth conditions but does not involve the supposed violation of general constraints on rule application.]

69.   [See now Evers (1975) for extensive arguments that Dutch and German have postlexical predicate raising.]

70.   See Gallagher (1970) for valuable observations about the meaning of *assassinate* which I have not touched on here.

71.   An additional difference not noted by Chomsky is that *colleague* is a symmetric relation but *henchman* is not: only the boss in a sinister undertaking can have henchmen.

72.   To take an example not given by Chomsky, the presupposition associated with BECOME in *No one has ever dissuaded Bill from doing anything* is 'Up to t Bill intend to do x', where t and x are the variables corresponding to *ever* and *anything*. It would make no sense to speak of 'Up to t Bill intend to do x' as being a presupposition of the whole sentence. See Lakoff (1971b: fn. 8) for discussion of further examples of this type. [See now Karttunen and Peters (1979) on the status of presuppositions involving a variable that is bound by a quantifier outside the constituent in question.]

73.   To avoid needless propagation of error, I have corrected one faulty detail of the structures that appear in McCawley (1968a) and Morgan (1969a); see McCawley (1973b) for reasons why the notion of causation involved in the semantic structure of *I killed John* is a relation between an event and an event, not (as the trees of the earlier papers imply) between a person and an event. The trees in (13) exactly fit paraphrases such as 'I did something which caused John to become almost not alive'.

74.   It is not clear whether Chomsky and Jackendoff wish to advance the 'extended lexical hypothesis' as a language universal or merely as a claim about English. The hypothesis could not be maintained for languages such as Japanese and Swahili, which have productive causative, potential, and other constructions that are most naturally described in terms of an underlying structure in which the causative (or potential, etc.) morpheme is the main verb and the 'basic' sentence is its complement, with Predicate-raising adjoining the verb of the embedded clause to the derivational morpheme. [See now Sadock (1980) for discussion of the wholesale interpenetration of syntax and derivational morphology in Greenlandic Eskimo.]

75.   See, however, Binnick (1971) for evidence that *bring* is inserted in place of CAUSE-*come* (that is a combination of a semantic predicate and the English word *come*) and thus that lexical insertion can replace a structure in which a lexical item has already been inserted.

76.   [Sanchez de Zavala (1974: 420–1) points out that in most varieties of Spanish (24a) is ungrammatical, the closest acceptable analogues to it being:

(i)   Mis padres son respectivamente al*to* y bajo. (that is both adjectives agreeing with the masculine gender of *padres*, though still singular)
(ii)   Mis padres son ella alta y él bajo. (literally 'My parents are she tall and he short')

He suggests that the dialects in which (i) is preferred to (24a) are the same as those in which (i′) is preferred to (24b):

(i′)   Mi madre y mi padre son respectivamente al*to* y bajo.

He points out that the sort of agreement found in (24a) is standard in Italian:

(iii) Miei genitori sono rispettivamente alta e basso.]

77.   Chomsky gives no reason for his reference to 'surface'; to determine which noun each adjective agrees with in ancient Greek, one must in fact refer to non-surface stages (Lakoff 1970b, Andrews 1971). [In these remarks, I assumed that Chomsky was referring both to agreement controlled by a linguistic antecedent that is determinate for all the relevant features and to agreement in which the choice among alternative agreement forms is based on knowledge about the purported referent rather than on morphological features of the antecedent. Chomsky may very well have intended his comment to apply only to the latter, even though his choice of words seems to take in agreement phenomena in general, and may have been referring only to the information conveyed in such cases by the choice of an agreement form and not also (as I had assumed) to determination of what constituent controls the agreement.]

78.   [Both Lakoff and I failed to consider an additional possibility that may in fact be what Chomsky had in mind, namely that the scope of the understood *many* is assigned not by the rule that assigns the scope of the *many* in the first conjunct but by an interpretive analogue to the VP-deletion transformation that simply copies all details of the semantic interpretation of the second VP (including the scopes of any quantifiers that occur in it) into the interpretation of the zero VP. Under such an approach, which is developed in Jackendoff (1972: 265–72), interpretation of understood elements of the zero VP need not make reference to any derivational stage other than surface structure. Jackendoff's approach is immune to the objection that leads me to ridicule later in this section a different

'interpretive' treatment of zero VPs that I incorrectly took to be the only alternative to a VP-deletion transformation; see, however, chapter 2 for discussion of some problems with his approach. Jackendoff allows empty VPs to be derived transformationally through movement of empty constituents into the VP, for example, the second conjunct of *Bill thinks he is admired by everyone, but he isn't* can be derived by passivization from a structure having an empty subject and an empty verb, resulting in a derived empty VP.]

79.   It is a fact of life that negative polarity items differ as to how closely they are 'tied' to their 'triggers'. Some must be preceded by the trigger in surface structure but others may follow it, and some require a trigger to be present throughout the derivation but others do not require a trigger if the polarity item is deleted:

That Sam has been here in weeks isn't likely.

*That Sam arrived until 2.00 isn't likely.

Sam hasn't been here in weeks, but Jack has.

*Sam didn't arrive until 2.00, but Bill did.

[For further discussion of the relationship of negative polarity items to their triggers, see now Ladusaw (1979) and Linebarger (1980).]

80.   Idioms of the form of *pull X's leg* appear to undergo the usual movement and deletion transformations, subject to the restriction that if either the noun or the verb is deleted, the other must be also, as illustrated in (32).

81.   In that case he has no basis for saying (fn. 29) that 'the regularity exhibited in [(34)] cannot be a matter of "output conditions" on surface or shallow structures . . . since it holds only prior to such transformations as passive'. Determiners and auxiliary verbs are just as freely combinable in the output of passive as in the input.

82.   This may not be such a great extent. See Lawler (1972, 1973) and R. Lakoff (1972) for some indication of how much about generics remains to be described and explained. [See now Carlson (1977) for a detailed analysis of the semantics of generic sentences in which they are treated as involving not quantified NPs but NPs that refer to 'kinds' rather than to individuals; the only quantifier-like entities that play a role in generics as Carlson analyses them are operators for deriving properties of kinds from properties of individuals. Carlson's approach is summarized and certain details of it criticized in McCawley 1981a: § 14.3.]

83.   [See in this connection Levi (1978: 33–7) and note 17 to this review.]

84.   [To my knowledge, no subsequent work has made any progress in specifying what words constitute anaphoric islands. Larry Gorbet (personal communication) suggests that the difference between (50b) and (50a) may be that the noun is more basic than the verb in (50a) but not in (50b), that is, that *answer*$_V$ means 'give an answer to' but *cook*$_V$ is not accurately paraphrased by anything containing 'a cook'.]

85.   [I now attach much less significance than I previously did to the question of whether quantifiers are predicates. Yet another proposal for the logical constituent structure of quantified sentences is adopted in McCawley (1981a): one in which the quantifier and the 'domain expression' (here, 'man *x*') are grouped into a single constituent; my sole (though not inconsiderable) reason for adopting that alternative is that the quantifier and the material of the domain expression make up a constituent in surface structure except when they are separated by the process of Quantifier-floating.]

86.   [For arguments that sentences like *John wants two children* have underlying sentential complements and undergo deletion of the verb of the complement, see McCawley (1974) and Ross (1976).]

87.   Chomsky's reference to this constraint as 'blocking such rules' misleadingly suggests that it is a constraint on rules rather than on derivations. The

example he treats on p. 185 makes clear that he meant it as excluding inadmissible derivations, since the discussion there deals with inadmissible applications of a rule that he assumes is a correct rule of English. The constraint excludes rules only in the derivative sense that it would prevent any rule that explicitly created the very characteristic of derivations that the constraint excludes from ever applying.

[In rejecting one particular version of a 'principle of strict cycle' here, I do not intend thereby to reject 'strict cyclicity' altogether: I accept the claim that a cyclic transformation can apply only on the smallest cyclic domain containing the material relevant to its application. This version of strict cyclicity does not exclude Quantifier-lowering, though, for example, it requires that in a derivation with (53) as logical structure the application of Quantifier-lowering that affects *few* is in the application of the cycle to the *few*-clause and cannot be postponed until the application of the cycle to the *many*-clause.

I leave open here the question of what the cyclic domains are: whether they are the Ss (as in *Aspects*), the S̄s and NPs (as in the volume under review here), or all constituents (as in Montague grammar; cf. McCawley (1977b). The last possibility has not been given serious consideration by transformational grammarians, with the notable exception of Williams (1974), probably in part due to its being in conflict with the SUBJACENCY PRINCIPLE of Chomsky (1973), according to which linguistic rules cannot influence elements that are embedded to a depth greater than one cyclic domain within the constituent to which the rule is applying. However, I see no reason why all cyclic domains should have to be 'subjacency domains', that is, if one wishes to accept a principle limiting the 'depth' to which linguistic elements can exert a syntactic influence, one is not forced to define the limits of the influence in terms of cyclic domains. There is in fact reason to take both S and 'S̄' to be cyclic domains, since explanations thereby become available for the fact that transformations to which complementizers are irrelevant (for example, Passive and Reflexivization) apply before transformations that involve complementizers (for example, WH-movement and imperative subject deletion; I assume here that imperatives, like questions, are marked as such in the complementizer) and of the fact that *want to* does not contract to *wanna* when the subject of the infinitive has been extracted by WH-movement (contraction would apply to the S, if it applies at all, under any version of a principle of strict cycle, and WH movement would apply to the S̄; note that under this suggestion traces are superfluous in explaining the failure of contraction).]

88.   [Here I failed to keep the various issues about pronouns separate the way I attempted to in § 3.2.4.5. Chomsky's claim here related not to whether a reflexive pronoun can have a given antecedent but to which form the reflexive pronoun takes, that is to the choice among *myself, yourself*, etc. There is nothing to prevent one from having deep structures in which the items that underlie reflexive pronouns are determinately reflexive but indeterminate with regard to person, number, and gender. Chomsky appears to have been saying that even if a reflexive pronoun could be assigned an antecedent in a higher clause, the rule choosing its surface form could not apply. I conjecture that it is accidental that in Japanese, where higher-clause antecedents of reflexives are common, the reflexive pronoun is invariant in form; the analysis alluded to in Chomsky's remarks implies that it is not an accident.]

89.   For a detailed discussion of 'suspension of presuppositions', especially those associated with 'scales', see Horn (1972).

90.   I cannot reconcile this passage with Chomsky's discussion of Equi-NP-deletion in terms of 'the subject relation' (see above, § 4.6.4).

91.   The methodological principle of Chomsky's that I discussed in § 4.2 cannot be used to justify the 'blindness' hypothesis since, given the lack of any constraints on what can be a SIR, the claim that all transformations are 'blind'

imposes a restriction only on the typographical form of grammars, not on their content.

92. [For my most recent ideas on language acquisition, see McCawley (1976a, 1977a, to appear b), and § 3 of Chapter 4.]

93. [For more recent expositions of Chomsky's ideas on syntax and semantics that greatly clarify his positions on many of the issues taken up here, see the subsequent works by him listed in the reference section of this volume.]

2 HOW TO GET AN INTERPRETIVE THEORY OF ANAPHORA TO WORK

1

Jackendoff (1972) argues for an account of anaphoric devices with the following characteristics: (i) All anaphoric devices are present *as such* in deep structures, rather than being derived transformationally from something else (such as a copy of the antecedent); moreover, distinctions among different kinds of anaphoric devices (for example, between reflexives and simple personal pronouns) are present in deep structure, rather than, say, reflexives being derived transformationally from non-reflexive personal pronouns. (ii) Transformations are sensitive only to syntactic information, not to semantic information, about their inputs.[1] (iii) Coreference information is treated as semantic rather than syntactic and thus plays no role in the application of transformations. (iv) There is a system of semantic interpretation rules (SIRs) that construct from any syntactic derivation the semantic representations that correspond to it. (v) Semantic representation consists of four parts: *functional structure*, which specifies what predicates are predicated of what arguments; a *coreference table*, which specifies what coreference relations hold among the nodes of functional structure;[2] *modal structure*, which is a specification of the scopes of logical elements (including 'world-creating' elements such as *want* and *dream*); and *topic–comment structure*. (vi) The stages of derivations relevant to the construction of the table of coreference are the *cyclic outputs*, that is those structures resulting from the application of the cycle of transformations to each of the Ss (and NPs) of the given deep structure. (vii) In the determination of the semantic representation, the cyclic outputs are processed *from bottom to top*, that is the application of the SIRs to any particular cyclic output presupposes their prior application to the cyclic outputs of all Ss and NPs contained in the given constituent. (viii) The conception of cycle assumed by Jackendoff incorporates the principle of the *strict cycle*: that no application of any transformation may be sensitive only to material that is entirely within a clause (or NP) to which the cycle has already applied.[3]

For example, for Jackendoff, (1a) would have the deep structure (1b) (ignoring auxiliaries and complementizers), and the coreference tables in the semantic representations associated with (1a) would be determined on the basis of the cyclic outputs (1c):

(1) (a) Bill is believed by his mother to be easy for his wife to
deceive.

(b)

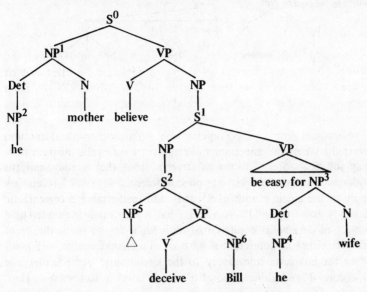

(c)

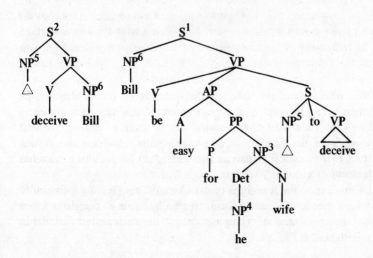

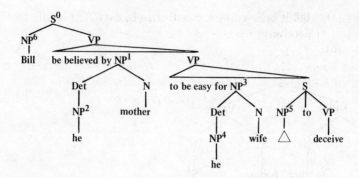

(The outputs from the NP cycles play no role below and are thus omitted.) When the anaphora rules apply to the cyclic output of S^2, they add '5 − coref 6' to the coreference table, that is, they mark the understood subject of *deceive* as noncoreferential with *Bill*.[4] When they apply to the cyclic output of S^1, they add to the table '5 coref 3' and either '4 coref 6' or '4 − coref 6' (that is they mark the understood subject of *deceive* as coreferential with *his wife* and mark the *he* of *his wife* either as coreferential with or as noncoreferential with *Bill*). When the anaphora rules apply to the cyclic output of S^0, they add '6 − coref 1' and either '2 coref 6' or 2 − coref 6' to the table. Thus, at least four semantic representations will be associated with (1a), containing respectively the four coreference tables shown in (2):

2. (a)	(b)	(c)	(d)
5 − coref 6	5 − coref 6	5 − coref 6	5 − coref 6
5 coref 3	5 coref 3	5 coref 3	5 coref 3
4 coref 6	4 − coref 6	4 coref 6	4 − coref 6
6 − coref 1	6 − coref 1	6 − coref 1	6 − coref 1
2 coref 6	2 coref 6	2 − coref 6	2 − coref 6

1.1

In this article I will not take up the question of the validity of the arguments that Jackendoff gives in support of this approach. Rather, I will be concerned with what it would take to make an approach of that type work in the face of certain problematic examples and certain features of Jackendoff's analysis that one might for reasons extraneous to Jackendoff's more basic assumptions wish to avoid.

I turn first to the reanalysis that Jackendoff says is forced on him of sentences that have generally been treated in terms of transformations of 'VP Deletion' and of 'Gapping', which delete repeated material in such sentences as (3a, b):

(3) (a) Fred got Sally to kiss him, but Sue refused to.
    (b) Mike brought the beer, and Larry the pretzels.

Jackendoff argues (1972: 268) that a VP Deletion transformation is inconsistent with his analysis of anaphora. Specifically, if VP Deletion applied in the derivation of (3a), its input would be (4):

(4)

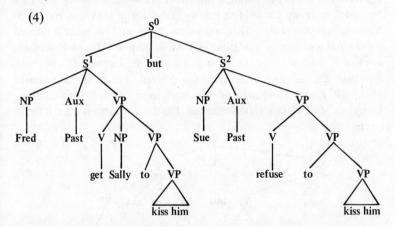

According to the conception of cycle that Jackendoff assumes, any transformation that applies freely to embedded Ss must be in the cycle. Since VP Deletion in fact does apply freely to embedded Ss (for example, *Bill told me that Marcia thinks that* [*Fred got Sally to kiss him but Sue refused to*]), under Jackendoff's analysis a VP Deletion transformation would have to be in the cycle. The lowest S that contains both the *Fred* of S^1 and the *him* of S^2 is S^0, and thus if all coreference assignments are to be determined on the basis of cyclic outputs, the determination that *Fred* and *him* are coreferential (or are not, as the case might be) would have to be made on the basis of the cyclic output of S^0. But in the cyclic output of S^0, VP Deletion would have already applied, and there would thus not be any *him* left in S^0 for the anaphora rules to mark as coreferential (or noncoreferential) with *Fred*. Therefore there cannot be any VP Deletion transformation.

Jackendoff then proposes the following account, which involves no VP Deletion transformation. Sentences having missing VPs have deep structures with empty nodes in the appropriate places; there is an SIR that assigns interpretations to the nodes of an 'empty VP'; and all the empty nodes in a sentence must receive an interpretation if the sentence is to be (syntactically and semantically) well-formed.

Sentences such as (5) have often been used as part of an argument for a VP Deletion transformation:

(5) (a)   Tom was arrested by the pigs, but Fred wasn't.
     (b)   Walt is tough to get along with, but Vera isn't.

Specifically, it has been argued that the missing constituents in (5) are transformationally derived (via Passive in the case of (5a), and via *Tough* Movement in the case of (5b)), and unless the second conjunct is derived from a full sentence by VP Deletion, Passivization and *Tough* Movement could not take place in the second conjunct. In Jackendoff's analysis, however, Passive can still apply in the derivation of both conjuncts of (5a), and *Tough* Movement in both conjuncts of (5b), without there being any VP Deletion transformation. His deep structures are:[5]

(6)   (a)

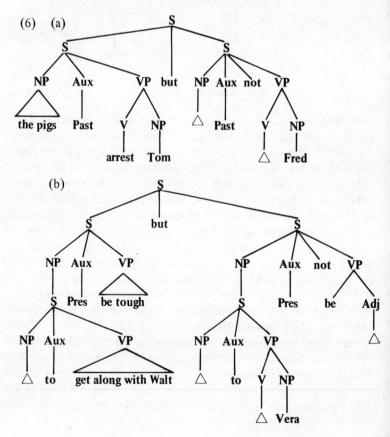

(b)

Application of Passive in both conjuncts of (6a) and Tough Movement in both conjuncts of (6b) yields (7a) and (7b), both of which contain 'empty VPs' to which the SIR proposed by Jackendoff will apply, yielding semantic representations in which the second conjunct of (6a) has the meaning of *Fred wasn't arrested by the pigs* and the second conjunct of (6b) has the meaning of *Vera isn't tough to get along with*:

(7)   (a)

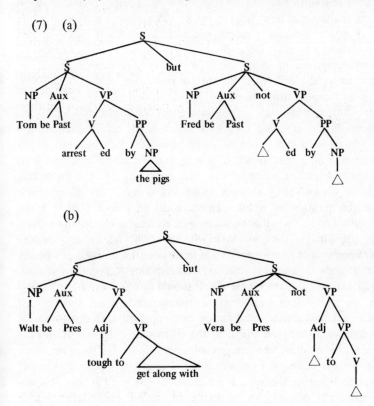

(b)

If the two conjuncts did not undergo parallel derivations, for example, if Passive applied in only one of the conjuncts of (6a), the conditions for the SIR would not be met, and the resulting structure would be ill-formed because of uninterpreted empty nodes. (If Passive applied only in the first conjunct, then the second conjunct would not have an 'empty VP'; if it applied only in the second conjunct, then the empty VP that results in the second conjunct would not be 'parallel to' the VP of the first conjunct, and the matching of corresponding pieces that the SIR calls for could not take place.)

1.2

Before going into the details of Jackendoff's SIR for interpreting empty VPs (henceforth, the *VP-Anaphora* rule), I should point out that the analysis that Jackendoff adopts robs his argument against VP Deletion of whatever force it had. In the analysis that he argues against, empty VPs have no surface realization at all, not even as empty nodes; however, in the analysis that he argues for, empty VPs appear in surface structure as VP nodes dominating empty nodes. Jackendoff has thus conflated two distinct issues: (i) Do understood VPs appear in surface structures as configurations of empty nodes or do they not appear in surface structure at all? and (ii) Is the surface realization of understood VPs, be it an 'empty' structure or nothing at all, derived from a 'full' constituent that is identical to the antecedent VP? Since the '→ ϕ' that appears in the standard notational schemes for transformations was introduced at a time when no distinction was made between empty nodes and no nodes at all, it is a mistake to simply interpret it as meaning 'delete' rather than 'turn into empty nodes'. If a distinction is to be drawn between empty nodes and no nodes at all, one must raise the questions of whether empty nodes are ever created by transformation and of whether nodes are ever eliminated entirely by a transformation; that is, the questions of whether a 'full' node in deep structure ever corresponds to an empty node in surface structure and of whether a 'full' node in deep structure ever corresponds to no nodes at all in surface structure. In the event that it should turn out that both 'emptying' transformations and 'deletion' transformations are necessary, it will be a trivial matter to adjust the notation for transformations so as to distinguish between them; in the event that only one of them is needed, '→ ϕ' should be interpreted correspondingly. However, there is at present no reason to assume that the empty nodes that Jackendoff takes to figure in the surface structures of (3) and (5) are not transformationally derived. An 'emptying' of one VP under identity with another would yield a cyclic output containing both empty anaphoric devices and (full or empty) potential antecedents, and thus a grammar with a VP-emptying rule would allow the same kind of interaction with the anaphora rules that provided the rationale for Jackendoff's rejection of the VP Deletion rule.[6]

1.3

Jackendoff's first approximation to the VP-Anaphora rule is (8) (1972: 268):

(8)   Associate with VP^2 the semantic representation of VP^1 if
     (a) VP^2 is Δ; and
     (b) VP^2 does not both precede and command VP^1.

Condition (b) is eventually separated out as a general condition on a multipart anaphora rule. Both conditions refer to the state of affairs in the cyclic output of the lowest cyclic node containing both VP^1 and VP^2. I will comment below on the interpretation of 'is Δ', which is not completely obvious, in that Jackendoff takes VPs such as those in (7) as meeting the condition 'is Δ' despite the fact that they contain such morphemes as *to*, *by*, and *-en*. The substance of the rule is contained in the explication that Jackendoff provides for the word *associate* (1972: 269–70): the 'semantic association' consists of 'inserting all semantic material mentioning parts of VP^1 into structurally parallel places in the reading of S^2; when an element of S^1 outside VP^1 is involved in a binary relation with an element of VP^1, the corresponding element of S^2 is substituted for it' (S^1 and S^2 here refer to the Ss of which VP^1 and VP^2 are immediate constituents). The rule thus adds nodes to the functional structure and adds relations to other parts of the semantic representation.

Jackendoff illustrates the VP-Anaphora rule with a derivation of the semantic structure of (3a). Applied to the first conjunct of (3a), the SIRs of his earlier chapters yield the structure shown in (9):[7]

(9)

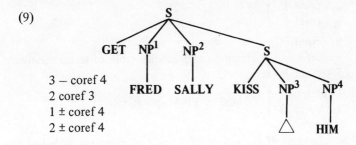

Jackendoff takes up only the case where nodes 1 and 4 are interpreted as coreferential; I will comment below on the other case, which in fact is the more problematic one.

I will argue below that consistency requires that the deep structure of the complement of *refuse* be '(for) $[\Delta]_{NP}$ to $[[\Delta]_V [\Delta]_{NP}]_{VP}$' rather than the '(for) $[\Delta]_{NP}$ to $[\Delta]_{VP}$' that Jackendoff actually gives. Assuming the correctness of this point, the result of applying the SIRs to the second conjunct of (3a) would be (10):

(10)

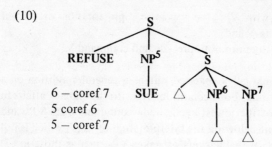

$$6 - coref\ 7$$
$$5\ coref\ 6$$
$$5 - coref\ 7$$

Application of the VP-Anaphora rule to the whole conjoined structure yields (11):[8]

(11)

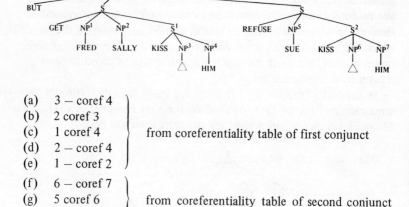

(a)	$3 - coref\ 4$	⎫
(b)	$2\ coref\ 3$	
(c)	$1\ coref\ 4$	⎬ from coreferentiality table of first conjunct
(d)	$2 - coref\ 4$	
(e)	$1 - coref\ 2$	⎭
(f)	$6 - coref\ 7$	⎫
(g)	$5\ coref\ 6$	⎬ from coreferentiality table of second conjunct
(h)	$5 - coref\ 7$	⎭
(i)	$1\ coref\ 7$	⎫
(j)	$2 - coref\ 7)$	⎬ added by VP-Anaphora rule

While Jackendoff gives '1 coref 7' as a specification added to the coreference table by the VP-Anaphora rule, his rule is not formulated in such a way that it could add that specification: it is formulated so as to add only relations between elements of VP^1 (that is 4) and elements of S^2 (that is 6 or 7). I conjecture that Jackendoff intended a formulation along the lines of: 'when an element outside of VP^1 is involved in a relation with an element of VP^1, the relation obtained by substituting the corresponding element of VP^2 is added to the semantic representation'. This revised rule would add '1 coref 7' (since

'1 coref 4' is already in the coreference table, 4 is in VP^1, and 7 is the element of VP^2 that corresponds to 4). Strictly speaking, this version of the rule would also add '2 coref 6' to the coreference table, thus yielding an inconsistent table implying that Sue = Sally. However, Jackendoff allows the VP-Anaphora rule to be overridden by a principle of 'sloppy identity': 'the rule apparently has the option of carrying over the table of coreference intact or substituting . . . the NP in the corresponding position' (1972: 271). This would allow '5 coref 6' to result instead of '2 coref 6', thus achieving a consistent coreference table in which the understood object of the empty VP is interpreted as referring to Fred.

This treatment raises two problems. First, it is not clear that VP^2 can be both 'parallel to VP^1' and 'empty' in cases where VP^1 involves a reflexive. Note that if VP^2 matches VP^1 constituent for constituent and is completely 'empty', its subject and its empty object will be marked as noncoreferential (as in (10)), since Jackendoff's coreference rule marks a nonreflexive NP as noncoreferential with its clausemates.[9] Thus unless either a distinction is somehow drawn between reflexive and nonreflexive empty nodes or VPs are allowed to count as empty even though containing reflexives (possibilities that I will take up below), (12a) will have the deep structure (12b), and the anaphora rule will assign to (12a) only an interpretation in which *Jake* and Δ are non-coreferential and will thus miss the most obvious interpretation of (12a), that in which the second clause means 'Jake didn't kick himself':

(12)   (a)   Larry kicked himself, but Jake didn't.

(b)

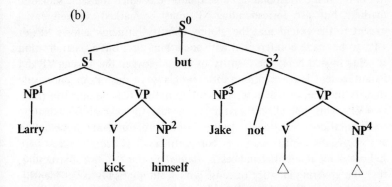

The 'sloppy identity' principle will not help here, since it applies only to information added when the VP-Anaphora rule applies to the S^0 cyclic output, whereas '3 − coref 4' is added to the coreference table when the anaphora rule applies to the S^2 cyclic output and thus remains in the coreference table regardless of what the VP-Anaphora rule does. The same problem arises with empty VPs whose antecedents involve other anaphoric devices that are subject to the same constraints as reflexives are. For example, for (13) to be assigned an interpretation in which the understood object in the second conjunct is a reciprocal that refers to Pat and Mike, either empty NPs must be allowed to bear the feature specifications of reciprocals or VPs containing *each other* plus empty material must be allowed to count as empty:

(13)　　Larry and Jake punched each other, but Pat and Mike didn't.

Second, the VP-Anaphora rule has false consequences when applied to the interpretation of (3a) in which *Fred* and *him* are noncoreferential. In that case, the VP-Anaphora rule would associate with (3a) a coreference table containing '1 − coref 4' and '1 − coref 7' but containing no information about whether 4 and 7 are coreferential, which means that they could be interpreted either way. However, a reading in which 4 and 7 are noncoreferential is completely impossible. Such a reading is precisely the sort of thing that a constraint against 'irrecoverable deletion' ought to rule out; however, for Jackendoff an appeal to recoverability would not be possible, since there is no deletion.

The second of these two problems appears to demand that there be an additional step in the 'semantic association' of VP^1 and VP^2: not only must corresponding constituents be assigned the same semantic markers, but also corresponding NPs must be marked as coreferential except to the extent that the 'sloppy identity' principle allows NPs or VP^2 to be made coreferential with something else. But a generalization is being missed here: the identity of sense between the missing VP and its antecedent is covered by a different clause of the VP-Anaphora rule than is the identity of reference between the NPs contained in those two VPs. This generalization is missed because, in Jackendoff's semantic representation, 'functional structure' and coreferentiality information are segregated into separate compartments. If coreference were indicated by referential indices *contained in* the functional structure, the rule covering identity of sense would automatically cover identity of reference of the included NPs.[10]

Regarding the first problem, one might suggest that it is simply an artifact of my assumption that (12) demands (14a) rather than (14b) as its deep structure within Jackendoff's framework:

(14) (a) Larry Past kick himself, but Jake Past not $[\triangle]_V [\triangle]_{NP}$
      (b) Larry Past kick himself, but Jake Past not $[\triangle]_{VP}$

If (14b) were the deep structure, there would be no empty NP to be marked noncoreferential with *Jake* when the anaphora rule applied to the second conjunct; then, when the VP-Anaphora rule applied to the whole structure, it could simply supply the meanings of *kick* and *himself* in interpreting the $\triangle$. However, if (as Jackendoff states) Gapping must be described by means of the same kind of interpretive rule as he proposes for missing VPs, the same problem can arise in cases where that solution is not available:

(15) (a) An Arab bought himself a watch, and a Turk a camera.
           [= . . . and a Turk bought himself a camera] [11]
      (b) Tom and Sally gave each other watches, and Dick and Jane lollipops. [= . . . and Dick and Jane gave each other lollipops]

The empty matter here does not form a constituent, and thus no use of $\triangle$'s can avoid assigning to (15) deep structures containing an indirect object NP that would be either nonempty or obligatorily marked as noncoreferential with the subject of its clause. Since the empty material has to match the antecedent material constituent-for-constituent in these cases, it would have to do so in all cases, since otherwise there would be a spurious proliferation of deep structures; for example, it would be possible to derive (3a) both from a deep structure with $[\triangle]_{VP}$ and from one with $[\triangle]_V [\triangle]_{NP}$.

1.4

Let us now turn to some possible solutions to these problems. Consider first the possibility of allowing empty nodes to bear feature specifications such as [+ Reflexive] and thus allowing (12a) to have a deep structure in which the second conjunct has an object NP that is both empty and reflexive. If empty nodes are constrained only by the requirement that they be interpreted, then that proposal has the egregiously false implication that all reflexives are optionally omissible, for example, that (16b) is fully grammatical and has the same interpretation as (16a):

(16) (a) John pinched himself.
      (b) ??John pinched.

In any sentence in which a nonempty reflexive allows a coherent semantic interpretation, an 'empty' reflexive would allow exactly the same semantic interpretation, according to Jackendoff's anaphora rules, and sentences like (16b) thus could not be excluded on the grounds of having uninterpreted constituents.

One might then propose distinguishing between two kinds of empty nodes: one that would figure in identity-of-sense anaphora and would be required not just to be interpreted but rather to be interpreted by a rule that matches parallel structures; and another kind that would not figure in identity-of-sense anaphora and would only be required to be interpreted. Only the former kind would be allowed to bear features like [+ Reflexive]. The former kind of empty nodes would be a ghostly intermediate stage between true emptiness and ordinary 'full' constituents; indeed, their emptiness would be the only clear distinction between them and 'full' constituents. A proponent (if such exists) of a theory that made a three-way distinction between completely empty nodes that were required only to be interpreted, feature-bearing empty nodes that were required to be interpreted by identity-of-sense anaphora rules, and 'full' constituents, would be obliged to show that that three-way distinction was necessary. However, I doubt that any such justification could be adduced that did not amount to fiat. For example, one might by fiat exclude 'emptying transformations' and then argue that there is no alternative to having feature-bearing empty nodes in the deep structure of (12): there must be an object NP node in the second clause when the VP-Anaphora rule applies; that node must be underlyingly empty, since there are no emptying transformations; and it must be [+ Reflexive], since otherwise (as argued above) it would be assigned the wrong interpretation. However, such a justification of feature-bearing empty nodes rests on the fiat exclusion of emptying transformations. If emptying transformations are allowed, then there is an alternative, conforming in all significant respects to Jackendoff's approach, in which no distinction is drawn between full constituents and feature-bearing empty constituents: the deep structures of both clauses of (12a) would contain *kick himself*, the anaphora rules would mark both reflexives as coreferential with the subjects of their clauses, an emptying transformation (applying in the S^0 cycle) would replace the terminal nodes of the second VP by empty nodes, and the VP-Anaphora rule would apply as before, though with no contradictions arising, since the coreference table would now contain '3 coref 4' rather than '3 − coref 4'.

Another possible solution is to broaden the interpretation of the notion 'empty'. Recall that in Jackendoff's treatment of (3), the 'empty VPs' that the VP-Anaphora rule interprets are not completely empty: they contain the 'grammatical morphemes' *to*, *by*, and *-en*, which must ultimately be deleted.[12] Perhaps by making this deletion explicit, a solution to the problems raised by (12)–(13) and (15) can be found: perhaps the VP-Anaphora rule is applicable even in the case of constituents that contain a (nonempty) reflexive or reciprocal pronoun, and those pronouns are ultimately deleted the same way that *to*, *by*, and *-en* are. However, it is not clear that those deletions will not amount to a degenerate form of VP Deletion. Note that reflexives and reciprocals in the company of empty nodes do not always delete:

(17) (a) Bill nominated Fred, Sam Pete, and Jake himself.
      (b) Dick and Jane denounced Mabel, and Bob and Carol each other.

For that matter, neither does *to*: note that *to* is deleted in (5b) but not in (3a). What the items that would have to be deleted have in common is that each is inside a VP that is parallel to but not in contrast with some other VP that precedes or commands it. As far as I can determine, the simplest rule that would delete reflexives and grammatical morphemes where Jackendoff's account would require that they be deleted is the same as the VP Deletion transformation, except that the deleted VP is not required to be identical to its antecedent but only nondistinct from it (that is, the difference between empty and full constituents would not count), though stressed reflexives must be taken as distinct not only from unstressed reflexives but even from each other, as in (18):

(18) Bill nominated Fred, Sam himself, and Jake himself.
      [= . . . Sam nominated himself and Jake nominated himself]

As far as I can see, the only alternative to having a VP Deletion or emptying transformation (either in its full glory or in a degenerate form) that duplicates part of Jackendoff's anaphora SIR, namely the condition that 'anaphoric device may not both precede and command antecedent', is to make the deletion/emptying more general than is required and rule out derivations where too much is deleted on the basis of their having uninterpreted empty nodes. If that alternative is adopted, then there is no reason for the emptying to be of anything less than the maximum conceivable generality: a rule that optionally turns any nodes whatever into empty nodes. Of course, under that proposal, there would be no reason to have the profusion of deep structure empty nodes that Jackendoff has: the nodes involved in empty VPs could just as well be derived from copies of the corresponding nodes in the antecedent VP.

Is there any empirical difference between a theory in which there is a 'blind' emptying rule plus SIRs that interpret empty VPs (likewise, other constituents, for example, $\bar{N}$, that allow anaphoric empty realization) in terms of antecedents to which they can be matched constituent-for-constituent, and a theory in which there is a transformation that deletes a VP under identity with another VP (and a transformation that deletes an $\bar{N}$ under identity with another $\bar{N}$, et perhaps cetera)? Given Jackendoff's other assumptions, the derivations corresponding to these two theories would differ somewhat. Because of the principle of the strict cycle, the 'blind' emptying would have to apply earlier than its 'seeing' counterpart. For example, in the derivation of (3a) from (4), the 'blind' emptying would have to apply on the S^2 cycle (since if it were postponed until the S^0 cycle, the principle of the strict cycle would be violated), whereas the 'seeing' emptying rule would have to apply on the S^0 cycle, since S^0 is the lowest node that contains both the emptied VP and its antecedent. The only way that that difference could have any empirical consequence would be if there were a rule other than the SIR under discussion that was sensitive to whether the nodes in question were empty prior to the end of the S^0 cycle. There are no obvious examples of transformations that *have to be* sensitive to the difference between full and empty constituents. Whether there are defensible SIRs other than those for the interpretation of empty constituents that must be sensitive to that distinction is not clear to me, since I am relatively unfamiliar with the analytic tradition in which such rules might be proposed. There is at least no obvious empirical difference between the theory with random emptying and the theory with emptying of VPs under identity with an antecedent VP.

1.5

Suppose that these considerations lead a proponent of Jackendoff's approach to the conclusion that he must at least *de facto* have a transformation deleting or emptying a VP under identity with another VP and that he might as well formulate the transformation directly in those terms. How much would he then have to give up of Jackendoff's assumptions and · policies? Is a generalization being missed through having both a VP-emptying transformation and a SIR for interpreting empty VPs, or is one of the two somehow predictable from the other and thus strictly speaking not part of the language-particular grammar?

At first, it might appear that the SIR could not be avoided, since it does work that is not done by deletion/emptying under identity; specifically, the SIR ensures that when the antecedent VP is ambiguous, the understood VP is given an interpretation that agrees with the interpretation of the antecedent VP. For example, (19) must be assigned only interpretations in which the overt occurrence and the understood occurrence of *the hunters* either are both subjects of *shoot* or are both objects:

> (19)   John was amazed at the shooting of the hunters, and so was Bill.

A deletion under identity would not by itself rule out spurious readings of (19) in which *the hunters* is the object of *shoot* in one conjunct and the subject of *shoot* in the other. However, in fact this extra work done by the SIR can be made a consequence of the VP-emptying transformation if a suitable revision is made in the familiar constraint against irrecoverable deletions. Suppose that deletions are restricted to deletion of a constant and deletion of an item under syntactic *and semantic* identity with another item. Semantic identity must here be understood as identity of all pieces of semantic structure corresponding to nodes of the two items, including coreference (and 'modal' and topic–comment) relations, subject, as usual, to the sloppy identity principle. This condition would block VP-emptying in (19) if one of the two occurrences of *the hunters* is the subject of *shoot* and the other one the object and would thus do the work of the SIR.[13]

This version of the recoverability condition is obeyed by all otherwise plausible deletion rules that I know of. For example, in (20), the ambiguous expression is always interpreted the same way in the understood material as in its overt occurrence:

> (20)   (a)   Susan denounced the shooting of the hunters, and Sam did so too.
>
>   (b)   Tom knows a man who denounced the shooting of the hunters, and Bill knows one too.
>
>   (c)   Frank is more annoyed at the shooting of the hunters than Titus is.
>
>   (d)   Marcia discussed his shooting with Brenda, and Nora with Nancy. [= ... and Nora discussed his shooting with Nancy]

       (e)   Tom thought that the shooting of the hunters was appalling, and Oscar thought so too.

In (21), the definite NPs of the understood matter are interpreted as coreferential with corresponding NPs of the antecedent:

    (21)   (a)   Susan wrote a nasty letter to Jack, and Sam did so too.
           (b)   Tom owns a cat that once belonged to Jack, and Bill owns two.
           (c)   Frank is more annoyed at Oliver's stupidity than Titus is.
           (d)   His wife wrote to Abby about his drinking, and his mother about his laziness.
           (e)   Tom thinks that Jack is incompetent, and Oscar thinks so too.

For example, in (21b), the *Jack* of the understood *cat that once belonged to Jack* must be the same Jack that is referred to in the first conjunct; in (21d), the mother's letter is directed to the same Abby as is the wife's letter. Note, incidentally, that the suggested recoverability condition does not imply that the NPs *a cat that once belonged to Jack* and *two* are coreferential in (21b): here the deletion is contingent on identity of $\bar{\text{N}}$s, not of NPs, and it is NPs rather than $\bar{\text{N}}$s that participate in coreference relations.[14]

    There are two points on which the revised recoverability principle conflicts with Jackendoff's premises: it allows transformations to be sensitive to semantic information, and it makes reference to the whole semantic representation in connection with rules that would be involved in arriving at the derivational stages from which the semantic representation is determined in Jackendoff's analysis. However, these two points do not necessarily lead to an analysis drastically different from Jackendoff's. Note that (i) an alternative conception of SIRs is possible, in which they are taken not as rules for constructing a semantic representation out of a syntactic derivation but as conditions that pairs (semantic representation, syntactic derivation) must satisfy in order to be admissible (see section 2.2 for some discussion of this alternative); and (ii) while the revised recoverability constraint gives transformations access to semantic information, it does not allow their formulations to mention semantic information, that is, whatever semantic constraints it imposes on a transformation are not part of the formulation of the transformation but are predictable from the syntactic conditions for its application. Thus, if it is possible to reformulate Jackendoff's coreference rules as constraints on (semantic representation, syntactic derivation) pairs, they could be combined consistently with deletions and/or emptyings that required not just syntactic but also semantic identity between the controlling item and the deleted/emptied item.

The adoption of the revised recoverability constraint would make it largely a matter of indifference whether the transformations of 'VP Deletion' etc. are emptyings or deletions, since no special SIR to interpret the empty nodes in question would now be needed. The only respect in which it might matter whether empty nodes or no nodes at all appear in the surface representations of understood VPs is that empty surface realizations of understood VPs might play a role in the interpretation of *other* nodes, particularly of anaphoric devices with 'missing antecedents' as in examples such as (22) (discussed in Postal and Grinder (1971)):

(22)   (a)   Frank didn't buy a car, but Shirley did, and she paid $3000 for *it*.

      (b)   Frank bought a car, and so did Shirley, and *they* both cost over $3000.

Whether positing a surface empty VP in the middle clause of these examples would facilitate specifying the reference of the pronoun in the last conjunct depends on a detail of these examples that has been largely overlooked, namely that the understood occurrence of *a car* in the middle clause has the dual function of bound variable (thus counting as 'identical to' *a car* in the first clause, whether or not that occurrence of *a car* is 'referential') and of constant (thus serving as antecedent for pronouns in subsequent clauses and providing a reference distinct from that of the first occurrence of *a car* when that is 'referential'; that is, the last clause of (22b) involves $they_{ij} = it_i + it_j$). Karttunen (1969) touches on this dual function of certain existentially quantified NPs and notes its relationship to the informal practice of mathematicians, who will often write a formula containing an existential quantifier (say, $(\exists e)$ $(\forall x)$ $(xe = ex = x)$) and then proceed to write formulas in which the existentially quantified variable (here, e) is treated as a constant, even though according to standard policies on the use of quantifiers and variables, those formulas are incoherent by virtue of having a variable (e) that is not in the scope of the quantifier that binds it (for example, the quantifier that binds e is in axiom 2, but e recurs in axiom 3). Karttunen's paper in fact provides grounds for institutionalizing the mathematicians' informal practice, that is, for treating existentially quantified NPs that are used 'referentially' as bringing into being constants that can serve as the references of anaphoric devices in the subsequent discourse.[15] If that suggestion is adopted, it is not obvious that surface nodes need play any role in the interpretation of pronouns with 'missing antecedents'; however, it is sufficiently unclear to me how to incorporate that suggestion into Jackendoff's scheme that I must leave this matter hanging in the air.

2

2.1

I now turn to a problem raised by Harada and Saito (1971). Since Jackendoff takes reflexives to be present *as such* in deep structure, the deep structure of (23a) would be (23b):[16]

(23)   (a)   Bill believes himself to be hard for Max to understand.

(b)

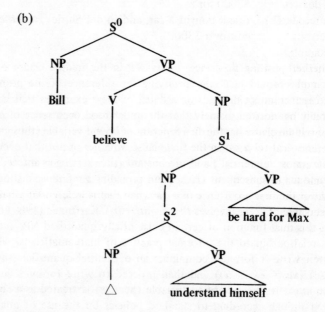

Since his coreference rule is obligatory and applies to cyclic outputs, it would mark *himself* as coreferential with △ when it applies to S^2. Since the △ would be marked coreferential with *Max* when the anaphora rules apply to S^1, *himself* would be coreferential with *Max*, contrary to the fact that (23a) only allows an interpretation in which *himself* is coreferential with *Bill*.

Harada and Saito have shown that there is a conflict between requiring reflexives to be present as such in deep structure and having coreference established on the basis of cyclic outputs. There are thus two principal ways in which one might try to revise Jackendoff's theory in order to meet Harada and Saito's objection: either (i) reformulate the coreference rules so that they determine coreference on the basis of some postcyclic stage of derivations (say, shallow structure or surface structure) or (ii) posit a transformation that derives reflexives from something non-reflexive and thus not yet have a reflexive in S^2 when the coreference rules apply to it.[17]

It is not obvious that (i) is a viable alternative. Jackendoff (personal communication) indicates that he favors it, though he has not to my knowledge given the appropriate reformulations of the coreference rules. (ii) could involve a much less drastic revision of Jackendoff's theory than might at first appear the case. A transformation deriving reflexives from nonreflexives need not derive them from copies of their antecedents (for example, it could derive them from corresponding personal pronouns) and need not be sensitive to coreference (for example, it could randomly and optionally convert personal pronouns into reflexives). The latter possibility would allow a correct assignment of coreference in (23a): the deep structure would be the same as (23b) except for having *him* in place of *himself*; Reflexivization (being optional) could be postponed until the S^0 cycle, when *him* had already been moved into S^0 via *Tough* Movement and Raising; and then the coreference rule would correctly mark *himself* as coreferential with *Bill*. Of course, a derivation in which Reflexivization applied on the S^2 cycle would have to be ruled out somehow, since with such a derivation *Max* would be marked as coreferential with *himself*, exactly as if the deep structure were (23b). I will show in the next section how this can be accomplished.

2.2

Jackendoff includes in his coreference rule the following condition on when a reflexive can be marked as coreferential to something (1972:136):

(24) NP^2 has not yet appeared on the right-hand side of the table.

Condition (24) allows Jackendoff to make the assignment of the antecedent to a reflexive obligatory and yet not have more than one antecedent assigned to any particular reflexive. For example, were (24) not imposed, both *Bill* and *John* in (25) would be marked as coreferential with the reflexive, and the coreference table would be inconsistent:

(25)   Bill asked John about himself.

This treatment involves two peculiarities in the way that the coreference rule is to apply: (i) it must be sensitive to the absence of information, that is, the rule applies only when certain entries in the coreference table are as yet blank, and (ii) different applications of an obligatory rule to a particular domain have to take place in random sequence, that is, one chooses at random whether *Bill* or *John* is to be made coreferential with *himself*, and either choice rules out the possibility of a subsequent application with the other as antecedent, by virtue of (24). Both of these characteristics could be avoided by modifying Jackendoff's system in a way parallel to Stanley's (1967) proposal for modifying earlier generative phonology.[18] Specifically, suppose that SIRs were treated as well-formedness conditions on a pair (semantic representation, syntactic structure) rather than as directions for constructing a semantic representation from the structures that appear in a given derivation. Instead of rules 'If condition *C*, then put *X* in the coreferentiality table', there would be rules 'If condition *C*, then *X* IS in the coreferentiality table', according to which a pairing of a given derivation and a given coreferentiality table is rejected if the former meets condition *C* and the latter does not contain *X*.[19,20]

[Besides insuring uniqueness of antecedents of reflexives, condition (24), in conjunction with Jackendoff's policy of having the anaphora rules be sensitive to the arrangements of items in cyclic outputs, incorporates a loose analogue to the requirement (Lees and Klima 1963) that a reflexive and its antecedent be clausemates. Jackendoff states condition (24) so that it applies not only to reflexive pronouns that have been specified as coreferential to something but also to nonreflexive pronouns that have been marked NONCOREFERENTIAL to something by prior application of the anaphora rules. Jackendoff is thus able (p. 204) to block application of his reflexive rule to the pair (*I, me*) in (26), thereby preventing those two items from being marked noncoreferential:

(26)   I expect Bill to examine me.

For Jackendoff, even if the derivation of (26) involves a step that eliminates entirely the complement subject and even if that makes

I and *me* count as surface clausemates by virtue of pruning of the lower S node, *me* is unavailable to be marked as noncoreferential to *I* since it has been marked noncoreferential to *Bill* in the application of the anaphora rules to the cyclic output *Bill to examine me* and condition (24) thus applies.]

[Since for Jackendoff, Ss and NPs both are cyclic domains, his rules account for the following well-known facts:

(27)   (a) Tom_i showed $Dick_j$ a picture of $himself_{i/j}$.
          (b) Tom_i showed $Dick_j$ $Harry_k$'s picture of $himself_{k/*i/*j}$.

The NP *a picture of himself* contains no NP that *himself* could be marked coreferential with, and thus when the anaphora rules apply to the cyclic output from the whole S, *himself* is still available to be marked coreferential with either *Tom* or *Dick* in (27a). In (27b), by contrast, *himself* is marked as coreferential with *Harry* when the anaphora rules apply to the cyclic output *Harry's picture of himself*, and it thus cannot be marked coreferential with either *Tom* or *Dick* when the anaphora rules apply to the cyclic output from the whole S.[21] Jackendoff's anaphora rules in their pristine form would thus not rule out reflexive subjects, as in (28), since the application of the anaphora rules to (28) would exactly parallel their application to (27a):

(28)   *Tom told Dick that himself was a genius.

Jackendoff accordingly added a condition to his rule (p. 136, condition (b)) to restrict its application to reflexives that are in the configuration (29):[22]

(29) $\{\bar{V}, \bar{N}\}$
           |
        (PP)
           |
      reflexive

This revision (or the alternative suggested in note 22) still allows a reflexive that is properly contained within a subject NP to have an antecedent in the next higher clause, as in (30), though with the defect noted in note 21 of making reflexivization in such sentences obligatory rather than optional:

(30)   That there is a picture of himself$_i$ in the post office bothers John$_i$.]

[To replace condition (24) by a well-formedness condition on (semantic representation, syntactic structure) pairs, it will be necessary first to remove one apparent inconsistency in Jackendoff's use of the term 'coreferential'. In his statement of (24), Jackendoff treats 'coref' as an asymmetric relation, in that the condition is activated only by the *b* of an entry [*a* ± coref *b*] in the table. However, elsewhere in the book he appears to treat 'coref' as symmetric, indeed as an equivalence relation. For example, in applying his noncoreferentiality rule ('If for any NP^1 and NP^2 in a sentence, there is no entry in the table *NP*^{1} ± coref *NP*^{2}, enter in the table NP^1 − coref *NP*^{2}' (p. 116), he treats it as entering 'NP^1 − coref NP^2' only if 'NP^1 coref NP^2' does not follow from the pre-existing entries in the table under the assumption that 'coref' is reflexive, symmetric, and transitive, for example, he takes it as adding to (31a) the entry in (31b) but not those in (31c):

(31)   (a)   John^1 said that Bill^2 had shot him^3
                2 − coref 3 (by reflexive rule)
                1 coref 3 (one of two options allowed by pronoun rule)
        (b)   1 − coref 2
        (c)   3 − coref 1
                1 − coref 1

In what follows I will assume that this inconsistency in Jackendoff's use of 'coref' has been rectified by the following steps, which allow the essential features of his analysis to be preserved: (i) the relations 'is coreferential with' and 'is antecedent of' are distinguished; (ii) 'is coreferential with' is reflexive, symmetric, and transitive, whereas 'is antecedent of' is anti-reflexive, anti-symmetric, and anti-transitive; (iii) the anaphora rules mark an item as antecedent of an anaphoric device rather than as coreferential with it;[23] (iv) if an NP is antecedent of an identity-of-reference anaphoric device, it is necessarily coreferential with it; (v) an anaphoric device can have only one antecedent (with a qualification for 'split antecedents', as in *John$_i$ asked Mary$_j$ when they$_{ij}$ should leave*); and (vi) the condition that a pronoun cannot precede and command its antecedent is imposed on the antecedent relation in all relevant syntactic structures, which in the present discussion will be the cyclic outputs. This will require that Jackendoff's α-rule for reflexives (which specifies a pair of NPs as coreferential if one of them is reflexive and noncoreferential if it is non-reflexive) be divided into two rules, one requiring a reflexive to have an antecedent meeting certain conditions and one stating that a nonreflexive pronoun is noncoreferential with (not just does not have as antecedent) certain other NPs.]

[The well-formedness condition on (semantic representation, syntactic structure) pairs that most closely simulates Jackendoff's reflexive rule is probably one that directly incorporates a requirement that the reflexive and its antecedent be 'cyclic domain mates', with an exception to allow for cases like (27a) and (30). Specifically, suppose that, as in Jackendoff's treatment, cyclic outputs are the syntactic structures that are relevant to determining the coreference possibilities for NPs, but instead of entries being added to a partially constructed coreference table on the basis of the syntactic configurations in each cyclic output, each cyclic output is simply checked against a fully specified coreferentiality table of antecedent relations, according to rule (32):

(32) (a) If NP^2 is reflexive and is preceded and commanded by at least one NP, then there is an NP^1 such that [1 antecedent 2].

     (b) If NP^2 is not a reflexive pronoun and is preceded by a cyclic domain mate NP^1, then [1 − coref 2].

Since each cyclic output is checked against the coreferentiality table, (32a) insures that a reflexive pronoun will have an antecedent in the lowest available cyclic domain: the same cyclic domain if it is preceded and commanded by an NP in the same cyclic domain, and the next higher cyclic domain otherwise. No condition 'NP^2 does not precede and command NP^1' need be included in (32a), since the requirement that anaphoric items should not both precede and command their antecedents is imposed on all cyclic outputs.] [24]

[The problem raised by Harada and Saito's example vanishes if (32) is adopted and there is a cyclic transformation that randomly converts simple personal pronouns into reflexives. The deep structure of (23a) will now differ from (23b) to the extent of having *him* in place of *himself*. If optional reflexivization applies to *him* on the S_2 cycle, inconsistent demands are made on the coreference table: *him* must be coreferential to $\triangle$ by virtue of what (32a) says about the S^2 cyclic output, but it must be coreferential with *Bill* by virtue of what it says about the S^0 cyclic output, which is impossible since $\triangle$ must be coreferential with *Max* and *Max* noncoreferential with *Bill*. If optional reflexivization applies on the S^1 or S^0 cycle,[25] the *him* that underlies *himself* will have to be noncoreferential with Δ (and thus with *Max*) by virtue of what (32b) says about the S^2 cyclic output, and *himself* will have to be coreferential with *Bill* in view of what (32a) says about the S^0 cyclic output. Thus, the applications of random reflexivization that correspond to a consistent coreferentiality table correspond to the right one for (23a).] [26]

3

In section 1, I have shown that even under fairly strict adherence to Jackendoff's assumptions, there is no real alternative to having a transformation that deletes a VP under identity with another VP, and I have argued that the way to incorporate such a transformation into a grammar that does a minimum of violence to Jackendoff's assumptions is to take SIRs to be conditions on the well-formedness of (semantic representation, syntactic derivation) pairs and adopt a revised version of the recoverability constraint, according to which deletion or emptying under identity is possible only when the deleted/emptied item is syntactically and semantically identical to its antecedent. In section 2, I have shown that such a 'static' reinterpretation of Jackendoff's SIRs forces one either to adopt a Reflexivization transformation or to revise the SIRs so that they refer only to postcyclic stages of derivations; I have also demonstrated that the problem raised by Harada and Saito concerning reflexives that originate in a lower clause also demands either a Reflexivization transformation or a revision of the SIRs so that either they refer only to postcyclic stages of derivations or they apply top-to-bottom.

Suppose that it can be shown that the alternatives of postcyclic anaphora rules and top-to-bottom anaphora rules are untenable. Would that mean that an 'interpretive' approach to anaphora must be rejected in favor of a 'generative' approach? I would like to close by maintaining that the question involves an assumption that is detrimental to any quest for an understanding of the subject at hand, namely the assumption that there is substance to the notions 'generative account' and 'interpretive account'. The various issues discussed in this article (and in Jackendoff's book) are to a large extent independent of each other, and there is no apparent conflict between the points that I have raised above and a number of important details of his treatment of anaphora; for example, the propositions that at least many kinds of anaphoric devices are not derived from copies of their antecedents, that transformations and SIRs form distinct systems of rules, and that there are SIRs that determine possible anaphora-antecedent relationships in the case of those anaphoric devices that are not derived from copies of their antecedents. The terms 'generative' and 'interpretive' have been applied to various theoretical positions not so much because of any inherent relationship between those positions as because certain positions have been associated (in fact or in popular caricature) with linguists who accept a distinction between 'transformation' and 'SIR', and other positions have been associated with linguists who reject that distinction. Actually, a wide variety of combinations of positions on the various issues can be found in the literature; for example, it is easy (McCawley (1975b)) to find attestations of all logically possible combinations of answers to the questions (i) Are all anaphoric pronouns derived from copies of their antecedents? and (ii) Are transformations sensitive to coreference? A 'generative' answer to one of the questions at issue need not commit one to 'generative' answers to other questions. In fact, the discussion on sections 1 and 2 should make it clear that the following views are mutually consistent: (a) the position that there are SIRs that relate syntactic configurations in cyclic outputs to coreference relations among the various NPs (an 'interpretivist' position); (b) the position that transformations are sensitive to coreference; and (c) the position that reflexive pronouns are derived from something nonreflexive by a transformation ('generativist' positions). A theory that combines (a), (b), and (c) must not be rejected merely for being 'bastardized' or for violation of an exogamy taboo; it is merely one of a large number of possible theories of anaphora and must stand or fall on its merits. The application of the terms 'generative' and 'interpretive' to positions on theoretical issues is pernicious in the same way that the application of the terms 'right' and 'left' to political issues is: it presupposes a somewhat capricious projection of a multidimensional space onto a one-dimensional space and makes the identification of real issues more difficult. I offer this article as a specimen of issue-identification carried out with relative disregard for the application of the labels 'generative' and 'interpretive', albeit with a certain amount of prejudice for many of the positions generally labeled as 'generative'.

Notes

1.   Jackendoff does not distinguish clearly between the claim that transformations may not refer to semantic information and the claim that transformations may not be sensitive to semantic information. It is possible to maintain the former

claim while rejecting the latter if one maintains that transformations are sensitive in a predictable way to semantic information. I will take up a specific proposal of this type in § 1.5.

2.   While Jackendoff does not exhibit his functional structures in tree format, the parenthesized formulas that he writes can be converted mechanically into a tree format, and for sake of clarity I will use such a format below. The following appear to be the principal systematic differences between Jackendoff's functional structures and the semantic structures given in such generative semantic studies as McCawley (1970a, 1972) and Lakoff (1971b): (a) For generative semanticists, referential indices fill the argument positions (other than sentential arguments), whereas for Jackendoff elements of sense rather than of reference appear in those positions, for example, where generative semanticists had 'LOVE (x_1, x_2)', Jackendoff might have 'LOVE (FRED, SHE)' in the functional structure plus an entry '1 − coref 2' in the coreference table, where '1' and '2' indicate the corresponding nodes of functional structure. (b) For generative semanticists, the 'scopes' of quantifiers, modal operators, etc. are indicated directly in the same tree structure that indicates what predicates are predicated of what arguments (specifically, quantifiers are treated as predicates, and the scope of a quantifier is the part of the tree that it commands), whereas for Jackendoff scope relations are indicated in a separate part of semantic structure, the 'modal structure'. (c) In Jackendoff's semantic structures, there are complex predicates consisting of a predicate *per se* and one or more 'modifiers' (which may be a predicate, a clause, or some other element), whereas generative semanticists have generally treated the content of Jackendoff's 'modifiers' as either conjoined with the structures they modify or as elements of higher clauses in which the modified item is embedded.

3.   [It was misleading for me to say 'THE principle of the strict cycle', since a number of distinct conceptions of strict cyclicity have been advanced. This particular version, which is due to Chomsky, applies to all transformations, not just the cyclic ones, and thus excludes the possibility of POSTCYCLIC transformations. While I reject this particular conception of strict cyclicity, I accept the alternative version that requires all applications of CYCLIC transformations to be on the smallest cyclic domain containing all the material to which that application of the transformation is sensitive. This does not exclude the possibility of postcyclic transformations applying to embedded structures; for a good example of a case where that possibility is needed, see Akmajian and Wasow's (1975) discussion of Tense hopping. Much confusion has been created by the deplorably prevalent confusion of the terms 'postcyclic' and 'last-cyclic'. A last-cyclic transformation is a transformation that is in the cycle but constrained to apply only on topmost Ss; the notion differs from Emonds's notion of 'root transformation' only in that it is neutral as to what transformation does, while Emonds's root transformations are required to move an item into a position as daughter of a topmost S node. Post-cyclic transformations presuppose prior application of the complete transformational cycle but are not in general restricted to applying to topmost clauses. For a refreshingly clear presentation of the issues relating to cyclic, postcyclic, and last-cyclic transformations, see Pullum (1976).]

4.   Note that the operation of the anaphora rule, and indeed of most of Jackendoff's SIRs, leans heavily on the notion of *corresponding node*. The coreference table is a set of relationships among nodes of functional structure, established on the basis of structural relationships among the corresponding nodes of the cyclic outputs.

5.   Jackendoff does not make clear why (6b) contains $[\Delta]_V$ and not, say, $[\Delta]_V [\Delta]_{Adv} [\Delta]_{Prep}$. Since he employs empty nodes in a similar way for sentences involving Gapping (1972: 268), in the deep structure of *Tom can't get along with Walt, nor Fred with Vera* the 'shadow' of *get along with* could not simply be $[\Delta]_V$.

6.   [Postal's (1970b) version of Equi-NP-deletion in effect involved an emptying transformation. His specific proposal was that deletion of a complement subject involves two steps: cyclic conversion of the complement subject into a pronoun marked '[+ DOOM]' and post-cyclic (indeed, post-everything) deletion of all items marked with that stigma. The derivation was to be ill-formed if the anaphoric device violated any of the constraints on how anaphoric devices may be related to their antecedents. Postal's proposal amounts to replacing a complement subject by an empty node that counts as an anaphoric device having the 'controller' NP as its antecedent; this is the earliest instance that I know of the device that has subsequently become known as a 'trace'.]

7.   [In my original version of (9) I inadvertently omitted some entries that Jackendoff's rules would add to the coreferentiality table. His rule for pronouns allows the option of adding either '2 coref 4' or '2 – coref 4' to the table, though only the latter yields a consistent table; with the latter specification in the table, the noncoreferentiality rule will add '1 – coref 2'. In (9)–(11) I have supplemented the entries that I originally gave with these additional entries, in so far as they yield consistent tables.]

8.   Since in chapter 2 Jackendoff gives a number of functional structures in which a semantically complex predicate is broken up into several semantic pieces, he may very well regard his KISS and REFUSE as mere makeshifts, pending a more thorough semantic analysis.

9.   [Actually, with its 'cyclic domain mates'. See § 2.2 for remarks on the counterpart in Jackendoff's system to the condition that a reflexive be a clause-mate of its antecedent.]

10.   This assumes, of course, that a 'sloppy identity' principle will apply under any alternative.

11.   Of necessity, any examples relevant to the point that I am making here will violate the 'No Ambiguity Condition' of Hankamer (1973), as these examples do. I take these examples to be in fact counterexamples to Hankamer's condition. See Channon (1975a, 1975b) for criticism of the No Ambiguity Condition.

12.   Jackendoff invokes the familiar rule of 'Agent Deletion' (1972: 269) to eliminate the *by* in (7a). However, the same kind of objection can be raised to that proposal as Jackendoff raises against VP Deletion: for Jackendoff, Agent Deletion would have to be in the cycle; thus, the *by* ∆, which would have to be present in the stage to which the VP-Anaphora rule applied if the sentence were to be interpretable, would have already been deleted; and thus the VP-Anaphora rule would be unable to apply. More importantly, the items deleted by Agent Deletion do not stand in the coreference relations that NPs in 'empty VPs' do. For example, *Steve was mugged, and so was Bert* is noncommittal as to whether the same mugger perpetrated both acts, in contrast with *Steve was mugged by him, and so was Bert*.

13.   If Perlmutter is correct in his claim (personal communication) that agreement consists in the copying of a pronoun, then deletion of unstressed subject (and object) pronouns in languages in which the verb agrees with the subject (and object) can be treated as a deletion under identity. In that event, deletion of 'constants' can be restricted to deletion of semantically empty items and deletion of semantically unmarked items such as the 'CAUSE', 'USE', and 'AT' whose deletion figures in the analysis of noun compounds and nonpredicate adjectives given in Levi (1974) [see now Levi (1978)]. Sentences such as *A parent shouldn't spank*, which Cantrall (1974: 30) has offered as counterexamples to the standard version of the recoverability constraint, may be amenable to a treatment involving deletion under identity followed by incorporation of indefinite object: *A parent of someone$_i$ shouldn't spank him$_i$ → *A parent of someone shouldn't spank → A parent shouldn't spank*. Deletion will of course have to be distinguished

from zero morphological realization, such as the zero pronoun that has been argued (Kuroda 1965) to be the only true personal pronoun in Japanese.

14.   Does the revised recoverability principle have the false implication that
    (i)   Bill bought a car and so did John.

only has an interpretation in which Bill and John bought the same car or that (21a) has only an interpretation in which Susan and Sam wrote the same letter? Whether it does depends on the specific details of the semantic representation of sentences involving logical bound variables. If *a car* is treated as an ordinary NP, capable of standing in the same sorts of coreferentiality relations as might *it* or *Harry*, then it does in fact have that catastrophic consequence. However, if *Bill bought a car* is analyzed as having a semantic structure in which an existential quantifier is external to a clause *Bill buy x*, which has the corresponding bound variable *as* the object NP, the recoverability principle would only require that each clause of (i) be interpreted as having a quantifier that binds a variable corresponding to the surface object. Even if the same index is used to represent the two variables, there is no coreferentiality between the NPs of the two clauses, since each quantifier binds only those occurrences of its variable that are in its scope. [See now Sag (1976), Williams (1977), and McCawley (1981c: 396–401) for discussion of the role of logical variables in linguistic identity.]

15.   [See McCawley (1979a, 1979b, 1981c: § § 9.6, 11.2) for further development of Karttunen's proposal.]

16.   Harada and Saito assign to (23a) a deep structure in which the VP of S^1 is *be hard* rather than *be hard for Max* and the subject of S^2 is *Max*. (23b), which conforms to Jackendoff's remarks about *Tough* Movement (1972: 154–6), presents exactly the same problems for his coreference rule as does the deep structure on which Harada and Saito based their argument.

17.   A third possibility, which I will not discuss further, since I do not understand its implications, would be to have the coreference assignment rules apply to cyclic outputs in top-to-bottom fashion; that is, the application of the coreference rule to any S would follow its application to all higher Ss. That proposal would avoid Harada and Saito's problem, since *Bill* would be marked coreferential to *himself* when the coreference rule applied to S^0, and the rule would be inhibited from marking *Max* coreferential with *himself*, by the clause that makes the rule inapplicable to an anaphoric device that has already been assigned an antecedent. [For the couple of other examples on which I have tried it out, such as *Realizing that he/John was unpopular didn't bother John/him*, top-to-bottom application of Jackendoff's rules yields the same results as bottom-to-top application.]

18.   One of Stanley's motivations for adopting 'morpheme structure conditions' was to avoid the spurious economies that are available when a morpheme structure can apply to a segment that is unspecified for one of the features to which the rule is sensitive. No analogue to that argument is possible here, since the examples discussed by Stanley involve the interaction of two rules $[+F] \rightarrow X$, $[-F] \rightarrow Y$, whereas Jackendoff's SIRs appear never to be contingent on a condition 'x − coref y'.

19.   Both this suggestion and Stanley's proposal conform to a more general methodological principle that excludes spurious stages in derivations. While the *whole* coreference table may well be psychologically real, I suspect that the various fragments of it that appear in Jackendoff's step-by-step construction of the table have no more psychological reality than do other fragments of the table that do not appear in his construction. The same consideration favors taking the base component of a transformational grammar to be a set of 'node admissibility conditions' (McCawley 1968c) rather than a 'phrase structure grammar' and is alluded to in Kiparsky's (1973) argument that rules of the form 'X $\rightarrow$ Y/Z' and 'X $\rightarrow$ W' apply disjunctively.

20. [The remainder of this section is newly written in an attempt to rectify my failure in the original version to recognize how condition (24) incorporated an analogue to the 'clausemate condition' of earlier treatments of reflexives such as Lees and Klima (1963).]

21. [This treatment incorrectly makes reflexivization obligatory rather than optional in sentences like (27a), that is, for *Tom showed Dick a picture of him* it would yield only a coreference table in which *him* was marked noncoreferential with both *Tom* and *Dick*.]

22. [Alternatively, one might rule (28) out on purely morphological grounds, namely that while the reflexive in (28) is in a configuration that demands a nominative case, English reflexives simply have no nominative form. It may be necessary to regard English genitive pronouns as ambiguous between a reflexive and a non-reflexive sense in order to allow *John loves his wife* to be ambiguous as to whether *his* refers to John. As Jackendoff's rules stand, they would make *John* and *his* noncoreferential unless *his* counted as reflexive. Other languages, such as Swedish, Russian, and Hindi, have morphologically distinct reflexive and nonreflexive possessives, for example

Per älskar hans mor. 'Peter$_i$ loves his$_j$ mother'
Per älskar sin mor.'Peter$_i$ loves his$_j$ mother']

23. [Lakoff (1968b) provides arguments for taking 'antecedent' rather than 'coreferential' as the basic notion in the analysis of anaphora. Note that the notion of 'antecedent' makes sense for both identity-of-sense anaphora and identity-of-reference anaphora, while the notion of 'coreferential' may make sense only for the latter.]

24. [The analysis sketched here fails to account for such reflexives as those in (i):

(i) (a) Which picture of himself did Susan say that John had sold?
     (b) How many photographs of himself did Susan say that John had taken?
     (c) The picture of himself that John found in the post office annoyed him.

Jackendoff's original analysis accounts for (ia–b) by virtue of the very feature of the analysis that assigns the correct interpretation to (23a), namely that the antecedent of a reflexive is assigned in the first cyclic output that provides a possible antecedent. Chiba (1972) has cited sentences such as (ic) in support of Brame's proposal that the head N (or better, $\bar{N}$) of a restrictive relative clause is derived by copying of a constituent inside the relative clause. Jackendoff (1972: 165) rejects the latter proposal on the grounds that it implies that sentences such as (ii) should be acceptable:

(ii)   *I painted a picture of himself$_i$ that John saw yesterday.

See also McCawley (1981b) for an argument that Brame's analysis is not tenable as a general account of restrictive relative clauses but serves as a 'patch' that extends a different analysis to cases to which it would otherwise be inapplicable. Cantrall (1974) argues that the possibility of using a reflexive in English depends not only on syntactic structure but also on 'viewpoint', that is, that reflexivization is favored when the clause can be interpreted as reflecting the viewpoint of the antecedent, as illustrated by such examples as:

(iii) The picture of him/himself that hangs in Nixon's study is impressive.
       The picture of him/*himself that hings in Lincoln's study is impressive.

[The astute reader will have noted the similarity between (32b) and the rule of noncoreferentiality that forms the basis of Lasnik's (1976) analysis of anaphora:

(32') If NP^1 precedes and kommands NP^2 and NP^2 is not a pronoun, then NP^1 and NP^2 are disjoint in reference, where A kommands B if the minimal cyclic node dominating A also dominates B.

The greater generality of (32') in relation to (32b) reflects a difference in the division of labor that Jackendoff and Lasnik posit between the 'basic' anaphora rules and a 'default' condition that allows or requires noncoreference in cases not covered by the 'basic' rules, for example, the noncoreferentiality of *John* and *the bastard* in *John said that the bastard was hungry* is accounted for by the 'basic' rule in Lasnik's system but is a side effect of the inapplicability of the 'basic' rule in Jackendoff's system. In much recent work (for example, Chomsky 1980), Lasnik's approach is formalized in terms of indexed NPs and a procedure that attaches to each NP a set of 'counter-indices' that specify what NPs the given NP must not overlap in reference with. In the version of this formalization adopted in Freidin and Lasnik (1981), NPs need not be assigned distinct indices and sameness of index corresponds to coreference. While Freidin and Lasnik speak of a procedure of random assignment of indices to the NPs of surface structure, there is no apparent reason why NPs could not bear indices throughout an entire syntactic derivation, in which case the assignment of indices would be essentially as in Chomsky (1965), except for the correction of Chomsky's error of treating indices as borne by Ns rather than by NPs.]

25.   [I do not exclude the possibility of reflexivization of the subject on the S^1 cycle, since if defective morphology is responsible for the absence of sentences like (28), as suggested in note 22, then such sentences should be permissible in intermediate stages of derivations, just as long as the offending reflexive is ultimately either deleted or moved to a position that calls for a form that its morphology allows.]

26.   Note also that the 'blind' version of reflexivization does not impose any tighter constraints on how reflexives can be related to their antecedents than does the 'seeing' version. While it might be claimed that the blind approach allows only cyclic outputs to be relevant to the reflexive–antecedent relation whereas a 'seeing' transformation could in principle be ordered before other transformations of the cycle, that observation merely reflects the historical accident that it was Jackendoff who first saw fit to impose a universal restriction that they refer only to cyclic outputs. Pronominalization transformations do not lend themselves any less than do anaphora SIRs to the imposition of a universal constraint that they be ordered after all (other) cyclic transformations. Actually, it is doubtful that either version of this putative universal can be maintained. Okada (1975) presents detailed arguments to show that the stages of the derivation that are relevant to the interpretation of reflexives and of empty complement subjects are not the cyclic outputs but the outputs of specific transformations of the cycle. Okada also notes that since Jackendoff's multipart anaphora rule would thus have to be broken up into at least three separate rules (one for empty complement subjects, one for reflexives, and one for nonreflexive pronouns), the constraint that the anaphoric device may not precede and command the antecedent cannot be part of those anaphora rules but must be a separate overall constraint on the anaphora–antecedent relation. This agrees with the conclusion of Lakoff (1968b) that some types of anaphoric devices must be derived from copies of their antecedents but other types cannot be, though all anaphoric devices are subject to the constraint that they not both precede and command their antecedents, which means that that constraint is thus not part of the rules that create the former type of anaphoric devices but is a general constraint on anaphora–antecedent relations.

3 LANGUAGE UNIVERSALS IN LINGUISTIC ARGUMENTATION

1. Introduction

I will begin this not very comprehensive survey of the ways in which language universals have figured and/or ought to have figured in linguistic argumentation by outlining certain assumptions and prejudices that will color what I say below.

First, I take the position that all language universals are implicational universals. Only under that assumption can one avoid arbitrary decisions as to what will count as a language. Most work on language universals has systematically ignored child language, written language, sign language, non-native language (pidgins, Roman Jakobson's English, etc.), and the language of aphasics and schizophrenics. For example, linguists happily accept the claim that all languages have nasal consonants[1] even though they are perfectly aware of languages that do not, for example, American Sign Language. It is of course reasonable for linguists to ignore ASL here: the universal relates to the vocal medium of spoken languages. However, the irrelevance of ASL to some language universals does not make it irrelevant to all discussion of language universals — it clearly is relevant to discussions of universals of constituent order or of semantic distinctions in the lexicon. If 'language' is understood broadly and universals are taken to be implicational, exclusion of any types of language from the domains of universals must be for cause: the antecedent of the implicational universal must give the grounds on which the particular varieties of language are to be excluded (for example, 'If the medium of expression of a language is vocal, it will have nasal consonants', excludes ASL by virtue of its medium of expression being nonvocal), and the linguist must attempt to state universals in their greatest generality, that is by specifying as narrowly as possible the conditions that would remove a variety of language from the applicability of the putative universal.[2]

Second, I wish to dissociate myself from an assumption that is so popular among linguists that it is difficult to find anyone who disputes it, namely the assumption that people who talk the same have the same linguistic competence. I have recently been advocating (McCawley 1976a; 1977a) a conception of language acquisition in which many details of acquisition are random or are influenced by ephemeral details of one's linguistic experience. Such a scheme for language acquisition need not lead to gross inhomogeneity in a linguistic community, since there is ample opportunity for revision of learning that has made the speaker grossly divergent from his neighbors. Moreover, it is easy to think of alternative linguistic rules and underlying forms that yield exactly the same well-formedness data and exactly the same pairings of meaning and expression; indeed, linguists are perpetually arguing about such alternative analyses, for example, the analysis in which the English regular plural ending is /iz/ and a rule deletes its vowel under one set of circumstances, versus the analysis in which the ending is /z/ and a rule inserts a vowel under other circumstances. Maybe for some people plurals work the one way and for other people the other way. The assumption that all normal adult members of a linguistic community have the same internalized analysis in such cases is gratuitous. In the rare cases where linguists have looked for interpersonal variation in language, they have generally found it. For example, Haber (1975) reports that speakers who ostensibly form English plurals the same way give a broad range of responses on tasks requiring the formation of plurals of novel words, with each speaker having his own ways of dealing with novel plurals. There is also considerable individual variation in the morphemic relations that speakers of English perceive, as one can readily verify by asking one's friends whether *pulley* is related to *pull* or *tinsel* to *tin*.

Third, and closely related to the last point, I claim conscientious objector status in the ongoing war against 'excessive power' of grammatical devices. We have all been taught to limit our descriptive devices as tightly as possible, preferably to those that were good enough for our scientific forefathers, since seemingly innocuous devices may turn out to harbor within them the dread Turing machine. It has accordingly become common for linguists to attempt to resolve disputes among competing analyses by drafting sweeping restrictions on grammars so as to give one of the competing analyses a legal monopoly. I will argue below that many proposed language universals have served only to allow linguists to construct cheap arguments for their favorite analyses and that those arguments have given the illusion of significance only because their alleged role in the war effort against 'excessive power' has obscured important respects in which they are extremely implausible.

2.   Universals as Self-serving Legislation

I will begin this largely negative survey of the use of language universals in linguistic argumentation by criticizing and recanting a couple of particularly bad arguments that I have offered in earlier works. In McCawley (1973c), I presented a number of arguments for treating vowel height in terms of a single 3 or 4 valued feature rather than in terms of two binary features such as Chomsky and Halle's (1968) [± high] and [± low]. The bulk of my arguments were based on phenomena in which constant increments of height played a role, for example, the raising of the first element of a long vowel by one degree of height in eastern Finnish dialects and the lowering of the second element of a long vowel by one degree in certain Lappish dialects. I then introduced my final argument by saying 'What would give a really crushing case for the nonbinary proposal would be to show some major restriction on rules which could be imposed under the nonbinary proposal but not under the binary proposal' and proceeded to discuss a supposed example of such a restriction: a requirement that phonological rules have a unitary 'structural change', that is a restriction excluding rules that specify changes in more than one feature specification at a time. Under the binary proposal, that universal would be violated by rules such as the Finnish and Lappish rules just discussed, whereas a nonbinary alternative involved a unitary structural change:

(1)   Eastern Finnish 'breaking'

(a)   binary version

$$\begin{bmatrix} - \text{ high} \\ \alpha \text{ low} \\ \beta \text{ front} \\ \gamma \text{ round} \end{bmatrix} \begin{bmatrix} - \text{ high} \\ \alpha \text{ low} \\ \beta \text{ front} \\ \gamma \text{ round} \end{bmatrix}$$

$$1 \rightarrow \begin{bmatrix} - \text{ low} \\ -\alpha \text{ high} \end{bmatrix}$$

(b)   nonbinary version

$$\begin{bmatrix} \alpha < 3 \text{ high} \\ \beta \text{ front} \\ \gamma \text{ round} \end{bmatrix} \begin{bmatrix} \alpha \text{ high} \\ \beta \text{ front} \\ \gamma \text{ round} \end{bmatrix}$$

$$1 \rightarrow [\alpha + 1 \text{ high}]$$

I also argued for reanalyses of certain apparent instances of rules involving changes of two or more feature specifications. Specifically, I argued that in cases such as the laxing, deaspiration, and despirantization of syllable-final consonants in Korean, the effects of the rule were predictable side effects of a unitary change (in this case, the rule basically just made all syllable-final consonants unreleased, and the other changes represented predictable concomitants of unreleased articulation) and showed how cases such as compensatory lengthening could be given a similar treatment, namely by taking the structural change not to be a change in the feature composition of segments but a change in the timing of phonetic events, in this case, postponement of the onset of a following consonant, with the changes of feature composition of the segments involved being predictable consequences of that single change of timing.

While I was thus able to present a fairly good case that one could impose a universal restriction that a phonological rule have a unitary structural change, I did not take up the question of whether that restriction had anything else to recommend it beyond its apparent viability as a universal. First, what that universal implies depends heavily on how one answers an extremely difficult question that linguists have said little about and are not in a position to say anything very coherent about, namely that of how one can justify a particular individuation of rules: how one can justify saying that a particular formula represents a single entry in the grammar rather than being merely a misleading way of representing several such entries (or perhaps, pieces of several such entries). To the extent that rules with multipart structural changes can be simulated by sets of rules with unitary structural changes (which is a large extent unless quite stringent additional constraints are imposed on what is allowed as a possible rule), the proposed universal is in effect merely a policy to divide among several rules the structural change of what one might otherwise have considered a single rule.[3] Second, if the structural change of a rule is to be related in any even indirect way to something that a speaker does or may do in the course of speech production, it is implausible to suppose that doing two such things together should be ruled out; if anything, structural changes that always go together ought to be kept together in the internalized grammar for maximum economy in the use of the grammar in production and comprehension.

A second place in which the putative universal that rules have unitary structural changes played a role in my argumentation is the paper that I published under the title 'English as a VSO language' (McCawley 1970c).[4] I pointed out there that a number of transformations require an additional step if they apply to SVO structures that is unnecessary if they apply to VSO structures.[5] For example, if *there*-insertion applies to an SVO structure, it must both move the underlying subject into a postverbal position and insert *there* in subject position, whereas if it applies to a VSO structure, it need only insert a *there* before the subject (the underlying subject will remain in postverbal position in surface structure, since only the first of the verb's sisters is moved into preverbal position by the rule that yields the surface SVO order):

(2)   SVO *there*-insertion   VSO *there*-insertion

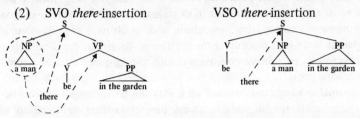

I ought to have argued against the SVO formulation of *there*-insertion on the grounds that it misses a generalization: all rules that create a new subject also demote the old subject to nonsubject status, and the SVO formulation of *there*-insertion makes the demotion of the old subject seem like an added complication of the phenomenon rather than a predictable side effect of the other part of the structural change.[6] What I did instead was argue for the VSO formulation on the grounds that it allowed one to enforce a universal restriction that transformations must have unitary structural changes. Besides sharing the implausibility of its phonological analogue, discussed above, this putative universal has the further defect of committing one to an analysis of the passive that has nothing to recommend it. As I pointed out in 'English as a VSO language', the SVO version of passive requires an extra part to its structural change that is unnecessary in the VSO version: not only must it move the underlying subject into the *by*-phrase but it must also move the underlying postverbal NP into subject position. However, if Passive is to have a unitary structural change, the markers of the passive (passive *be* and the *by*) must not be inserted by the Passive transformation but must be present as such in the input to Passive. Underlying structures in which those elements are present have in fact been proposed widely (an underlying *by* is proposed in Lees (1964) and Chomsky (1965) and assumed in Chomsky's subsequent works; an underlying *be* is adopted in Hasegawa (1968), R. Lakoff (1971), and, I am ashamed to say, McCawley (1970c)). However, the arguments that have been given for such underlying structures rest on preposterous premises, particularly the assumption that transformations cannot 'build structure'. Thus, for example, the argument that Chomsky (1965) seemed to find the weightiest for having passive *by* present in deep structure is that, given his policy on where node labels come from (namely that they must be the labels of corresponding deep structure nodes), that is the only way he can get the *by*-phrase to be a prepositional phrase or even a syntactic constituent. What little substance these arguments might have vanishes if one adopts Anderson's (1966) position that principles of syntactic category assignment relate not just to deep structure but to all stages of a derivation (for example, anything consisting of a preposition and an NP is a PP, regardless of what it is derived from) and the further position that transformations apply so as to achieve conformity with the language's surface target configurations.[7]

Another highly dubious universal that has been pressed into service in arguments for linguistic analyses that allow that universal to be enforced is the putative universal that no quantifiers need be used in formulating rules. For example, in Bach's (1970) otherwise superbly argued case for deriving the surface SOV word order of Amharic from an underlying VSO order, the following argument appears. In Amharic, restrictive relative clauses precede the head noun and are marked by a prefix $yə$ – on the final verb of the relative clause. Bach maintains (and let us grant him these assumptions, since it is a different point of the argument that I wish to attack) that, regardless of whether Amharic has underlying VSO, SVO, or SOV word order, in deep structure the relative clause must precede the noun as it does in surface structure (a reasonable assumption) and $yə$ – must precede the relative clause (a not so reasonable assumption).[8] Bach notes that VSO underlying order allows one to formulate the $yə$ – attachment rule without the use of quantifiers (its structural description is simply [X $yə$ V Y]), whereas with SOV word order the structural description of $yə$ – attachment must make use of a quantifier to specify that the material after the verb to which $yə$ – is attached contains no verb, that is, that $yə$ – is attached to the last verb (the last verb in SOV order being, of course, the first verb in VSO order). (3) gives a sample derivation according to Bach's preferred analysis:

'The house that Mr. Kəbbədə had'

A restriction excluding rules whose formulations include quantifiers would of course significantly narrow the class of possible grammars. However, it would narrow the class to such an extent as to make language impoverished in comparison with other cognitive domains, such as visual perception. A condition such as 'where X contains no V' in a rule with a structural description [... X V Y] or [Y V X ...] amounts to an instruction to match the symbol V to the first V or the last V in the given domain. The sketches of perceptual mechanisms given in Miller and Johnson-Laird (1976) involve wide reliance on searches through structured domains, especially searches for the first or last element that meets a given condition. While I am in no position here to propose any specific integration of psychological mechanisms in perception and in language use, I hold that it is implausible to suggest that organizational features that figure widely in perception and in non-linguistic knowledge are systematically excluded from language.

3. Universals and Underlying Constituent Order

A much more promising use of language universals in argumentation, one also illustrated in Bach's Amharic paper, is the use of implicational universals and tendencies as the basis for assigning to languages that appear to violate the universals an underlying order different from their surface order. For example, Bach makes much of the atypical status of Amharic among surface SOV languages, for example, that it has more prepositions than postpositions and that it has forwards Gapping. Amharic can be made less of an anomaly by treating it as having VSO word order for the bulk of its syntax (and thus acting like a VSO language with regard to most of its syntactic rules), with only relatively superficial syntactic rules presupposing an SOV order that is derived from VSO order by a transformation moving each verb to the end of its clause.

I have one serious objection to such invocations of language universals in establishing deep constituent orders, namely that they involve a gratuitous assumption that there *is* a deep constituent order. I attribute the prevalence of that gratuitous assumption to two principal causes: first, a hasty and mistaken judgement that unordered structures are out-landish abominations (this judgement may in many instances be a symptom of DENDROPHOBIA, a malady that is manifested in a tendency to think in terms of strings rather than of trees whenever possible, and at times even when not possible; Chomsky appears to suffer from chronic congenital dendrophobia), and second, a mistaken application of Postal's (1968) 'naturalness principle', according to which underlying linguistic structures have the same formal nature as superficial structures. Postal's principle provides a rationale for taking underlying forms of morphemes to be composed of segments and for taking those segments to be composed of specifications of values for features that also occur in surface phonology, rather than, say, having underlying segments be indivisible units or involve 'abstract' features that have no phonetic correlates. However, the principle only excludes units and structural characteristics that do not figure in superficial linguistic structure − it does not require that all the units and structural characteristics found in superficial structures also occur at deeper levels of linguistic structure. Thus, for example, the principle does not rule out underlying forms in which some or all phonological segments are unspecified with regard to voicing or length. In McCawley (1976b), I have argued that constituents of underlying syntactic structures must be allowed to be unspecified for morphological characteristics (such as person, number, case, or definiteness) that they must have determinate specifications for in surface structure. For example, I argued that underlying structures must be allowed in English in which nouns are indeterminate with regard to number, in view of the fact that while there is as much reason to derive (4a) by conjunction reduction from conjoined NPs as there is to employ conjunction reduction in anything else, corresponding NPs in which conjunction reduction has not applied must be determinate as to whether each of the two composers wrote one or more than one quartet:

(4)   (a)   The quartets of Eierkopf and Misthaufen
      (b)   The quartet(s) of Eierkopf and the quartet(s) of Misthaufen

By all applicable tests for ambiguity, (4a) is unspecified rather than ambiguous as to whether each composer wrote more than one quartet,[9] and thus the nouns in the structure to which conjunction reduction applies to derive (4a) must be unspecified for number, though if conjunction reduction does not apply there must be a number specification on each noun. Postal's naturalness condition, as I understand it, would not exclude an underlying structure for (4a) in which both conjuncts are unspecified for number. Nor would it exclude analyses involving underlying structures that are unspecified for anything else for which surface structures are determinate, such as, in particular, constituent order.

Thus, a fair proportion of arguments that have been offered for underlying word orders different from surface word order are at best arguments that if the language has an underlying word order at all, it is the one that the argument claims to give support to. Accordingly, there is a serious question as to what claims about underlying word order can be justified without reliance on the gratuitous assumption that there is one, and as to the extent to which proposed implicational universals about word order can be given interpretations that will make them applicable to underlying structures that in some cases are wholly or partially unordered. I will make no attempt to answer the latter question here, though I commend it to the attention of my fellow linguists. On the former question, the best I can do at the moment is to cite two reasonably clear cases, one of an argument for an underlying word order different from surface order that is independent of the assumption that there is an underlying word order, the other of a well-known argument for a specific underlying word order for which an alternative analysis is available that requires no linear order of constituents at any level other than surface structure.

Of Bach's arguments for underlying VSO order in Amharic, the following are the strongest, in that it is difficult to attribute the distribution of the morphemes in question to anything other than the underlying constituent order that Bach proposes. Bach argues that the *yə* — relative clause marker and the *yə* — genitive marker are the same morpheme, on the basis of a shared morphological idiosyncracy, namely that both delete when preceded by a preposition. While *yə* — is prefixed to the last verb of a relative clause, it is prefixed to the first word of a genitive NP:

(5) *yə-yohannis bet*   'John's house'
     [*yə-tillik šum*] *bet*   'the house of a big chief'
     GEN-big   chief house

This is predicted by Bach's proposed underlying word order as long as his hypothesized relative clause reduction in genitive NPs (that is, deletion of 'which . . . has', for example, 'which John has' → 'John's') applies before *yə*-attachment.[10] After deletion of the hypothesized 'have' and before movement of the verb to the end of the relative clause, the first word of the relative clause is the verb in the case of a full relative clause, but is the first word of the genitive NP if the relative clause has been reduced to a genitive NP. Furthermore, no factor other than word order appears to be shared by the words to which *yə* — is attached; for example, there is no generalization in terms of the notion 'head', since while the verb can most plausibly be regarded as the head of the full relative clause, the first word of a multiword genitive NP is never the head of either the genitive NP or the relative clause from which the genitive NP is derived. The facts are exactly parallel for the definite accusative marker *-n*, which is suffixed to the first word of an NP that begins with anything other than a (full) relative clause but is suffixed to the last word (the verb) of a relative clause that begins the NP:

(6)   *liju-n*   'the child'
      tilliḳu-n konjo lij   'the big beautiful child'
      tilliḳinna konjo y∂-hon∂wi-n lij   'the child who is big and
                                               beautiful'

Under Bach's proposed analysis, the word to which *-n* is suffixed is the word with which the NP begins after relative clause reduction but before movement of the V to the end. Again, no alternative factor such as the head/adjunct distinction provides any apparent basis for a generalization as to what word gets the suffix.

On the other hand, the considerations that Koster (1974, 1975) gives as grounds for analyzing Dutch as having SOV deep constituent order can be reconciled with an analysis that agrees in essentials with Koster's but makes no reference to constituent order in anything but surface structure. In Dutch, adverbs and prepositional phrases following the verb in a main clause can often occur in either order (7a), though when they precede the verb in a subordinate clause they can occur in only one of the two orders (7b):

(7)   (a)   *Jan dacht tijdens de pauze aan zijn vader.*
            Jan dacht aan zijn vader tijdens de pauze.
            'Jan thought of his father during the intermission'
      (b)   *Piet zei, dat Jan tijdens de pauze aan zijn vader dacht.*
            *Piet zei, dat Jan aan zijn vader tijdens de pauze dacht.
            'Piet said that Jan thought of his father during the inter-
            mission'

Koster explains this odd fact on the basis of the possibility of these elements following the verb in subordinate clauses. Specifically, either or both may follow the verb, but when both do they are in the opposite order to that which they exhibit when they precede the verb:

(8)   *Piet zei, dat Jan aan zijn vader dacht tijdens de pauze.*
      Piet zei, dat Jan tijdens de pauze dacht aan zijn vader.
      Piet zei, dat Jan dacht aan zijn vader tijdens de pauze.
      *Piet zei, dat Jan dacht tijdens de pauze aan zijn vader.

With SOV deep constituent order, the facts about main clauses can be seen as paralleling those about subordinate clauses: the second sentence in (7a) arises not through permutation of the prepositional phrases but through movement of one of them to the right of the (basically final) verb, as in the first sentence of (8). Movement of the verb into second position then leaves the two prepositional phrases adjacent but in the opposite of their original order.

However, the generalization that the word order possibilities in main clauses reflect the possibility of putting material after the verb in subordinate clauses can be incorporated into an analysis that involves unordered constituents in all derivational stages but surface structure. Suppose that, as in de Haan (1976) and in distinction to Koster, we treat adverbial elements as sisters of their respective VP's and treat the occurrence of *tidjens de pauze* after the verb and the occurrence of *aan zijn vader* after the verb as resulting from two different processes: in the one case an analogue to English adverb placement, allowing an adverb to either precede or follow its sister VP, and in the other case an analogue to English heavy-NP-shift, allowing a sufficiently 'heavy' daughter of a VP node to appear at the end of that VP. In terms of Koster's underlying constituent order, the derivational possibilities could then be summed up in the following diagram:

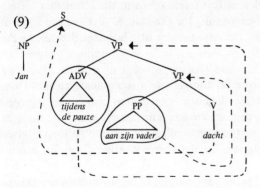

The movement of the V into second position in main clauses involves a change in constituent structure. This is particularly clear from consideration of sentences in which something other than the subject appears in first position, for example, *Tijdens de pauze dacht Jan aan zijn vader*, in which *dacht Jan aan zijn vader* presumably is not a VP and thus the V must be something other than a daughter of a VP node. Note then that Dutch word order can be described in the following terms, which involve no reference to underlying word order: (i) in a main clause, one NP or adverbial expression is made a daughter of the S node; (ii) in a main clause, the finite verb is made a daughter of the S node; (iii) if a VP node directly dominates a V, the V is last within the VP, except that a heavy daughter of the VP node may optionally follow the V, (iv) if a VP node directly dominates a VP and an adverb, they may occur in either order, and (v) if an S node directly dominates a V, a VP, and something else, then the V is second and the VP third.[11] This alternative analysis is in the spirit of Koster's, in that the structure of subordinate clauses is more basic than that of main clauses, but it takes the difference between them as basically one of constituent structure rather than of word order.

4. Language Universals and the Notion 'Explanation'

Koster's analysis provides an EXPLANATION of the facts that prepositional phrases following the verb in a Dutch main clause can occur in more orders than are possible when they precede the verb in a subordinate clause. An explanation purports to show why things are the way they are, that is, to show why some range of alternative states of affairs are not manifested. Any purported explanation of linguistic phenomena thus carries with it implications to the effect that certain types of language are impossible, for example, Koster's explanation of the Dutch facts implies the impossibility of a language that allows the same possibilities as Dutch for word order in subordinate clauses, but only allows adverbs in main clauses to occur in an order that they could have if they preceded the verb in a subordinate clause. Thus, the status of a putative linguistic explanation should be regarded as shaky unless an appropriate cross-linguistic survey has been done, in which languages sharing the factors allegedly responsible for the given phenomena are investigated to determine whether they also exhibit those phenomena.

Regrettably few supposed explanations of linguistic phenomena have been accompanied by appropriate cross-linguistic data. One well-known 'explanatory' device that comes to grief when one tries to test it cross-linguistically is rule schemata such as Chomsky's (1970) $\overline{\overline{X}} \to \text{Spec}_X \ \overline{X}$, which collapses several phrase-structure rules in a single formula (NP → Det $\overline{N}$, 'Pred P' → Aux VP, AP → Degree $\overline{A}$). The claim that language is acquired in terms of such rule schemata supposedly explains the fact that determiners, auxiliaries, and degree expressions in English all occur to the left of their heads. If the notation (as part of a language-acquisition faculty) provides a real explanation of that fact, then a cross-linguistic survey should reveal a tendency for determiners, auxiliaries, and degree expressions all to occur on the same side of their heads (that is either all before the head or all after the head). There is in fact no such correlation. While there are many languages in which determiners precede nouns and auxiliary verbs precede main verbs, as in English, there are also many languages where determiners precede nouns and auxiliary verbs follow main verbs (for example, Japanese and Turkish) and many languages where determiners follow nouns and auxiliary verbs precede main verbs (for example, Malay and Swahili), but there are few languages (Somali and Basque are two examples) in which determiners follow nouns and auxiliary verbs follow main verbs. This suggests that what Chomsky's schema supposedly explains is not really a 'fact' but a conjunction of several unrelated facts that by accident share similarities.

One exemplary instance in which a cross-linguistic survey is used to verify an explanation of language-particular facts is provided by Cole (1974). Cole disputes Postal's (1972) claim that the question (10a) and the relative clause in (10b) are bad for the same reason, namely that an item is moved over something coreferential to it:

(10)   (a)   *Who$_i$ did the claim that he$_i$ is a fraud surprise?
       (b)   *The man who$_i$ the claim that he$_i$ is a fraud surprised
             has left town.

Cole maintains that (10a) is ungrammatical because its derivation involves a stage in which there is backwards pronominalization with indefinite antecedent and is thus ungrammatical for the same reason as are such examples as (11):

(11)   *The claim that he$_i$ was a fraud surprised $\begin{cases} \text{someone}_i. \\ \text{every member}_i \text{ of} \\ \text{the committee.} \end{cases}$

That cannot be the reason for the ungrammaticality of (10b), since relative pronouns are presumably definite and thus at no stage of the derivation of (10b) is there backwards pronominalization with an indefinite antecedent. Cole proposes to account for the ungrammaticality of (10b) by invocation of a device that linguists have tended to reject out of hand as a cop-out and a failure to capture a generalization, namely a 'rule of analogy' whereby relative clauses like that of (10b) are ungrammatical simply by virtue of their looking like ungrammatical questions.

Indeed, if only facts about the variety of English treated by Postal are considered, it is hard to see how any support for Cole's analysis could be found. However, Cole's proposal carries with it cross-linguistic implications that Cole proceeded to investigate and which yielded extremely solid support for his analysis. Specifically, if Cole is correct as to what is responsible for the ungrammaticality of (10b), then in languages that have WH-movement and do not allow backwards pronominalization with indefinite antecedent, sentences like (10a) should always be bad, but sentences like (10b) should be bad only if the language provides a basis for the analogy to which Cole attributes the ungrammaticality of (10b), that is, analogues to (10b) should be good in languages in which relative clauses do not look like questions (and thus, all such languages should provide counterexamples to Postal's putative explanation of the English facts), whereas they may be bad in languages whose relative clauses do look like questions (though they need not be bad in all such languages — the fact that a language provides the basis for a given analogical rule does not imply that the language must have the rule). And in fact, in languages whose relative clauses do not look like questions, for example, German and Chinese, relative clauses like that of (10b) are good. Moreover, the split does not go along genetic lines, for example, English behaves like French and unlike German.[12]

5.   The Cleansing Power of Universality

The most common responses to embarrassing facts have generally been to ignore them and to dispute them. In recent years a third response has in certain linguistic circles come to rival those two responses in popularity, namely the response of claiming that the embarrassing facts are universal. This ploy, which might be summed up in the slogan 'Make the dirty stuff universal' is illustrated by the following passages:

(12)   Notice that if the filter in question belongs to U[niversal] G[rammar], then its proper formulation is irrelevant to the theory of filters; that is, it will have no bearing on the question of the proper format for presenting filters and restrictions on possible filters. (Chomsky and Lasnik 1977: 451)

Notice, incidentally, that this conclusion [that the Specified Subject Condition requires a formulation in terms of the semantic notion of 'Agent' rather than the syntactic notion

> of 'Subject'], if correct, would not affect the hypothesis
> that transformations do not refer to semantic relations
> but only to bracketing of phrase markers (see the opening
> discussion) even if the semantic notion of 'agency' plays a
> role in determining the applicability of transformation.
> (Chomsky 1973: 124)

Chomsky (both solo and with Lasnik) is willing to allow the applicability
of transformations to depend on nonsyntactic factors and is willing to
admit filters of grossly different types from those countenanced by
the 'theory of filters' that he promises to develop, just as long as the
otherwise offensive conditions and filters are universal.[13]

I take Chomsky at his word when he suggests elsewhere that language
universals are genetically determined. Note, though, that both universal
characteristics within a species and individual variation involve genetic
determination. Typically, gross anatomical structures are universal but
fine details of structure are subject to genetically determined individual
variation, for example, all normal human beings have two arms involving
humerus, ulna, and radius, connected to hands having the standard
numbers and arrangement of carpals, metacarpals, and phalanges, but on
the other hand no two persons have the same fingerprints. Williams (1956)
provides a useful survey of details of human anatomy in which there
is considerable genetically determined individual variation, for example,
the shape, capacity, and location of the stomach. The moral to be drawn
from these considerations is that genetically determined universals
provide loci for individual variation, even of genetically determined
individual variation, and no realm of structure can be regarded as immune
to individual variation in its finer details. I conclude from this that if
biology is as deeply implicated in language as Chomsky says it is, then
individual variation (and presumably also differences between populations) should be possible in any realm of linguistic structure. If, for
example, Chomsky's suggestion is correct that a version of the Specified
Subject Condition involving the notion 'agent' is universal and if that
universal is genetically determined, then it would be surprising not to
find variation among individuals or between populations as to its fine
details, for example, as to how broadly 'agent' must be interpreted.

6.   Benediction

In this paper, I have suggested at several points that there may be
more diversity in language than linguists generally allow for. This does

not mean that there are fewer interesting linguistic universals than linguists have generally suggested there are or that there is any conflict between the search for universals and the search for diversity. Indeed, the characteristic of language universals that I regard as most valuable is that they make it possible for the linguist to focus his attention in such a way as to identify specific types of diversity that would otherwise go unnoticed.

Notes

1.   For expository purposes, I ignore here a couple of languages indigenous to the state of Washington that may in fact be real counterexamples to this claim.

2.   [For highly insightful discussion of the appropriate scope of general propositions and the status of putative counterexamples to general propositions, see Lakatos (1976), which, though concerned directly with philosophy of mathematics, is of direct applicability to many questions of linguistics.]

3.   Compare here the fact that a putative universal that all grammars must contain an even number of rules could be enforced simply by adopting a policy of adding a vacuous rule to any grammar that has an odd number of rules.

4.   It could more appropriately have been called 'English as not an SVO language': the bulk of the arguments were at best arguments that certain rules applied to structures in which the subject and the remaining material were not on opposite sides of the verb; thus the arguments were consistent with SOV order. The one argument that was specifically directed towards establishing verb-initial order does not provide a clear case for that conclusion (see McCawley (1973d: 226-7) for details).

5.   I could of course have said 'SOV structures' instead; cf note 3.

6.   This is in fact the insight that lies at the bottom of the relational grammar treatment of relation-changing transformations; see Perlmutter and Postal (1977).

7.   Under this position, as contrasted with the 'structure preserving' framework of Emonds (1976), there can be gross discrepancies between the allowable deep structure configurations and the allowable surface configurations. My principal criticism of Emonds's approach is that it rests on a gratuitous assumption that language-particular combinatoric restrictions (= 'base rules') relate to deep structures rather than, for example, to surface structures and that it thus forces one to adopt highly specific and otherwise unmotivated deep structures in order to account for phenomena to which, as far as I can see, deep structure is irrelevant. For example, the phenomenon of Affix-hopping is a reflection of the morphological fact that English verbal affixes are suffixes. Emonds's position requires him to set up deep structures containing empty affix positions so that Affix hopping can be structure-preserving, which, by elimination, it must be in his rule typology. (I should, by the way, say 'the phenomena of Affix-hopping', in view of Akmajian and Wasow's (1975) demonstration that *-en* and *-ing* must be attached to verbs by a rule that applies under different conditions and at a different stage of derivations than the rule that attaches tenses to verbs.)

8.   Bach in this argument displays the common tendency of transformational grammarians to place disproportionately heavy emphasis on whether an affix is a prefix or a suffix. I maintain that the status of a bound morpheme as a prefix or suffix is a matter of its morphology rather than of syntax and that syntactic

rules should be neutral as to whether morphemes that they introduce or move are prefixes or suffixes: the rule should attach the bound morpheme to the relevant item, with its morphology determining whether it emerges as a left sister or a right sister of the item to which it is attached. Indeed, while Bach underplays the suffix -*n*, to be discussed below, and concentrates instead on the prefix *yə*-, the facts about -*n* provide an even solider argument for underlying verb-first order, since the argument about -*n* does not rest on a possibly vulnerable claim of morphemic identity the way that the argument about *yə*-(as we will see in section 3) does.

Note, incidentally, that a suffix may be positioned in terms of the beginning of a complex constituent with which it is combined. For example, Latin -*que* 'and' is suffixed to the first word of the conjunct in which it appears, as in *senatus populusque romanus* 'the senate and the Roman people'. This fact provides one of several arguments that -*que*, like *et*, basically precedes the conjunct but is adjoined to the immediately adjacent word of that conjunct and, by virtue of its morphological status as a suffix, appears at the end of that word.

9.　It is of course ambiguous with respect to another distinction, that between individual authorship (cf. *the operas of Verdi and Puccini*) and joint authorship (cf. *the operettas of Gilbert and Sullivan*). This ambiguity is manifested more clearly in the NP *the operas of Verdi and Boito*. (Boito was both a composer of operas and one of Verdi's librettists.)

10.　This condition need not involve any extrinsic rule ordering: it is equivalent to the condition that *yə*- must appear on a word that appears overtly in the relative clause.

11.　This sketch is an oversimplification, for example, I have not taken up word order in questions. The rule of Verb-raising (Evers 1975), which adjoins a nonfinite verb to the next higher verb, requires some complication in this analysis, since the lower verb must become a right sister of the higher verb. This means that if the imposition of a word order is to be postponed until surface structure, the word order rules must have access to information distinguishing the roles of the two sister verbs, for example, identification of one of them as head and the other as adjunct.

12.　[For a test of the apparent cross-linguistic implications of certain analyses involving 'traces', see Pullum (1980a).]

13.　[See Iwakura (1979) for a detailed study of problems with the specific surface filters that Chomsky and Lasnik propose. Iwakura notes, for example, that Chomsky and Lasnik's filter *[NP NP tense VP], which is to exclude both complement Ss that lack a complementizer and relative clauses that have lost both their complementizer and a subject relative pronoun, also excludes such quite innocuous things as dependent subject-questions (for example, *Who wants the money isn't clear*); the moral that I draw from Iwakura's examples is that the source of the oddity of the two kinds of surface structures that the filter is supposed to block is not a particular configuration of syntactic categories but the absence of any mark of subordination in a structure involving subordination.]

4 THE NONEXISTENCE OF SYNTACTIC CATEGORIES[1]

1. The State of Argumentation about Syntactic Categories

The syntactic structures that have figured in analyses by generative grammarians of all varieties involve many kinds of details that can be and have been argued about: what elements they involve, how those elements are grouped into larger units, the left-to-right ordering among the items, and the syntactic categories to which the items are assigned. In the first three of these areas, it has been reasonably clear what was being argued about and how one can argue about it. For example, in arguing about constituent structure, one is arguing about whether various combinations of items act as a unit or do not act as a unit with regard to various linguistic phenomena (cf. Zwicky 1978), and the disagreements about constituent structure have revolved mainly about disagreements as to what the facts are, as to which facts instantiate broader phenomena, and as to what one should do in the absence of acceptable arguments (that is, what constitutes a 'null hypothesis').

There is a large and much-discussed body of literature in which arguments about syntactic category assignments have been presented and/or criticized. For example, a large part of *Aspects of the Theory of Syntax* is devoted to refining the notion of syntactic category by employing certain very specific types of features so as to eliminate much of the profusion of 'unanalyzed' categories that was typical of earlier transformational grammar. Lakoff (1965) and a number of subsequent works by Lakoff, Ross, Bach, and myself devoted much effort to arguing that the inventory of syntactic categories could be drastically reduced by the employment of rule exception features and a theory of rule government. Various works by Chomsky, Bresnan, Jackendoff, and Wasow have presented arguments against these latter claims and in favor of the 'X-bar' conception of syntactic category and the fairly large inventory of categories that it admits.

It is remarkable that in this genre, which makes up a large proportion of the polemical writings of generative grammarians, it is impossible to find clear statements of what is being argued about. Not only is there no generally accepted conception of syntactic category, but it is difficult to find ANY explicit statements of what it is for two things to belong to the same syntactic category. Much of the argumentation for and against various systems of categories and assignments of items to categories presupposes the existence of certain categories, as when Ross (1969c: 359) takes the possibility of topicalization as a test for whether the item moved into topic position is an NP. At other times, a general policy has been adopted according to which sameness of category corresponds to whether the items are in some sense 'treated alike' by rules of grammar, though little attention is given to the problem of choosing an appropriate interpretation of 'treated alike' and justifying the choice.

It is a fact of life that one transformation may treat alike two items that another does not treat alike. For example, *that*-clauses and dependent questions are alike in that both can be extraposed but unlike in that Preposition-deletion is obligatory before the one but only marginal before the other:

(1)   It's likely that Bill will get the job.
      It's not clear who will get the nomination.
      Tom's afraid (*of) that Bill will accept the job.
      Tom's worried about /?φ who will get the nomination.

The principal ways in which different linguists have lived with this fact of life (one that everyone seems to be aware of) are (a) to take things that are ever treated differently by a transformation as belonging to different categories, as when Jackendoff (1972: 100) takes the existence of transformational differences between modal auxiliary verbs and main verbs as reason to put them in different categories; (b) to treat things that are ever treated alike by a transformation as belonging to the same category, as when Ross (1969c) argues that adjective phrases[2] are NPs on the grounds that there are transformations such as Topicalization that treat APs and NPs alike; (c) to treat categories as 'squishy', for example, to take the facts cited in (1) as showing that dependent questions are less sentence-y than *that*-clauses and that Extraposition and Preposition-deletion differ with regard to the degree of S-hood that they require of the affected clause (Ross 1972b, 1973); and (d) to treat categories as complexes of features.

Neither of the first two positions is satisfactory. (I will take up the third and fourth positions later in this paper.) The first position stacks the cards in favor of a profusion of categories, and the second stacks them in favor of a paucity of categories, since the first provides necessary but not sufficient conditions for sameness of category, while the second provides sufficient but not necessary conditions. Moreover, both make gratuitous assumptions about the relation between categories and transformations that ought long ago to have been submitted to critical reappraisal.

To clarify this last remark, I must digress into the history of formalism in transformational grammar. In early transformational grammar, the 'structural description' of a transformation was formulated in terms that were not very structural: a string of category names and variables, or a complex formula constructed from such strings by the use of parentheses and curly brackets. Both the formulation of each trans-formation and the statement of how transformations in general applied were given in string terms rather than in tree terms. A transformation was taken as applying to a string of 'formatives' that could be factored into substrings, each of which is a member of the category that appeared as the corresponding term of the structural description.

In the mid 1960s, many linguists started indicating additional details of structure through the use of subscripted brackets in the structural descriptions, but the notational system remained basically that of *Syntactic Structures.* If transformations are formulated in that notation, the transformation must mention the category of the affected item.[3] This is because variables need not be matched to constituents, and hence it is impossible to insure that a term in a structural description will match a constituent unless its category is mentioned. In the form-ulation of the transformation, categories must be employed so as to in effect provide an algorithm for finding the right item for the trans-formation to affect. Note, however, that the more syntactic structure that structural descriptions are allowed to mention, the less need there is for them to mention syntactic categories. For example, if one admits structural notions like 'sister' and 'daughter' in the formulation of transformations, one can formulate a Raising transformation without mentioning the category of the item that becomes subject of the higher clause, in that only that item can be sister of the VP that is daughter of the lower S node, that is, only that item can fill the circled position in the following structure:

Note that a formula such as X VP VP would not uniquely identify the relevant constituents, since the X need not be matched to a constituent and thus could be matched to more than the subject of the lower S (for example, if the embedded S were *Fred try to lose weight*, the X could be matched to *Fred try* or *Fred try to* as well as to *Fred*). In this case there is some reason to prefer a formulation of the transformation in terms of the location or the structural role of the affected item, since items that can occur in that position appear to undergo Raising regardless of their category:

(2)   Under the bed seems to be a good place to hide the money.
         Carefully seems to be the best way to handle that plutonium.

Whether one takes the existence of sentences like these to have any implications for the syntactic category of prepositional phrases like *under the bed* depends on whether one takes the conditions for the application of Raising to involve the category of the raised item. Only on the gratuitous assumption that its category is relevant to the applicability of Raising do these examples provide an argument that PPs and NPs belong to the same category.[4]

Schachter (1973) makes the point that some of the phenomena on which Ross (1969c) based his arguments that APs are NPs do not provide a clear test for the syntactic category of the affected items. Thus, while Ross maintained that 'Equative deletion' factors out an NP from parallel Ss and used that observation in arguing that the predicate AP of (3b) is an NP, Schachter notes that items that it would be much harder to bring oneself to call NPs are treated the same way (3c-f):

(3)   (a)   Rodney built what I wanted him to build: a golden igloo.
         (b)   Tom is what his brother will never be: totally fearless.
         (c)   Billy slept where I would never sleep: under the desk.
         (d)   Helen sang the way she always sings: flat.
         (e)   The stock market moved in the direction John hoped it
                 would: downward.
         (f)   Ed attends classes as often as he needs to: about once
                 every two weeks.

Schachter does not address the question of whether the conditions for formation of this construction need mention the category of the focused item, but his discussion directly suggests that question. While the focused item in this construction cannot be just anything, for example, cannot be an article or a preposition, it is not obvious that the formulation of the rules for this construction need mention the category of the focused item — the restriction may simply be that that item must be something that can stand alone as an entire phrase.

One case in which the applicability of a transformation fairly clearly depends on a property of the affected item other than syntactic category as normally understood is the preposing found in such examples as (4):

(4) (a) Into the opera house raced Harpo.
     (b) Off came Harpo's fake beard.
     (c) Home raced Jack.

Jackendoff (1973: 347) gives examples such as these in support of his claim that 'particles' as in (4b) are objectless PPs. While I am inclined to accept that conclusion (see in this regard also the similar conclusion of Jespersen (1924: 88)), this particular argument for it is weak in view of examples like (5), taken from Jackendoff, in which the preposed items show little similarity to PPs:

(5) Buried here lies the producer of *A night at the opera*.
     Screaming down the hall ran two celebrated linguists.

There are in addition many cases in which particles and PPs cannot undergo this preposing:

(6) (a)   *About child labor in Upper Volta spoke John.
     (b)   *Off goofed Harpo.
     (c)   *Home wrote John.
     (c')   Home rode John.
     (d)   *Into the canyon fired the sheriff.
     (d')   Into the canyon rode the sheriff.
     (e)   *At the calendar looked Fred.

The condition for this preposing appears to be that the preposed expression gives location or direction OF THE SUBJECT. Thus, (6d') differs from (6d) with regard to whether it is the sheriff or merely the bullets that go into the canyon, and (6c') differs from (6c) with regard to whether it is John or John's letter that goes home; in (4b), *off* tells where the fake beard moved to, but in (6b) it says nothing about Harpo's movements.

The assumption that the syntactic categories of the affected items must be mentioned in the formulations of transformations is in fact one of a large number of gratuitous assumptions that have been made both by generative semanticists arguing for a paucity of categories and by interpretive semanticists arguing for a profusion of categories. I maintain that the apparent conflict between the conclusions of these two sets of arguments is due largely to the assumptions that their proponents have shared plus the general lack of overlap between the sets of facts with which the two sets of linguists have combined their shared theoretical premises. The facts that interpretive semanticists have used in arguing for a profusion of categories have been facts about phenomena in or close to surface structure, and the facts that generative semanticists have used in arguing for a highly restricted set of categories have been facts relating to structures that are closer approximations to semantic structure than to surface structure. What allowed both camps to continue blithely ignoring the facts that the other's categories were supposed to figure in an account of was a second shared gratuitous assumption, namely that syntactic categories remain constant throughout derivations. The disputes over categories thus had the character of a dispute between two persons, one of whom argues that a pound sterling is worth $1.90 and bases his conclusions on facts about transactions in New York involving American dollars, the other of whom argues that a pound sterling is worth $11 and bases his conclusions on facts about transactions in Hong Kong involving Hong Kong dollars, who disagree only in virtue of their sharing the assumption that an American dollar is the same as a Hong Kong dollar. The assumption that syntactic categories remain constant throughout a derivation (that is, that a constituent in surface structure must have the same syntactic category as the constituents that correspond to it in all earlier stages of the derivation) is a close analogue to the assumption that an American dollar is the same thing as a Hong Kong dollar: without that assumption there would be no conflict between the conclusions that surface structures involve a great variety of syntactic categories and that the deepest structures of derivations involve only a small number of categories. In speaking of the claim that categories remain constant as 'gratuitous', I am rejecting a set of assumptions normally made by transformational grammarians that make that proposition not gratuitous but inevitable. These assumptions (which are 'metaphysical' in the sense of Collingwood (1940): while embodying no factual claim, they influence the way in which their adherents think) are (a) Platonism: surface structure (in the sense of *Aspects*, rather than of Chomsky's most recent work) is merely a distorted image of an 'abstract' level that provides the more important and more 'real' units and combinatoric regularities; (b) linguistic rules are operations; and (c) strings (rather than trees or other topological objects) are the preferred units of both object language and metalanguage.

In accordance with (a) and (b), the terminology of transformational grammar has consistently been chosen so as to fit the metaphor of a grammar as a procedure for assembling structures on a 'basic' level and converting them into corresponding structures on other levels:[5] the terms 'base rules' and 'base structures' suggest a 'foundation' on which the other structures are erected and without whose support those structures could not stand, and 'derivation' suggests priority of 'input' structures over 'output' structures. Moreover, notwithstanding the frequency with which transformational grammarians have emphasized that they use 'generate' in its mathematical sense ('X generates Y' means 'Y is the set corresponding to X', where X is something that serves as a characterization of a set), they often use it in ways that are intelligible only if it is taken to mean 'produce', for example, 'we must provide . . . a general account of how these grammars function, that is how they generate SDs and assign to them phonetic and semantic interpretations' (Chomsky 1966: 8); if 'generate' is used in the mathematical sense, asking how grammars generate SDs is as incoherent as asking how Euclid's axioms imply the theorems of Euclidean geometry. In accordance with (a)–(c), syntactic categories were taken to be 'nonterminal symbols' that figure in a procedure for constructing deep structures, and a deep structure was taken to be a string of terminal symbols, various of whose substrings are assigned to a category on the basis of having been derived from the nonterminal symbol corresponding to that category. Within that conception of a grammar, then, items owe their category to the way that the 'base rules' function in the assembling of the deep structure. From the perspective provided by that conception of grammar, the idea of an item changing its category in the course of a derivation is as absurd as the idea of a person changing his date of birth in the course of his life.

2.   An Alternative to 'Categories'

In the remainder of this article, I will approach the question of syntactic category from the vantage point of an alternative conception of transformational grammar that is non-Platonistic, takes linguistic rules to be templates rather than operations, and takes linguistic structures to be graphs (generally, trees)[6] rather than strings. In this conception, the idea of a 'derivation' as a sequence of structural analyses of a linguistic object is retained, but the idea of the 'deepest' stage of the derivation as a 'starting point' or an 'origin' of the derivation is rejected; the rules of the grammar are constraints on what can occur at various stages of the derivation and on how the different stages of the derivation can or must differ from one another; and these constraints can be sensitive to factors outside of the derivation, for example, to information about the speaker and addressee and their shared background knowledge.

Before sketching the conception of syntactic category that I wish to combine with the conception of a grammar as a system of derivational constraints, I would like to describe briefly an alternative to the standard position on syntactic categories that has generally been ignored though it has had a great influence on my thinking in this area. I refer to the proposal of Anderson (1966) to separate two functions that had been conflated in the base rules of the *Aspects* theory: that of specifying how elements may combine in deep structures and that of assigning items to categories. For Anderson, the second function was fulfilled by a set of largely universal definitions that were applicable not just to deep structure but to all stages of derivations. For example, according to this position, anything consisting of a determiner and a noun is an NP, regardless of whether it corresponds to a deep structure NP. While the standard position on categories in transformational grammar requires that a surface instance of any category always correspond to a deep structure constituent of that same category, Anderson's policy allows new instances of categories to arise in the course of the derivation and indeed allows categories to appear in surface structure that do not occur at all in the deep structures of the given language. For example, if 'prepositional phrase' is universally characterized as 'consists of P and NP', then Anderson's policy allows a language to have surface PPs without necessarily also having deep structure PPs: all that is necessary is that in the course of the derivation constituents be formed by the adjunction of a preposition to an NP, since such a constituent then meets the (universal) criterion for being a PP.

Or at least, that is the case if one interprets 'is a preposition' in the most obvious way, so that, for example, if *of* is adjoined to an NP, the result is a PP because *of* is a P and the NP is an NP, and the result of the adjunction thus consists of a P and an NP. The usual policy in transformational grammar, however, has been the quite different one of treating transformationally inserted constants (such as the *of* that is generally agreed to be transformationally inserted in such nominalizations as *the destruction of the city*) as having no syntactic category whatever, in accordance with the claim that surface occurrences of a category must be traceable back to deep occurrences of the same category. In addition, because of the standard policy of treating the category and the lexical item that fills it as two distinct items (for example, in the deep structure of *The cat sat on the mat*, there is a node labeled 'V' that dominates a separate node labeled *sit*), treating a transformationally inserted constant as having a category would violate the widely (though uncritically) accepted prohibition against 'structure building': the step would involve the addition to the tree of not only a terminal node (here labeled *of*) but also a nonterminal node (labeled P). The separate nodes for V and *sit* are forced on the orthodox trans-formational grammarian not by any considerations of how language works but by the metaphor of rules as operations, since in the 'operation' conception of base rules, *sit* arises through the replacement of V by *sit* in a string NP V PP. If one gives up that metaphor (in favor of the 'template' metaphor that corresponds to the conception of linguistic rules as derivational constraints), the need to treat the lexical item and the category as corresponding to separate nodes in the structure vanishes: the category can be treated as part of the lexical item, and a 'base rule' like ⟨VP: V PP⟩ (that is 'a node labeled VP may directly dominate a node labeled V followed by a node labeled PP') will admit a configuration like the circled one in (7), under the assumption that the rule requires of the left daughter of the VP node only that it have the label V, not that it have no other labels in addition:

(7)

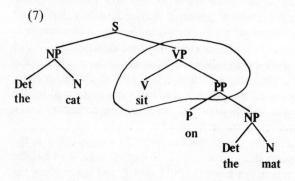

Under this alternative policy, which I will assume in the remainder of this article, transformationally inserted constants can be taken to belong to particular categories, and Anderson's category definitions will treat them the same way that they treat anything of those categories.

The position on syntactic categories that I will elaborate in the rest of this article is one according to which, as in Anderson's approach, the changes in the composition of an item over the course of the derivation can give rise to changes in its syntactic category. It differs from Anderson's approach principally in that it avoids the notion of syntactic category as such, operating instead directly in terms of a number of distinct factors to which syntactic phenomena can be sensitive; in this view, syntactic category names will be merely informal abbreviations for combinations of these factors. This might at first seem merely to amount to the proposal that syntactic categories are complexes of features, as is proposed in 'X-bar syntax'. There is an important difference, however, in that I take the various syntactically relevant factors as leading existences of their own, in particular, as existing independently of any role that they might play in 'base rules' (I regard only some of the syntactically relevant factors as having any role in any analogue to 'base rules') and as not necessarily being purely syntactic in nature.

I will describe this approach by giving a partial inventory of factors to which syntactic phenomena can be sensitive, and giving for each some indication of what sorts of linguistic rules can be sensitive to it. The first factor in this list is LOGICAL CATEGORY. There is a minimum set of categories ('sentence', 'predicate', and 'argument') in terms of which the gross combinatorics of logical structure can be characterized.[7] Subject to a qualification to be taken up in § 4, the putative syntactic categories S and NP can be identified with the logical categories 'sentence' and 'argument' respectively, in the sense that syntactic constituents belong to those categories if and only if the corresponding constituents of logical structure are sentences or arguments respectively. Putative demonstrations were offered by Lakoff (1972), Ross (1969c), Bach (1968), and myself (1972) that syntactic category was identical to logical category, in particular, that elements corresponding to predicates in logical structure were all of the same syntactic category regardless of whether they were nouns, verbs, adjectives, etc. These arguments all rested on the gratuitous assumption that syntactic category remains constant throughout derivations and that syntactic categories can be identified with the combinatoric categories of the deepest stage of syntactic derivations. The most that I would now take these arguments to have shown is that logical combinatoric categories play a role in some syntactic phenomena and that the deepest level of syntactic derivations is identical to logical structure. Those conclusions, of course, imply nothing about syntactic categories in surface structure unless they are supplemented by the gratuitous assumptions just mentioned. Some respects in which I would identify logical categories as playing a role in syntax include: (i) the sentences of logical structure provide domains for the cycle of transformations to apply to (see, for example,

McCawley (1981a) for an explanation on the basis of this assumption for the fact that passive *be* follows all other auxiliary verbs);[8] (ii) predicates, regardless of lexical category, determine which governed transformations apply to the sentence that the predicate is the head of (Lakoff 1965); and (iii) predicates in English, regardless of lexical category, precede their nonsubject arguments.

The proposition that logical category plays a role in syntax is neutral with regard to whether other factors also play a role. A second factor that clearly is relevant to syntax is LEXICAL CATEGORY, that is, the difference among noun, verb, adjective, and a few other classes of lexical items. In view of the apparent irrelevance of this factor to logical combinatorics,[9] this factor did not figure directly in the conception of syntactic category espoused by me and other generative semanticists around 1970; I will comment below on the way in which we proposed distinguishing among items of different lexical category and my reasons for now rejecting that attempt to explain lexical category away. The area of syntax to which lexical category differences are most clearly relevant is that of constraints on surface combinatorics, that is 'output constraints' or 'target structures'. For example, noun, verb, and adjective differ sharply with regard to their possibilities for combining with NP (as opposed to PP) in surface structure. While a V in English can have up to two NPs as sisters, only a highly restricted set of As (for example, *like* and *worth*) allow even a single NP sister, and combinations of an N with even one NP sister are excluded altogether (other than combinations of an N and a preceding genitive NP, in which case, as should be clear from discussion below, I regard the NP as an aunt or cousin of the N and not as its sister):

(8)

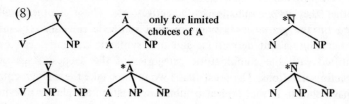

In surface structure, an S in English may consist of NP V̄ but not of NP Ā or NP PP, etc.

Lexical category differences are commonly but not always reflected in morphological differences, for example, English verbs are inflected for tense, for agreement with subject, and for the contrast between independent and various dependent (participle) forms; nouns are inflected for number; adjectives are inflected for comparative and superlative degree. Not all items that are normally assigned to a given lexical category can take the inflections characteristic of that category (for example, *beware* is generally regarded as a verb even though it has no participle or past tense forms nor any overt mark of agreement (cf. J. D. Fodor 1972); the *future* of *his future wife* is generally regarded as an adjective even though it has no comparative or superlative forms), and languages that are largely lacking in morphology (for example, Chinese) still have lexical category distinctions. I conjecture that for membership in a particular lexical category, allowing inflections characteristic of that category is not a necessary condition but IS a sufficient condition; this conjecture plays a significant part in the conception of language acquisition that I sketch below in § 3 and in greater detail in McCawley (to appear b).

In (8) I have labeled the mother nodes with complex symbols whose components are the lexical category of the head and a superscript bar. I take the bar to indicate that the constituent consists of a predicate element plus that element's nonsubject arguments. That notation implies that such constituents share significant properties but can differ in ways that correspond to the lexical category of the head of the constituent. This in fact appears to be the case, for example, the nonfinite complements of verbs are $\bar{X}$s of different types, with different verbs allowing different choices of X:

(9)   Fred seems eager to win.
      John felt ashamed to himself.
      They appointed Alice director of the accounting department.
      *Fred seems trying to win.
      *John felt hating himself.
      *They appointed Alice responsible for the accounting department.

To prevent confusion, I should indicate some significant differences between the use of the superscript bar here and the bars of orthodox X-bar syntax (for example, Chomsky 1970, Jackendoff 1977). In Chomskyan X-bar syntax, multiple bars are used as parts of category names, indicating the depth to which the head of the constituent is embedded within the constituent, and NP is identified as N plus some fixed number of bars (two for Chomsky, three for Jackendoff). I find both of these characteristics of X-bar syntax objectionable in view of the dilemma into which they force one (as argued in McCawley (1981b) and Verkuyl (1981)), whereby one must either accept a demonstrably wrong constituent structure for structures with stacked modifiers (as in (10a), taken from Jackendoff 1977)[10] or allow bars to multiply without limit (as in (10b), taken from Verkuyl (1981)):

(10)

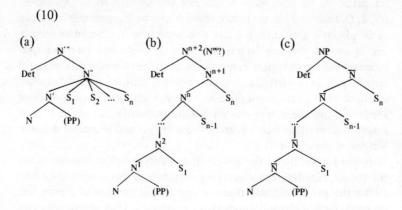

(a)   (b)   (c)

In the conception of syntactic categories adopted here, the constituent structure and labeling are as in (10c), since each of the constituents labeled as $\bar{N}$ in (10c) has an N as its head, includes the nonsubject arguments of that N, and does not itself make up the argument of a predicate and is thus not an NP. There in fact appears to be no syntactic difference among the various things labeled $\bar{N}$ in structures like (10c), for example, *theory of light*, *theory of light that Newton advanced*, and *theory of light that Newton advanced that was refuted by Fresnel* can all serve as antecedents of *one*.

Nothing that I have said so far requires that heads of constituents remain constant throughout derivations, for example, nothing in the above is inconsistent with the derivational steps familiar in the generative semantics literature of around the 1970s in which the head of a constituent is replaced (through a step of lexical insertion) or in which the given constituent becomes an adjunct to a new head that is inserted by, say, copula-insertion. I take symbols like $\bar{V}$ to have no existence other than as informal abbreviations for the combinations of information that they stand for. Suppose that the verb *like* and the adjective *fond* are fully synonymous, and are alternative realizations of a predicate FOND. The conception of syntactic category being developed here then allows for the following derivations of *John likes Mary* and *John is fond of Mary:*[11]

(11)

Here '0' is a makeshift device to indicate 'has no lexical category'; I assume that elements of logical structure are without lexical category. Then $\bar{0}$ will be an informal abbreviation for 'consists of head without lexical category, plus its nonsubject arguments'. Lexical insertion can replace FOND by either the verb *like* or the adjective *fond*. The constituent of which FOND was head thereby becomes respectively a $\bar{V}$ or an $\bar{A}$, since its head is now a V or an A and the constituent still consists of the head and its nonsubject arguments. (Note that there is no step of replacing $\bar{0}$ by $\bar{V}$ or $\bar{A}$: $\bar{0}$, $\bar{V}$, and $\bar{A}$ strictly speaking are not node labels but are informal indications of information about the constituents in a tree that could be regarded as unlabeled except for its terminal nodes.) The adjunction of *of* to the NP *Mary* and of *be* to the $\bar{A}$ result in a $\bar{P}$ and a $\bar{V}$ respectively, simply because *of* is a preposition and anything consisting of a preposition and an NP is a $\bar{P}$, and because *be* is a verb and anything having a verb as its head and consisting of an S minus its subject is a $\bar{V}$.

A fourth factor to which syntactic phenomena can be sensitive, and which has figured sporadically in previous approaches to syntactic categories, is that of 'grammatical relations', both 'nexus' relations (to reintroduce Jespersen's (1924, 1937) term) such as 'subject of' and 'direct object of', and relations such as 'modifier' and 'head' that are based on notions of dependency. The notion of 'head' figures implicitly in such category names as $\bar{N}$, $\bar{V}$, $\bar{A}$, in which the lexical category mentioned is that of the head of the constituent. While the head in many cases expresses a predicate of which the adjuncts express arguments (and thus to some extent the grammatical relation 'head' is predictable from logical category and logical constituent structure), there are also derived heads (such as the *be* inserted in the first derivation in (11)) that correspond to nothing in logical structure, as well as derived grammatical relations between items and predicates of which they are not arguments in logical structures (as in the phenomena referred to in relational grammar as 'ascensions', in which a constituent of an item takes over that item's grammatical relation in the course of the derivation).

As a fifth syntactically relevant factor, with which I will conclude but not complete this list, I will mention exception features, that is, differences among lexical items with regard to whether they do or do not allow application of a given transformation or whether they make a normally optional transformation obligatory. For example, *want* differs from most verbs that take *for–to* complement objects in triggering a transformation that deletes the *for* if it immediately follows the verb:

(12)   I want (*for) the rain to stop.
        I want very much for the rain to stop.
        What I want is for the rain to stop.
        I intend for/?ϕ Fred to empty the garbage.
        What I intend is for Fred to empty the garbage.

The difference between auxiliary and non-auxiliary verbs in English can be localized in the exceptional behavior of auxiliaries in undergoing a transformation combining them with an immediately c-commanding tense, thereby forming a unit that remains intact in inversion, negative placement, $\bar{V}$-deletion and other phenomena:[12]

(13)

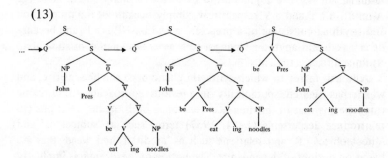

In the theory of exceptionality presented in Lakoff (1965), exception features are extremely limited in the role they can play in syntax: only bounded transformations can have exceptions, exceptional application or nonapplication of a transformation must be due to an exception feature in the predicate element of the S in question, and each exception feature plays a role only in the applicability of the transformation that it indicates exceptionality in. In particular, exception features played no role in phrase structure rules, that is items with the same exception features were supposed to occur in the same gross deep structure configurations. Because categories in all versions of transformational grammar were identified with the combinatoric units of deep structure, exception features were regarded as not constituting syntactic category distinctions. I now regard that policy as a mistake: exception features are simply one of several factors that play a role in syntax, and there is no justification for giving factors that are involved in deep structure combinatorics any privileged position in an account of the notion 'syntactic category'. The well-known attempt by Lakoff, Ross, Bach, and myself to reduce lexical category differences to exception features was presented as an attempt to reduce the inventory of syntactic categories to a set identifiable with the combinatoric categories of logic. In accordance with what I have just said, I now regard the analyses offered as part of that program not as having eliminated differences among categories but only as having localized those differences. Thus, Lakoff's proposal that verbs differed from predicate elements of other lexical categories in not triggering a transformation of copula-insertion (so that in effect 'verb' could be identified with $[- \textit{be}\text{-insertion}]$) implied that all other differences between verbs and other lexical categories should correlate with the different derived syntactic configurations in which verbs and items of other lexical categories appear subsequent to copula-insertion, for example, a transformation affecting items in the configuration $[\text{NP} [_{-} \text{X}]]_S$ would affect only verbs, since copula-insertion would have caused items of other categories no longer to be in that configuration.

This account of lexical category differences has been denounced by Bresnan (1972: 195–200), Brame (1976: 24–6), and Wasow (1976: 289) on the grounds that it makes the syntax 'irregular' and that it prevents one from capturing 'deep structure regularities' that can be expressed only in terms of lexical category differences. While I now reject the exception feature account of lexical categories (for reasons that I will give shortly), I regard the arguments against it offered by Bresnan *et al.* as mistaken in three important respects. First, contrary to what they suggest, their analysis and the 1970 generative semanticists' analysis differ not in whether irregularity plays a role in it but in where the irregularity is localized. Any unpredictable difference among lexical items is an irregularity, whether it is a difference in lexical category, in applicability of governed transformations, or in morphology. Second, the analysis with exception features and no lexical categories actually invokes less irregularity than do the alternatives endorsed by Bresnan *et al.*, since the former limit the direct influence of irregularity to the transformations that putatively provided the basis of the category distinctions, whereas for Bresnan *et al.* the lexical category distinctions could in principle figure in the formulation of any base rule or transformation. Third, Bresnan *et al.* make the gratuitous assumption that deep structure is the locus of the 'regularities' that they claim are missed under the rule-exception approach; I maintain that it is in fact surface structure rather than deep structure to which combinatoric regularities involving lexical category distinctions apply; see in this regard the discussion below of the status of *the destruction of the city* as an instance of the $[_{\bar{N}}\text{ N PP}]$ pattern.

I now reject the rule-exception approach to lexical categories for the following reasons, which appear not to have been noticed previously either by its proponents or by its opponents. First, derived structure configuration does not provide an adequate basis for identifying the lexical category of items, since things of different category in many cases occur in parallel surface configurations, for example, the adverbs of sentences like (14a) and the verbs of sentences like (14b):

(14) (a)   Bill CAREFULLY lit the fuse.
      (b)   Bill TRIED lighting the fuse.

In both cases the indicated item is in the surface configuration $[\text{NP } [_{-}\bar{V}]_{\bar{V}}]_S$. Only the adverb can be moved into S-initial or $\bar{V}$-final position, and thus that configuration could not by itself serve as the condition for the application of those transformations. Second, instances of a given lexical category may (under assumptions generally accepted by generative semanticists) enter derivations in any of several ways (for example, verbs may replace predicates of logical structure or may be inserted in such processes as copula-insertion), but in all cases they are subject to the same surface combinatoric restrictions, for example, a V has to be leftmost in its $\bar{V}$ regardless of how it entered the derivation. The policy of reducing lexical category distinctions to rule-exception features thus does not in principle rule out such non-languages as a language that is just like English except that copula *be* is at the right rather than the left of the $\bar{A}$, NP, or PP that it is a sister of.

3.   Surface Combinatoric Rules in Synchronic and Developmental Syntax

What then WOULD rule out such non-languages? For one thing, the approach of Emonds (1976), in which items can be inserted only in place of an item of the same category: under that approach, if the base rules allow Vs only in $\bar{V}$-initial position, then Vs can be inserted only in that position. Emonds's approach rules out a $\bar{V}$-final *be* because it forces surface structures to conform to much of the gross combinatoric restrictions that his base rules impose on deep structures.[13] The given non-language would thus also be excluded if gross syntactic combinatoric restrictions were restrictions purely on surface structure, having no connection whatever with deep structure. I in fact see no reason why the gross combinatoric restrictions embodied in such rules as S → NP $\bar{V}$ should be taken as applying to deep structure. The principal reason that they have in fact been taken as applying to that level of structure is that the community in which they have been proposed has been committed to metaphysical assumptions that require grammars to contain full combinatoric specifications for deep structures. The many arguments that Emonds has advanced for his 'structure preserving' framework have provided many cases in which transformational outputs must conform to gross combinatoric restrictions peculiar to the specific language, but in none of those cases has Emonds provided any real case that deep structures must be subject to the same constraints. There is in fact at least one clear case in which deep structures must not conform to a gross combinatoric constraint to which surface structures are subject. Consider the *of* of such nominalizations as *the destruction of the city*. There is general agreement that that element is absent from structures underlying the nominalization; indeed, this conclusion is shared by all parties to the dispute as to whether nominalizations have underlying structures involving embedded sentences. In particular, transformational insertion of the *of* is an essential part of Chomsky's (1970) lexicalist treatment of nominalizations, in which Ss and corresponding nominalizations are to have parallel deep structures that differ with regard to whether a V or an N fills a certain position, as in (15):

(15)　(a)　　　　　　　　　(b)

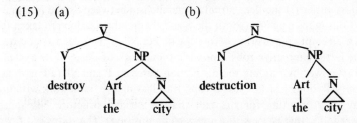

(The absence of *of* from underlying structures proposed by generative semanticists is for the quite different reason that it is semantically empty). In virtue of his assumption that transformations cannot build structure, Chomsky takes the result of inserting *of* in (15b) to be (16a) rather than (16b):

(16)   (a)   (b)

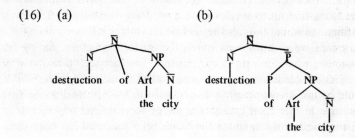

But in fact, *of the city* forms a constituent by any applicable test of constituent-hood. For example, it permutes with adverbs and PPs exactly the same way that any PP does, exhibits the same Pied-piping phenomena, and undergoes Right-node-raising:

(17)   the enemy's destruction yesterday of three cities
        *the enemy's destruction of yesterday three cities
        the destruction by the enemy of the city
        *the destruction of by the enemy the city
        Of which cities is the destruction imminent?
        the shooting yesterday and the stabbing today of several policemen

Treating *of the city* as anything but a PP would require one to admit a difference in surface structure between these nominalizations and unquestioned surface instances of [$_{\bar{N}}$ N $\bar{P}$] without there being any difference in their syntactic behavior. Insertion of the *of* will not conform to Emonds's particular conception of structure preservation unless either (i) the deep structure parallelism between Ss and nominalizations is given up or (ii) both the S and the nominalization are taken to have an empty preposition before the object NP in their deep structures. The latter alternative robs Emonds's framework of much of its explanatory power by eroding the distinction between $\bar{P}$ and NP (a $\bar{P}$ with an empty P looks just like an NP) and thus leaving the framework with no way of accounting for the fact that in surface structure NPs must precede $\bar{P}$s (that is, $\bar{P}$s with a non-zero preposition). The status of *of the city* as a $\bar{P}$ ceases to pose any problem if the combinatoric rule that $\bar{N}$ may consist of N $\bar{P}$ is made to apply to surface structure and if movement and insertion transformations are required to yield outputs that conform to the surface combinatoric constraints: the *of* must be adjoined to the object NP as a left sister, since that is the only way of adding a preposition to the $\bar{N}$ so that the output has a shape that English allows $\bar{N}$s to have; moreover, if there is an underlying structure $[_{\bar{N}} \text{N NP}]$, something must apply to it, since that configuration is not a permissible surface configuration in English. Exactly the same treatment of the *of* is required even if one treats *the destruction of the city* as having an underlying structure containing a sentence *NP destroy the city*, with a nominalization transformation extracting the verb from that S and combining it with a nominalization morpheme: there still is an intermediate derivational stage involving N NP, and the subsequent derivation must still convert that somehow into a surface structure that conforms to the restrictions that English imposes.

I accordingly take it as well established that a grammar of a language must contain syntactic combinatoric rules (roughly, 'phrase structure rules', though I wish to leave their exact formal nature open here) for surface structure, or at least, for some linguistic level close to surface structure, whereas I see no reason for believing that any such rules are required for any more remote syntactic level. In saying this, I must emphasize the following points, which are essential for its interpretation. First, my remark relates only to specifically syntactic combinatoric rules (for example, the English rule that a $\bar{V}$ may consist of a V followed by up to two NPs followed by any number of $\bar{P}$s) and not to purely semantic combinatoric rules, which exist in addition to syntactic combinatoric rules. The issue addressed in my remark is only that of whether syntactic 'phrase structure rules' constrain the inputs to a system of transformations or the outputs. Second, the remark relates only to gross combinatoric restrictions, not to conditions on where particular lexical items can be used. Transformational grammarians have generally made the gratuitous assumption that both 'gross' and 'petty' combinatoric restrictions (see note 7) must relate to the same level and have accordingly jumped to the conclusion that there must be phrase structure rules for a level of deep syntactic structure, when their arguments have only showed that the strict subcategorization and selectional properties of lexical items relate to something 'deeper' than surface structure. My remark thus should not be taken as implying that the conditions on the use of particular lexical items must be formulated in terms of surface structure.[14] Third, my remark is neutral as to whether there is a level of syntactic deep structure. For there to be a 'deepest level of syntactic structure', there doesn't have to be a system of gross combinatoric rules for that level, any more than for there to be a level of surface structure there has to be a system of surface gross combinatoric rules. Fourth, the qualification that the level to which gross combinatoric rules apply is 'at least . . . close to surface structure' reflects my recognition of the possibility that the gross combinatoric rules do not take into account phenomena such as parenthetical placement and Heavy-NP-shift that, as I argue in McCawley (to appear a), alter constituent order without altering constituent structure (thus giving rise to discontinuous structure when the order of non-sisters is altered); for example, I wish to admit the possibility that English has a system of gross combinatoric rules whereby the NPs of a $\bar{V}$ must precede the PPs, with Heavy-NP-Shift allowed to create deviations from that word order (for example, *He left in his room the book that he had intended to return to the library*).

The approach to syntactic categories sketched in § 2, in conjunction with the claim that syntactic combinatoric rules refer to surface structure, allows one to develop an approach to language acquisition that makes the acquisition of syntax seem far less mysterious than it is generally made to sound. The factors that play a role in syntax can to a large extent be learned independently of one another, for example, one can learn what a word means without at the same time learning its lexical category, and vice versa. Whatever syntactically relevant information a child has learned at a given point in his development, he can use that information in tabulating syntactic configurations that he has succeeded in identifying, for example, a child learning English can identify a syntactic configuration $[_{\bar{\sigma}} \text{O NP}]$ if he has learned to identify subject, predicate, and nonsubject argument, even if he cannot yet identify lexical categories. The child will use his inventory of configurations in understanding speech, in that he will take what he hears as instantiating already learned configurations whenever possible. Each addition to his knowledge will expand the class of utterances that he can interpret. Suppose, for example, that he has reached the point of being able to identify lexical categories (on the basis of, say, what they are inflected for) and has identified a syntactic configuration $[_{\bar{V}} \text{V} \bar{V}]$ (for example, *try eating oatmeal*); then as soon as he identifies the emphasized elements in *He* WAS *eating oatmeal* and *The boys* HAVE *eaten the oatmeal* as verbs, he is in a position to identify those sentences as exemplifying the $[_{\bar{V}} \text{V} \bar{V}]$ configuration also.[15] Thus, under this highly programmatic sketch of language acquisition, a child will assign a right-branching constituent structure with nested $\bar{V}$s to auxiliary verbs even if he has not yet learned the restrictions on auxiliary verbs that are responsible for the nonoccurrence of the impermissible sequences of them. More generally, this approach predicts that a child will be able to assign quite specific surface structures to a considerable body of sentences even if his syntactic knowledge is still fairly fragmentary. The learning of transformations and/or semantic interpretation rules will accordingly be one dimension more constrained than it is usually assumed to be: rather than having to learn a grammar as a whole, with his knowledge of surface structure being a side effect of that global learning task, he has only to learn to relate in a systematic way the surface structures and semantic structures that he has learned already largely as a side effect of his learning of the meanings and morphology of words. The possibility of such a scheme of language learning depends, of course, on the replacement of the standard notion of syntactic category by the idea of a set of syntactically relevant factors that can be learned separately from one another and from the syntactic constructions in which they play a role.

4. Some Additional Issues

In § 1 I mentioned in passing the notion of 'squishy grammar', as developed in Ross (1972b, 1973), but did not devote any attention to it in my discussion of the question of what it is for things to be of the same syntactic category. Justifying a particular choice of syntactic categories is at least as much of a problem in squishy grammar as in discrete grammar. Existing work in squishy grammar has in fact largely ignored the problem of justifying the choice of categories and has simply assumed the appropriateness of certain widely recognized categories and argued that membership in them is not absolute but a matter of degree.[16] I wish to suggest here that the awesome problem of justifying a particular choice of squishy categories can plausibly be replaced by the more tractable problem of determining what factors play a role in syntax at all and what sources of possible squishiness there are for each of those factors. The squishes that I find best substantiated are those that can be described in terms of degree of deviation from the most prototypic correlations among the factors identified in § 2 or between them and details of semantic structure. For example, NP-hood is greatest in those constituents which (i) correspond to arguments in logical structure; (ii) are in surface positions in which items corresponding to arguments typically occur; and (iii) have the surface constituent structure most typical of items meeting (i) and (ii), namely [Det $\bar{N}$]. Thus, existential *there* meets criterion (ii) but not criteria (i) and (iii) and thus is only weakly an NP; extraposed complement Ss meet only criterion (i), whereas non-extraposed complements meet both (i) and (ii) and are thus closer to being hard-core NPs, a judgement that is confirmed by Higgins's (1973: 159) observation that only the latter may be topicalized (*That you are right, I don't think (*it) is obvious*). A basis for squishiness of lexical categories is provided by markedness principles relating to what predicates are most typically expressed in which lexical category, as in the approaches of Dixon (1977) and Lyons (1977: 423-30). Dixon gives a set of implicational universals defining a range of possible systems of adjectives, including such universals as that if a language allows adjectives denoting 'human propensities' (for example, *kind, clever*), then it allows adjectives denoting colors. I conjecture that the meanings that a language allows to be expressed in more than one lexical category are always among those having characteristics that different markedness principles associate with different lexical categories, for example, the meaning expressed by *like*$_V$ and *fond*$_A$ is a stative 2-place predicate; for 2-place predicates, V is unmarked and A marked, for stative predicates, A is unmarked and V marked, and thus no matter whether this predicate is expressed by an A or a V, it will be marked in one respect and unmarked in another.

In conjunction with this position on degree of category membership, the analysis of predicate nouns that I have argued for elsewhere (1981b) implies that the constituent following the copula in *Scott was the author of Waverley* is only loosely speaking an NP: if *author* corresponds to a predicate of which *Scott* and *Waverley* are the two arguments, then *the author of Waverley* has the surface position and internal structure that are typical of NPs that correspond to logical arguments, but does not itself correspond to an argument and thus meets only two of the three criteria given above for being a core NP. I have maintained that the article on predicate nouns serves principally to achieve conformity with the surface combinatoric rules, that is, insertion of a semantically empty[17] article serves to replace the impermissible $*[_{\bar{V}} \text{ V } \bar{\text{N}}]$ configuration by the permissible $[_{\bar{V}} \text{ V NP}]$. If requirements calling for an NP in a particular position can be met by creation of a less than full-fledged NP in that position, something must be said about what it takes to fulfill the requirements of surface syntactic combinatorics. In this case, the best that I can do is suggest that such somewhat peripheral NPs are taken as meeting a syntactic demand for an 'NP' only because there is no way to meet the demand more fully: inserting the article makes a constituent that is in an NP position look like a hard-core NP, but it cannot make it have the meaning of a hard-core NP. Accordingly the identification of the syntactic category NP with the logical role of argument must be weakened: nonarguments can count as NPs if their properties are otherwise typical of constituents that correspond to arguments.

What I have just said raises the question of whether the notion 'NP' can be defined in terms of basic factors only disjunctively (for example, 'has form [Det $\bar{N}$] or corresponds to argument of logical structure'). I will not attempt to answer that question here, which could be done only on the basis of a more thorough survey than I have yet made of syntactic phenomena that purportedly call for 'NP'. I wish, however, to comment on the parallelism that this question points to between the possibilities for the status of the notion of 'syntactic category' in syntax and the possibilities for the status of the notion 'boundary' in phonology. Pyle (1972) adopted a position on boundaries that is very close to that which I have taken here on syntactic categories: he attempted to do away with references to boundary markers as such and to state rules in terms of more primitive notions, namely in terms of the wordhood or phrasehood of the constituents that the segments were at the beginning or end of in surface structure. Selkirk (1976) has argued against Pyle's position and in favor of analyses involving 'abstract boundaries'. Her arguments, which I find impressive, deal with boundary phenomena in French and modern Greek where several clearly distinct rules are all inhibited by the same unusual combination of phonological, morphological, and syntactic factors. Selkirk interprets this state of affairs as implying that the rules are directly sensitive not to those factors but to a boundary and that the odd combination of factors is simply the condition for the insertion of that boundary. The disputes about categories and about boundaries are not completely parallel, since proponents of 'abstract' boundaries (like Selkirk) are happy to have all boundaries inserted by rules, whereas the proponents of abstract syntactic categories have without exception taken them to be present as such throughout the syntactic derivations rather than being 'created by rules' on the basis of something else.

There are thus three possibilities for the status of syntactic categories: (i) they are like Pyle's conception of phonological boundary: they never need figure as such in derivations, and all invocations of them can satisfactorily be replaced by invocations of more basic factors; (ii) they are like Selkirk's conception of phonological boundary: they are predictable on the basis of other factors, but the rules on the basis of which they are predicted can be highly idiosyncratic, and it is the categories rather than those factors that play a direct role in syntactic rules; (iii) they conform to Chomsky's conception of syntactic category:

they figure as such in all stages of derivations and are not predictable from anything more basic. Of the three, (i) is clearly the one that most tightly constrains the role of syntactic categories in grammar: it implies that syntactic categories have no independent existence and that the syntactic behavior of items is determined completely by characteristics of them that are either nonsyntactic or noncategorial. It is accordingly the conception of syntactic category which I choose to pursue until I am overwhelmed by clear instances of what I suggested that the surface category NP might be: a unitary category definable only disjunctively in terms of the sorts of factors listed above. In that case I would be forced to reject (i) in favor of the weaker (ii). The only sort of argument for (iii) that I can imagine would be an argument from ignorance plus hindsight: an argument that all attempts to make (i) or (ii) work have failed and that by elimination, only (iii) remains viable. However, it will be a long time before linguists have the hindsight that it would take to make such an argument convincing.

Notes

1.   This is an extensively revised and enlarged version of a paper read at the 1977 Michigan State University Metatheory Conference. I am grateful to Frederick J. Newmeyer for his remarks as commentator at that conference, and to Newmeyer and Valerie F. Reyna for valuable comments on a preliminary draft of this revision.

2.   Ross claimed to be showing that ADJECTIVES are NPs, but the arguments that he gave actually apply to adjective phrases (combinations of an adjective and whatever 'object' adjuncts it may have) rather than to adjectives, for example, when an adjective does not make up an entire AP, it is the whole AP rather than the adjective that can appear in predicate position in a pseudo-cleft construction:

What he has never been is *ashamed of his past*.

*What he has never been of his past is *ashamed*.

3.   This takes in the case of a transformation that mentions a specific lexical item, for example, a transformation deleting *will* or moving *for* + NP; the item can be regarded as comprising a one-member category.

4.   This statement in turn involves the gratuitous assumption that all the things commonly identified as PPs belong to the same syntactic category. I have not to my knowledge seen any discussion of whether the PPs that can themselves serve as objects of prepositions (for example, *from under the bed*) should be assigned a different syntactic category from those that cannot (**from despite his anger*).

5.   This metaphor does not commit one to conceiving of a grammar as a model of speech production. One can regard a grammar as having the form of a procedure for assembling deep structures and converting them into structures on other levels without holding that that particular procedure is executed in speech production. Moreover, one can regard a grammar as a procedure for speech production without regarding it as involving any subprocedure for the assembly of structures on one privileged level (Lakoff and Thompson (1975) comes close to this position).

6.   One case in which I am fairly sure that a non-tree must be allowed as a syntactic structure is the surface structure of Right-node-raising constructions, for example, *Alice owns, and Fred hopes that some day he too will own, a Rembrant etching*. I argue in McCawley (to appear a) that the constituent at the end of the sentence is a surface constituent of all the conjunct clauses, so that the surface structure contains a node with multiple mothers.

7.   Here, as in McCawley (1981a), I distinguish between GROSS COMBINATORICS (principles determining what overall shapes constituents can have, for example, that an NP in surface structure can consist of a Det followed by an N̄ or that a proposition in logical structure can consist of a predicate and any number of arguments) and PETTY COMBINATORICS (restrictions on what structures particular items can appear in, for example, that in deep structure *put* must be the head of a constituent [_ NP PP] or that in logical structure the predicate BECOME must be combined with one argument, which must be a proposition).

I do not assume that logical structure is FIRST-ORDER predicate logic. I take predicates to be subcategorized with respect to the Russellian 'types' of their arguments; thus, predicates of individuals, predicates of propositions, predicates of predicates of individuals, etc. are regarded here as all of the category 'predicate' though of different 'logical type'. I also assume that logical structure involves not only predicates and the various kinds of referential indices that can serve as arguments but also at least two 'operators': a set-formation operator (generally written { } and employed in defining sets by enumeration or by description) and an abstraction operator (generally written λ and used in defining non-atomic predicates). As I argued in McCawley (1972), quantifiers and sentential coordinating conjunctions can be treated as predicates that are predicated of expressions denoting sets of propositions; however, the general approach to categories presented in this paper in no way depends on acceptance of that analysis of quantifiers and coordinating conjunctions.

8.   Newmeyer (1976) and Dowty (1979) argue that the 'word-formation' transformations (such as Predicate-raising) posited in the generative semantic literature would have to apply precyclically, since otherwise, for example, cyclic transformations such as *there*-insertion could apply prelexically in cases like **Bill provoked there a riot* (cf. *Bill caused there to occur a riot*). Their conclusions could be taken as showing that the embedded Ss posited in generative semanticists' lexical decompositions do not in fact serve as cyclic domains. An alternative account is possible in view of the facts that Newmeyer's and Dowty's examples of transformations that must not apply prelexically are all MOVEMENT transformations that change grammatical relations and that (as argued in Aissen (1974)) such transformations cannot even provide inputs to POSTLEXICAL word-formation transformations such as the postlexical Predicate-raising involved in the productive causative constructions of Japanese and Turkish. I thus prefer an alternative account of Newmeyer's and Dowty's observations in which all the Ss of semantic structure are cyclic domains but derivations are subject to a global constraint embodying the suggestion by Lakoff (1965), discussed in note 5 to my review of Chomsky (1972) (in this volume), that word-formation rules cannot apply to structures involving items that have derived grammatical relations. More precisely, the constraint should exclude derivations in which word-formation rules apply to a predicate to which any item stands in multiple grammatical relations, that is, the constraint should not exclude derivations in which one application of a word-formation rule feeds another or in which a 'feature-change' rule like Reflexive feeds a word-formation rule, but only derivations in which word-formation rules affect an item that has an underlying subject or object distinct from its 'current' subject or object. See also Pullum (1976) for criticism of Newmeyer's arguments.

9.　An excellent case is made in Gupta (1980) for treating nouns as making a different contribution to logical structure than do lexical items of other categories. For Gupta, nouns and only nouns define the domains over which bound variables range. I am not convinced, however, by Gupta's arguments that nouns form a separate LOGICAL category from predicates, rather than simply being a particular variety of predicates.

10.　Jackendoff appears to adopt the constituent structure (10a) simply in order to avoid the derivation from pristine X-bar syntax that would be involved in admitting configurations like $[_{\bar{N}}$ N S] ; he avoids such configurations at the price of converting his base rules into schemata that involve (S)* and having a semantic interpretation rule that makes semantic constituents out of combinations of an N̄ and one or more immediately following S̄s (Jackendoff 1977: 185–90). It is not clear to me why this is any less of a deviation from pristine X-bar syntax than would be the admission of configurations like $[_{\bar{N}}$ N̄ S] (more generally, configurations in which 'modifiers' combine with items of a given category to yield items of the same category) as a systematic exception to the principle that the number of bars increases as one ascends the tree, since an exception to that principle has to be made anyway so as to allow for coordinate structures.

11.　For ease of exposition, tense is omitted from the structures given here. In addition, I have treated the Ss of logical structure as having NP X̄ form, that is, as having the subject as a sister of the rest of the S. I know of no strong reason for preferring one of the following ways of distinguishing among the arguments of a multi-place predicate over the other two: (i) taking linear order in logical structure to be significant and identifying the particular arguments of a predicate as corresponding to specific positions in that linear order; (ii) taking logical structures to contain explicit indications of grammatical relations between the various arguments and the predicate, as in relational grammar, and (iii) taking grammatical relations as indicated indirectly by constituent structure, for example, taking the 'subject' to be a separate constituent from the rest of the S:

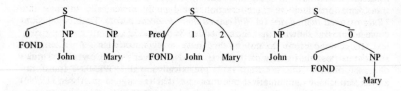

I see no justification for the prejudice that I displayed in many of my earlier works in favor of (i) as a way of distinguishing the arguments in logical structure. On the other hand, I can see no particular objection to (i): while English surface structures clearly have a form like (iii), in which the (surface) subject is a sister of the rest of the clause and the latter constituent is of category V̄, logical structures of the form (i) are available at the easily affordable price of a transformation that extracts the first argument from each S, yielding (in virtue of what the 'bar' means) a derived structure of the form (iii).

12.　I take the output of 'attraction to tense' in (13) to involve '*be* + Pres' rather than 'Pres + *be*', since I see no reason for allowing structures in which the adjunction of a bound morpheme to a word results in an order of morphemes conflicting with that demanded by the morphology of the language. See McCawley (1981a) for discussion of the point that the 'Affix-hopping' rule of Chomsky's analysis of auxiliary verbs conflates two mechanisms that should be kept separate:

one determining what word a particular morpheme is adjoined to and one determining whether that morpheme appears as a prefix, a suffix, etc. in the resulting word. Only the morphology and not the syntax of English would be different if the prefix of Old English past participles had been lost and the suffix retained (yielding, for example, *i-stole* in place of *stol-en*) rather than vice versa.

The set of verbs that undergo the transformation under discussion here is not completely identical to what are usually called auxiliary verbs: it includes all uses of *be*, whether as an auxiliary or as a main verb, and in many dialects it includes the 'possession' sense of *have*, as in *He has some money*.

13.   Contrary to popular misconception, however, Emonds's approach does not require that surface or shallow structures conform to his base rules, in that his approach imposes no constraint on deletion (thus, it allows derived structures in which constituents are absent that base rules require to be present) and the 'Pied-piping' condition that he accepts allows non-Ss to appear in derived structures in positions in which the base rules allow only Ss (for example, his version of 'heavy NP shift' moves an S into an S position, carrying along the rest of an NP in which the moved S was contained).

14.   While I regard 'strict subcategorization' as generally not applying to surface structure, I note that certain restrictions on the type of object allowed by a verb apparently relate to surface structure. For example, *ignore* allows underlying but not surface sentential objects:

*He ignored that the law was widely violated.

He ignored the fact that the law was widely violated.

What he ignored was that the law was widely violated.

15.   In saying this, I am begging an important question: when a child identifies *have* or *be* as belonging to the lexical category V on the basis of its tense or agreement inflection, has he necessarily also identified it as semantically a predicate, as my definition of $\bar{X}$ requires it to be if it is to be eligible to be the head of an $\bar{X}$? I conjecture that the child moves from (relatively) known to unknown, taking lexical category as a clue to semantic category when he is dealing with items whose semantic role is not yet clear to him. I note also that the identification of auxiliary verbs, especially modal auxiliaries, as verbs is more difficult than in the case of 'main' verbs, because they are normally unstressed or contracted and have irregular (and in the case of modals, defective) inflection.

16.   Gazdar and Klein (1978) argue that Ross's data fail an important statistical test that they take to be a necessary condition for degree of category membership to function as a factor in syntactic rules. I take their result as discrediting not the enterprise of fuzzy grammar but only Ross's assumption that there is a one-dimensional scale linking his opposed poles. In the alternative version of fuzzy grammar that I suggest but do not elaborate in this paper, fuzzy categories are defined in terms of multiple dimensions on which items can deviate from the 'core' of the category, and 'closeness to the core' is a partial, not a total, ordering of the peripheral members of the category.

17.   The choice between definite and indefinite article in predicate NPs is made, however, on the basis of a semantic consideration: that one is chosen which would be less misleading if the article were interpreted as having its usual sense. For an insightful treatment of the semantics of NPs in a language (Modern Greek) in which there is a three-way contrast among definite article, indefinite article, and no article at all, see Pentheroudakis (1977).

REFERENCES

Abbott, B. (1979) 'Deletion rules and Emonds' structure preserving constraint', paper read at annual meeting, Linguistic Society of America, Los Angeles

Aissen, J. (1974) 'Verb raising', *Linguistic Inquiry, 5*, 325-66

Akmajian, A. (1968) 'The analysis of cleft sentences', unpublished paper, MIT

—— (1969) and R. S. Jackendoff (1970) 'Coreferentiality and stress', *Linguistic Inquiry, 1*, 124-6

—— and T. Wasow (1975) 'The constituent structure of VP and AUX and the position of the verb *be*', *Linguistic Analysis*, 1, 205-45

—— S. Steele and T. Wasow (1979) 'The category AUX in universal grammar', *Linguistic Inquiry*, 10, 1-64

Anderson, S. (1966) 'Concerning the notion "base component of a transformational grammar"', MIT internal memorandum, reprinted in McCawley (1976c) *Notes from the Linguistic Underground*, Academic Press, New York, pp. 113-28

—— (1972) 'How to get *even*', *Language, 48*, 893-906

Andrews, A. (1971) 'Case agreement of predicate modifiers in ancient Greek', *Linguistic Inquiry, 2*, 127-51

Bach, E. (1968) 'Nouns and noun phrases' in E. Bach and R. T. Harms (1968), *Universals in Linguistic Theory*, Holt, Rinehart and Winston, New York, pp. 90-122

—— (1970) 'Is Amharic an SOV language?', *Journal of Ethiopian Studies, 8*, 9-20

Baker, C. L. and M. Brame (1972) 'Global rules: a rejoinder', *Language, 48*, 51-75

Becker, A. and D. Arms (1969) 'Prepositions as predicates', *Papers from the Fifth Regional Meeting, Chicago Linguistic Society*, 1-11

Berman, A. and M. Szamosi (1972) 'Observations on sentential stress', *Language, 48*, 304-25

Binnick, R. I. (1971) '*Come* and *Bring*', *Linguistic Inquiry, 2*, 260-7

Boertien, H. (1979) 'The double modal construction in Texas', *Texas Linguistic Forum, 13*, 14-33

Bolinger, D. (1971) 'Semantic overloading: a restudy of the verb *remind*', *Language, 47*, 522-47

Brame, M. (1976) *Conjectures and Refutations in Syntax and Semantics*, North Holland, Amsterdam

Bresnan, J. (1970) 'On complementizers: towards a syntactic theory of sentence types', *Foundations of Language,* **6**, 297-321

—— (1971) 'Sentence stress and syntactic transformation', *Language,* **47**, 257-81

—— (1972) 'Theory of complementation of English syntax', unpublished PhD thesis, MIT

Cantrall, W. (1974) *Viewpoint, Reflexives, and the Nature of Noun Phrases,* Mouton, The Hague

Carlson, G. (1977) *Reference to Kinds in English,* PhD thesis, University of Massachusetts at Amherst; also Garland Press, New York (1980)

Channon, R. (1975a) 'The NAC, and How Not to Get It', *Papers from the Fifth Annual Meeting of the North Eastern Linguistic Society,* Harvard University, Cambridge, Mass., 276-98

—— (1975b) 'Acceptable Ambiguity', *Proceedings of the First Berkeley Linguistic Society Conference,* Berkeley Linguistic Society, Berkeley, Ca., 37-46

Chiba, S. (1972) 'Another Case for "Relative Clause Formation Is a Copying Rule"', *Studies in English Linguistics,* **1**, 1-12

Chomsky, N. (1957) *Syntactic Structures,* Mouton, The Hague

—— (1965) *Aspects of the Theory of Syntax,* MIT Press, Cambridge, Mass.

—— (1966) *Topics in the Theory of Generative Grammar,* Mouton, The Hague

—— (1970) 'Remarks on nominalization' in R. Jacobs and P. S. Rosenbaum (eds.), *Readings in English Transformational Grammar,* Ginn, Boston, pp. 184-221; reprinted in Chomsky (1972) *Studies on Semantics in Generative Grammar,* Mouton, The Hague pp. 11-61

—— (1973) 'Conditions on transformations' in S. Anderson and P. Kiparsky (eds.), *A Festschrift for Morris Halle,* Holt, Rinehart and Winston, New York; reprinted in Chomsky (1977) *Essays on Form and Interpretation,* pp. 81-160, North Holland, Amsterdam, pp. 81-160

—— (1976) 'Conditions on rules of grammar', *Linguistic Analysis,* **2**, 303-5; page references to reprint in Chomsky (1977), pp. 163-210

—— (1980) 'On binding', *Linguistic Inquiry,* **11**, 1-46

—— and M. Halle (1968) *The Sound Pattern of English,* Harper and Row, New York

—— and H. Lasnik (1977) 'Filters and control', *Linguistic Inquiry,* **8**, 425-504

Cole, P. (1974) 'Backward pronominalization and analogy', *Linguistic Inquiry*, 5, 425–43

Collingwood, R. G. (1940) *An Essay on Metaphysics*, Regnery, Chicago

Dixon, R. M. W. (1977) 'Where have all the adjectives gone?', *Studies in Language*, 1, 19–80

Dougherty, R. C. (1974) 'The syntax and semantics of *each other* constructions', *Foundations of Language,* 12, 1–47

Dowty, D. (1978) 'Governed transformations as lexical rules in a Montague grammar', *Linguistic Inquiry*, 9, 393–426

—— (1979) *Word Meaning in Montague Grammar*, Reidel, Dordrecht

Elliot, D. (1971) 'The grammar of emotive and exclamatory adjectives in English', *Ohio State Working Papers in Linguistics,* 8, 1–110

Emonds, J. (1970) 'Root and structure-preserving transformations', unpublished PhD thesis, MIT (Extensive revision published as Emonds, 1976)

—— (1976) *A Transformational Approach to English Syntax*, Academic Press, New York

Epée, R. (1976) 'A counterexample to the Q replacement and COMP substitution universals', *Linguistic Inquiry,* 7, 677–86

Evers, A. (1975) 'The transformational cycle in Dutch and German', unpublished PhD thesis, University of Utrecht

Feyerabend, P. K. (1975) *Against Method*, New Left Books, London

Fiengo, R. (1974) 'Semantic conditions on surface structure', unpublished PhD thesis, MIT

—— and H. Lasnik (1973) 'The logical structure of reciprocal sentences in English', *Foundations of Language*, 9, 447–68

Fillmore, C. J. (1966) 'A proposal concerning English prepositions', Georgetown University *Monograph Series on Languages and Linguistics, 19*, 19–34

—— (1968) 'The case for case', in E. Bach and R. T. Harms (eds.), *Universals in Linguistic Theory,* Holt, Rinehart and Winston, New York, pp. 1–88

—— (1971a) 'Some problems for case grammar', Georgetown University *Monograph Series on Languages and Linguistics,* 21 35–56

—— (1971b) 'Verbs of judging' in C. J. Fillmore and D. T. Langendoen *Studies in Linguistic Semantics,* Holt, Rinehart and Winston, New York, pp. 273–89

Fodor, J. A. (1970) 'Three reasons for not deriving "kill" from "cause to die"', *Linguistic Inquiry,* 1, 429–48

Fodor, J. D. (1972) 'Beware', *Linguistic Inquiry*, 3, 528–35

Fraser, B. (1971) 'An analysis of *even* in English' in C. J. Fillmore and
D. T. Langendoen *Studies in Linguistic Semantics*, Holt, Rinehart
and Winston, New York, pp. 150-78

Freidin, R. and H. Lasnik (1981) 'Disjoint reference and *Wh*-trace',
Linguistic Inquiry, 12, 39-53

Gallagher, M. (1970) 'Does meaning grow on trees?' in J. Sadock and
A. Vanek, *Studies Presented to Robert B. Lees by his Students*,
Linguistic Research Inc., Edmonton, pp. 79-93

Gazdar, G. (1981) 'Unbounded dependencies and coordinate structure',
Linguistic Inquiry, 12, 155-84

—— (in press) 'Phrase structure grammar' in P. Jacobson and G.
Pullum (eds.), *The Nature of Syntactic Representation,* Reidel,
Dordrecht

—— and E. Klein (1978) 'Review of Keenan (ed.), *Formal Semantics
of Natural Language*', *Language*, 54, 661-7

—— G. Pullum and I. Sag (forthcoming) 'A phrase structure grammar
of the English auxiliary system', *Language*

Gordon, D. and G. Lakoff (1971) 'Conversational postulates', *Papers
from the Seventh Regional Meeting, Chicago Linguistic Society*,
pp. 63-84; also in P. Cole and J. L. Morgan (eds.) (1975), *Speech
Acts (Syntax and Semantics* 3), Academic Press, New York, pp.
83-106

Grinder, J. and P. M. Postal (1971), 'Missing antecedents', *Linguistic
Inquiry*, 2, 269-312

Gruber, J. (1965) 'Studies in lexical relations', PhD thesis, MIT; forms a
part of Gruber (1976)

—— (1976) *Lexical Structure in Syntax and Semantics,* North Holland,
Amsterdam

Gupta, A. (1980) *The Logic of Common Nouns*, Yale University Press,
New Haven

Haan, G. de (1976) 'Regelordening en domainformuleringen op trans-
formaties' in G. Koefoed and A. Evers (eds.), *Lijnen van taaltheore-
tisch onderzoek*, H. D. Tjeenk Willink, Groningen, pp. 279-302

Haber, L. (1975) 'The muzzy theory',*Papers from the Eleventh Regional
Meeting, Chicago Linguistic Society*, pp. 240-56

Halle, M. (1959) *The Sound Pattern of Russian*, Mouton, The Hague

Hankamer, J. (1972) 'Analogical rules in syntax',*Papers from the Eighth
Regional Meeting, Chicago Linguistic Society*, 111-23

—— (1973) 'Unacceptable ambiguity', *Linguistic Inquiry*, 4, 17-68

Harada, S. and S. Saito (1971), 'A non-source for reflexives',*Linguistic
Inquiry*, 2, 546-57

Harman, G. (1963) 'Generative grammars without transformational rules', *Language,* **39**, 597-616

Harris, Z. (1946) 'From morpheme to utterance', *Language,* **22**, 161-83

Hasegawa, K. (1968) 'The passive construction in English', *Language*, **44**, 230-43

Higgins, F. R. (1973) 'On Emonds's analysis of Extraposition', *Syntax and Semantics* 2, pp. 149-95

Hofmann, T. R. (1966) 'Past tense replacement and the English modal system', Harvard University Computation Laboratory Report NSF-17; reprinted in McCawley (1976c) *Notes from the Linguistic Underground,* Academic Press, New York, pp. 85-100

Horn, L. (1972) 'On the semantic properties of logical operators in English', unpublished PhD thesis (distributed by Indiana University Linguistics Club)

Ikeuchi, M. (1972) 'Adverbial clauses in noun phrases', *Studies in English Linguistics,* **1**, 96-101

Ioup, G. (1974) 'The treatment of quantifier scope in a transformational grammar', PhD thesis, City University of New York

Inoue, K. (1979) 'An analysis of the English present perfect', *Linguistics,* **17**, 561-89

Iwakura, K. (1979) 'On surface filters and deletion rules', *Linguistic Analysis,* **5**, 93-124

Jackendoff, R. S. (1969) 'An interpretive theory of negation', *Foundations of Language,* **5**, 218-41

—— (1972) *Semantic Interpretation in Generative Grammar,* MIT Press, Cambridge, Mass.

—— (1973) 'The base rules for prepositional phrases' in S. Anderson and P. Kiparsky (1973) *A Festschrift for Morris Halle*, Holt, Rinehart and Winston, New York, pp. 345-56

—— (1977) *X-bar syntax,* MIT Press, Cambridge, Mass.

Jacobson, P. and P. Neubauer (1976) 'Rule cyclicity: evidence from the intervention constraint', *Linguistic Inquiry,* **7**, 429-61

Jespersen, O. (1924) *The Philosophy of Grammar,* Allen and Unwin, London

—— (1937) *Analytic Syntax*, Allen and Unwin, London

Johnson, D. and P. M. Postal (1980) *Arc Pair Grammar*, Princeton University Press, Princeton

Karttunen, L. (1969) 'Discourse referents', paper read at COLING conference, Sanga-Säby, Sweden; in J. McCawley (1976), *Notes from the Linguistic Underground*, Academic Press, New York pp. 363-85

—— and P. S. Peters (1979) 'Conventional implicature' in C.-K. Oh and D. Dinneen (eds.), *Presupposition* (*Syntax and Semantics* 11), Academic Press, New York, pp. 1–56

Katz, J. J. and J. A. Fodor (1963) 'The structure of a semantic theory', *Language,* 39, 170–210

—— and P. M. Postal (1964) *An Integrated Theory of Linguistic Descriptions*, MIT Press, Cambridge, Mass.

Kiparsky, P. (1973) '"Elsewhere" in phonology' in S. Anderson and P. Kiparsky (eds.), *A Festschrift for Morris Halle*, Holt, Rinehart and Winston, New York pp. 93–106

Koster, J. (1974) 'Het werkwoord als spiegelcentrum', *Spektator,* 3, 601–18

—— (1975) 'Dutch as an SOV language', *Linguistic Analysis,* 1, 111–36

—— (1978) *Locality Principles in Syntax*, Foris, Dordrecht

Kuno, S. (1971) 'The position of locatives in existential sentences', *Linguistic Inquiry,* 2, 333–78

Kuroda, S.-Y. (1965) *Generative Grammatical Studies in the Japanese Language*, Garland, New York (1979)

—— (1969) 'Attachment transformations' in D. A. Reibel and S. A. Schane *Modern Studies in English*, Prentice Hall, Englewood Cliffs, NJ, pp. 331–51

—— (1970) 'Some remarks on English manner adverbials', in R. Jakobson and S. Kawamoto, (eds.), *Studies in General and Oriental Linguistics,* the TEC Corp., Tokyo, 378–96

—— (1971) 'Two remarks on pronominalization', *Foundations of Language,* 7, 331–51

Ladusaw, W. (1979) *Polarity Sensitivity as Inherent Scope Relations,* PhD thesis, University of Texas at Austin; distributed by Indiana University Linguistics Club

Lakatos, I. (1970) 'Falsification and the methodology of research programmes' in I. Lakatos and A. Musgrave (eds.), *Criticism and the Growth of Knowledge*, Cambridge University Press, Cambridge, pp. 91–196

—— (1976) *Proofs and Refutations*, Cambridge University Press, Cambridge

Lakoff, G. (1965) *On the Nature of Syntactic Irregularity*, Harvard University Computation Laboratory Report NSF-16; reprinted 1970 under the title *Irregularity in Syntax*, Holt, Rinehart and Winston, New York

—— (1968a) 'Instrumental adverbs and the concept of deep structure', *Foundations of Language,* 4, 4–29

—— (1968b) 'Pronouns and reference', Indiana University Linguistics Club, Bloomington. Reprinted in McCawley (1976), pp. 275-335

—— (1969a) 'On derivational constraints', *Papers from the Fifth Regional Meeting, Chicago Linguistic Society*, 117-39

—— (1969b) 'Presuppositions and relative grammaticality', *Journal of Philosophical Linguistics*, **1**, no. 1, 103-16; also in D. Steinberg and L. Jakobovits (1971) *Semantics*, Cambridge University Press, London and New York, pp. 329-40, under the title 'Presuppositions and relative well formedness'

—— (1970a) 'Repartee', *Foundations of Language*, **6**, 389-422

—— (1970b) 'Global rules', *Language*, **46**, 627-39

—— (1971a) 'On generative semantics' in D. Steinberg and L. Jakobovits (1971), *Semantics*, Cambridge University Press, London and New York, pp. 232-96

—— (1971b) 'Linguistics and natural logic', *Synthese*; also appears in D. Davidson, and G. Harman (1972) *Semantics of Natural Language*, Reidel, Dordrecht, pp. 545-65

—— (1972a) 'The arbitrary basis of transformational grammar', *Language*, **48**, 76-87

—— (1972b) 'The global nature of the nuclear stress rule', *Language*, **48**, 285-303

—— (1973) 'Some thoughts on transderivational constraints', in B. Kachru *et al.*, (eds.), *Issues in Linguistics: Papers in Honor of Henry and Renée Kahane*, University of Illinois Press, Urbana and Chicago, 442-52

—— and J. R. Ross (1972) 'A note on anaphoric islands and causatives', *Linguistic Inquiry*, **3**, 121-5

—— and H. Thompson (1975), 'Introducing cognitive grammar', *Papers from the First Annual Meeting, Berkeley Linguistic Society*, pp. 295-313

Lakoff, R. (1971) 'Passive resistance', *Papers from the Seventh Regional Meeting, Chicago Linguistic Society*, pp. 149-62

—— (1972) 'The pragmatics of modality', *Papers from the Eighth Regional Meeting, Chicago Linguistic Society*, pp. 229-46

Langendoen, D. T. (1970) 'The *can't seem to* construction', *Linguistic Inquiry*, **1**, 25-35

Lasnik, H. (1976) 'Remarks on coreference', *Linguistic Analysis*, **2**, 1-22

Lawler, J. (1972) 'Generic to a fault', *Papers from the Eighth Regional Meeting, Chicago Linguistic Society*, pp. 247-58

—— (1973) 'Studies in English generics', University of Michigan dissertation

Leech, G. (1969) *Towards a Semantic Description of English,* Longmans, London, and Indiana University Press, Bloomington

Lees, R. B. (1960) *The Grammar of English Nominalizations,* Mouton, The Hague

—— (1964) 'On passives and imperatives in English', *Gengo Kenkyu,* **46**, 28–41

—— and E. S. Klima (1963) 'Rules for English pronominalization', *Language,* **39**, 17–28; also in D. A. Reibel and S. A. Schane (1969) *Modern Studies in English,* Prentice Hall, Englewood Cliffs, NJ, pp. 145–59

Levi, J. (1974) 'On the alleged idiosyncrasy of nonpredicate NPs', *Papers from the Tenth Regional Meeting, Chicago Linguistic Society,* pp. 402–15

—— (1978) *The Syntax and Semantics of Complex Nominals,* Academic Press, New York

Linebarger, M. (1980) *The Grammar of Negative Polarity,* PhD thesis, MIT; distributed by Indiana University Linguistics Club

Lounsbury, F. G. (1964) 'The structural analysis of kinship terms' in H. Lunt (ed.), *Proceedings of the Ninth International Congress of Linguists,* Mouton, The Hague, pp. 1073–90

Lyons, J. (1977) *Semantics,* Cambridge University Press, Cambridge

Matthews, P. H. (1967) 'Review of Chomsky, *Aspects of the Theory of Syntax',* *Journal of Linguistics,* **3**, 119–52

McCawley, J. D. (1968a) 'Lexical insertion in a transformational grammar without deep structure', *Papers from the Fourth Regional Meeting, Chicago Linguistic Society,* pp. 71–80; also in (1973d) *Grammar and Meaning,* Taishukan, Tokyo, and Academic Press, New York, pp. 155–66

—— (1968b) 'The role of semantics in a grammar', in E. Bach and R. T. Harms (1968) *Universals in Linguistic Theory,* Holt, Rinehart and Winston, New York, pp. 124–69; also in (1973d) *Grammar and Meaning,* Taishukan, Tokyo, and Academic Press, New York, pp. 59–98

—— (1968c) 'Concerning the base component of a transformational grammar', *Foundations of Language,* **4**, 243–69; also in (1973d) *Grammar and Meaning,* Taishukan, Tokyo, and Academic Press, New York, p. 35–58

—— (1970a) 'Semantic representation' in P. M. Garvin (ed.) *Cognition: A Multiple View,* Spartan Books, New York, pp. 227–47; also in (1973d) *Grammar and Meaning,* Taishukan, Tokyo, and Academic Press, New York, pp. 240–56

—— (1970b) 'Where do noun phrases come from?' in R. Jacobs and P. S. Rosenbaum (1970) *Readings in English transformational grammar*, Ginn, Boston, pp. 166-83; also in (1973d) *Grammar and Meaning*, Taishukan, Tokyo, and Academic Press, New York, pp. 133-54

—— (1970c) 'English as a VSO language', *Language*, **46**, 286-99; also in (1973d) *Grammar and Meaning*, Taishukan, Tokyo, and Academic Press, New York, pp. 211-28

—— (1971a) 'Prelexical syntax', *Monograph Series on Languages and Linguistics*, Georgetown University, Washington, DC, vol. 24, pp. 19-33; also in (1973d) *Grammar and Meaning*, Taishukan, Tokyo, and Academic Press, New York, pp. 343-56

—— (1971b) 'Tense and time reference in English' in C. J. Fillmore and D. T. Langendoen (1971) *Studies in Linguistic Semantics*, Holt, Rinehart and Winston, New York, pp. 96-113; also in (1973d) *Grammar and Meaning*, Taishukan, Tokyo, and Academic Press, New York, pp. 257-72

—— (1972) 'A program for logic' in D. Davidson and G. Harman (1972) *Semantics of Natural Language*, Reidel, Dordrecht, pp. 498-544; also in (1973d) *Grammar and Meaning*, Taishukan, Tokyo, and Academic Press, New York, pp. 285-319

—— (1973a) 'External NPs vs. annotated deep structures', *Linguistic Inquiry*, **4**, 221-40

—— (1973b) 'Syntactic and logical arguments for semantic structures' in O. Fujimura (ed.), *Three Dimensions of Linguistic Theory*, TEC Corp., Tokyo, pp. 259-376

—— (1973c) 'The role of notation in generative phonology', in M. Gross, M. Halle, and M. Schutzenberger (eds.), *The Formal Analysis of Natural Languages*, Mouton, The Hague, pp. 51-62; also in (1979a) *Adverbs, Vowels, and Other Objects of Wonder*, University of Chicago Press, Chicago, pp. 204-16

—— (1973d) *Grammar and Meaning*, Taishukan, Tokyo, and Academic Press, New York

—— (1974) 'On identifying the remains of deceased clauses', *Language Research*, **9**, 73-85; also in (1979a) *Adverbs, Vowels, and other Objects of Wonder*, University of Chicago Press, Chicago, pp. 84-95

—— (1975a) 'Verbs of bitching' in D. Hockney *et al.* (eds.), *Contemporary Research in Philosophical Logic and Linguistic Semantics*, Reidel, Dordrecht, pp. 313-32; also in (1979a) *Adverbs, Vowels, and Other Objects of Wonder*, University of Chicago Press, Chicago, pp. 135-50

—— (1975b) 'Review of Chomsky, *Studies on Semantics in Generative*

Grammar', *Studies in English Linguistics*, **3**, 209–311; also in this volume.

—— (1976a) 'Some ideas not to live by', *Die neueren Sprachen*, **75**, 151–65; also in (1979a) *Adverbs, Vowels, and Other Objects of Wonder*, University of Chicago Press, Chicago, pp. 234–46

—— (1976b) 'Morphological indeterminacy in underlying syntactic structure', *Papers from the 1975 Mid-America Linguistics Conference*, University of Kansas Linguistics Department, Lawrence, Kansas, pp. 317–26; also in (1979a) *Adverbs, Vowels, and Other Objects of Wonder*, University of Chicago Press, Chicago, pp. 113–21

—— (1976c) *Notes from the Linguistic Underground*, Academic Press, New York

—— (1977a) 'Acquisition models as models of acquisition', in R. Fasold and R. Shuy (eds.), *Studies in Language Variation*, Georgetown University Press, Washington, DC, pp. 51–64

—— (1977b) 'Evolutionary parallels between Montague grammar and transformational grammar', *Papers from the Seventh Annual Meeting, Northeastern Linguistic Society*, University of Massachusetts at Amherst, pp. 219–32; also in (1979a) *Adverbs, Vowels, and Other Objects of Wonder*, University of Chicago Press, Chicago, pp. 122–32

—— (1978) 'World-creating predicates', *Versus*, *19/20*, 79–93

—— (1979a) *Adverbs, Vowels, and Other Objects of Wonder*, University of Chicago Press, Chicago

—— (1979b) 'Presupposition and discourse structure' in C.-K. Oh and D. Dinneen (eds.), *Presupposition (Syntax and Semantics* 11), Academic Press, New York, pp. 371–88

—— (1981a) 'An un-syntax' in E. Moravcsik and J. Wirth (eds.), *Current Approaches to Syntax (Syntax and Semantics* 13), Academic Press, New York, pp. 167–93

—— (1981b) 'The syntax and semantics of English relative clauses', *Lingua*, **53**, 99–149

—— (1981c) *Everything that Linguists have always Wanted to Know about Logic (but were Ashamed to Ask)*, University of Chicago Press, Chicago, and Blackwell, Oxford

—— (1981d) 'Review of F. J. Newmeyer, *Linguistic Theory in America'*, *Linguistics*, **18**, pp. 911–30

—— (1981e) 'Notes on the English present perfect', *Australian Journal of Linguistics*, **1**, pp. 81–90

—— (to appear a) 'Parentheticals and discontinuous constituent structure', *Linguistic Inquiry*

—— (to appear b) 'Towards plausibility in theories of language acquisition', *Cognition and Communication*

McCawley, N. A. (1972) 'A study of Japanese reflexivization', unpublished PhD thesis, University of Illinois

Miller, G. and P. N. Johnson-Laird (1976) *Language and Perception*, Belknap, Cambridge, Mass.

Morgan, J. L. (1969a) 'On arguing about semantics', *Papers in Linguistics*, **1**, 49-70

—— (1969b) 'On the treatment of presupposition in transformational grammar', *Papers from the Fifth Regional Meeting, Chicago Linguistic Society*, pp. 167-77

Morreall, J. (1979) 'Possible words', *Linguistic Inquiry*, **10**, 724-6

Musgrave, A. (1976) 'Why did oxygen supplant phlogiston? Research programmes in the Chemical Revolution' in C. Howson (ed.), *Method and Appraisal in the Physical Sciences*, Cambridge University Press, Cambridge, pp. 181-209

Newmeyer, F. J. (1976) 'The precyclic nature of predicate raising' in M. Shibatani (ed.), *The Grammar of Causative Constructions (Syntax and Semantics* 6), Academic Press, New York, pp. 131-64

Okada, N. (1975) 'Notes on interpretive semantics', *Studies in English Linguistics*, **3**, 182-208

Partee, B. H. (1971) 'Linguistic metatheory' in W. O. Dingwall, *A Survey of Linguistic Science*, University of Maryland, pp. 650-79

Pentheroudakis, J. (1977) 'Reference and Indefinite Descriptions in Modern Greek', unpublished PhD thesis, University of Chicago

Perlmutter, D. M. (1970) 'Surface structure constraints in syntax', *Linguistic Inquiry*, **1**, 187-256

—— (1971) *Deep and Surface Structure Constraints*, Holt, Rinehart and Winston, New York

—— (in press) *Studies in Relational Grammar*, University of Chicago Press, Chicago

—— and P. M. Postal (1977) 'Toward a universal characterization of passivation', *Papers from the Second Annual Meeting*, Berkeley Linguistic Society, pp. 394-417

Postal, P. M. (1968) *Aspects of Phonological Theory*, Harper and Row, New York

—— (1969) 'Anaphoric islands', *Papers from the Fifth Regional Meeting, Chicago Linguistic Society*, pp. 205-39

—— (1970a) 'On the surface verb *remind*', *Linguistic Inquiry*, **1**, 37-120; also in C. J. Fillmore and D. T. Langendoen (1971) *Studies in Linguistic Semantics*, Holt, Rinehart and Winston, New York, pp. 180-270

—— (1970b) 'On coreferential complement subject deletion', *Linguistic Inquiry,* **1**, 439-500

—— (1972) 'The best theory' in P. S. Peters, *Goals of Linguistic Theory,* Prentice Hall, Englewood Cliffs, NJ

—— (1974) *On Raising,* MIT Press, Cambridge, Mass.

—— (Ms) 'The derivation of English pseudo-adjectives'

—— and J. Grinder (1971) 'Missing antecedents', *Linguistic Inquiry,* **2**, 269-312

Pullum, G. K. (1976) *Rule Interaction and the Organization of a Grammar,* PhD thesis, University of London; slightly abridged version published by Garland, New York (1979)

—— (1980a) 'Languages in which movement does not parallel bound anaphora', *Linguistic Inquiry,* **11**, 613-20

—— (1980b) 'Syntactic relations and linguistic universals', *Transactions of the Philological Society,* 1-39

—— and D. Wilson (1977) 'Autonomous syntax and the analysis of auxiliaries, *Language,* **53**, 741-88

Pyle, C. (1972) 'On eliminating BM's', *Papers from the Eighth Regional Meeting, Chicago Linguistic Society,* pp. 516-32

Querido, A. (1971) 'Predicate agglomeration, predicate agglutination, and lexical synthesis', duplicated, Université de Montréal

Rosenbaum, P. S. (1967) *The Grammar of English Predicate Complement Constructions,* MIT Press, Cambridge, Mass.

Ross, J. R. (1967a) 'On the cyclic nature of English pronominalization', *To Honor Roman Jakobson,* Mouton, The Hague, pp. 1669-82; also in D. A. Reibel, and S. A. Schane (1969) *Modern Studies in English,* Prentice Hall, Englewood Cliffs, NJ, pp. 187-200

—— (1967b) 'Constraints on variables in syntax', unpublished PhD thesis, MIT

—— (1969a) 'Auxiliaries as Main verbs', *Journal of Philosophical Linguistics,* **1**, 77-102

—— (1969b) 'Guess who?', *Papers from the Fifth Regional Meeting, Chicago Linguistic Society,* pp. 252-86

—— (1969c) 'Adjectives as noun phrases', in D. A. Reibel and S. A. Schane (1969) *Modern Studies in English,* Prentice Hall, Englewood Cliffs, NJ, pp. 352-60

—— (1970) 'On declarative sentences', in R. Jacobs and P. S. Rosenbaum (1970) *Readings in English transformational grammar,* Ginn, Boston, pp. 222-72

—— (1972a) 'Act', in D. Davidson and G. Harman (1972) *Semantics of Natural Language,* Reidel, Dordrecht, pp. 70-126

——— (1972b) 'The category squish: Endstation Hauptwort', *Papers from the Eighth Regional Meeting, Chicago Linguistic Society*, pp. 316-28

——— (1973) 'Nouniness' in O. Fujimura (ed.), *Three Dimensions of Linguistic Theory*, TEC Corp, Tokyo, pp. 136-257

——— (1976) 'To have have and not to have have' in M. Jazayery, E. Polomé and W. Winter (eds.), *Linguistic and Literary Studies in Honor of A. A. Hill*, Vol. 1, de Ridder, Lisse, pp. 263-70

Rudin, C. (1981) '"Who what to whom said?": an argument from Bulgarian against cyclic WH-movement', *Papers from the Seventeenth Regional Meeting, Chicago Linguistic Society*, pp. 353-62

Sadock, J. (1970) 'Whimperatives' in J. Sadock and A. Vanek (1970), *Studies Presented to Robert B. Lees by his Students*, Linguistic Research, Inc., Edmonton, pp. 223-38

——— (1980) 'Noun incorporation in Greenlandic', *Language*, **56**, 300-19

Sag, I. (1976) 'Deletion and logical form', unpublished PhD thesis, MIT

Sanchez de Zavala, V. (1974) *Semántica y sintaxis en la lingüística transformatoria*, Alianza Editorial, Madrid

Sanders, J. (1971) *Invariant Ordering*, Indiana University Linguistics Club, Bloomington

Schachter, P. (1973) 'On syntactic categories' in P. Schachter and G. Bedell (eds.), *Critiques of Syntactic Studies*, Vol. 2, UCLA Linguistics Department, Los Angeles, pp. 138-92

Schiebe, T. (1970) 'A global constraint involving quantifiers in German', *Linguistic Inquiry*, **1**, 351-7

Schmerling, S. (1971) 'Presupposition and the notion of normal stress', *Papers from the Seventh Regional Meeting, Chicago Linguistic Society*, pp. 242-53

——— (1976) *Aspects of English Sentence Stress*, University of Texas Press, Austin

Selkirk, E. (1976) 'Concerning bracketing and boundaries in phonological representations', paper read at 1976 conference of Northeastern Linguistic Society

Seuren, P. (1972) 'Predicate raising and dative in French and sundry languages', mimeographed, Oxford

Shibatani, M. (1972) 'Lakoff and Ross on the anaphoric island constraint', paper read at annual meeting, Linguistic Society of America

Staal, J. F. (1967) *Word Order in Sanskrit and Universal Grammar*, Reidel, Dordrecht

Steinberg D. and L. Jakobovits (1971) *Semantics*, Cambridge University Press, London and New York

Vendler, Z. (1957) 'Verbs and times', *Philosophical Review,* **66,** 143–60; also in Z. Vendler, (1967), *Linguistics in Philosophy,* Cornell University Press, Ithaca, pp. 97–121

Verkuyl, H. (1981) 'Numerals and quantifiers in X̄-syntax and their semantic interpretation' in J. Groenendijk *et al.* (eds.), *Formal Methods in the Study of Language*

Wachowicz, K. (1974) 'Against the universality of a single WH-question movement', *Foundations of Language,* **11,** 155–66

Wasow, T. (1976) Review of McCawley, *Grammar and Meaning, Linguistic Analysis,* **2,** 279–301

—— (1977) 'Transformations and the lexicon' in P. Culicover, A. Akmajian and T. Wasow (eds.), *Formal Syntax,* Academic Press, New York, pp. 327–60

Williams, E. (1974) 'Rule ordering in syntax', unpublished PhD thesis, MIT distributed by Indiana University Linguistics Club

—— (1977) 'Discourse and logical form', *Linguistic Inquiry,* **8,** 101–39

Williams, R. (1956) *Biochemical Individuality,* Wiley, New York

Zwicky, A. M. (1978) 'Arguing for constituents', *Papers from the Fourteenth Regional Meeting, Chicago Linguistic Society,* 503–12

INDEX